LEVEL II PRACTICE EXAMS – VOL

SCHWESER 2018 LEVEL II CFA® PRACTICE EXAMS VOLUME 2

©2017 Kaplan, Inc. All rights reserved.

Published in 2017 by Kaplan, Inc.

Printed in the United States of America.

ISBN: 978-1-4754-5986-9

HOW TO USE THE LEVEL II PRACTICE EXAMS

Thank you for purchasing the Schweser Practice Exams. We hope that you find this volume effective and user-friendly. The following suggestions are designed to help you get the most out of these practice exams and prepare for the actual Level II Exam.

Be ready for a new format. The format of the Level II exam is different from Level I. The exam consists of item sets, which are vignettes or short cases followed by six multiple-choice questions (CFA Institute calls these "mini-cases"). There will be 20 item sets (120 questions) on the exam: 10 item sets (60 questions) in the morning and 10 more item sets (60 more questions) in the afternoon. Each question is worth 3 points (and is allocated 3 minutes), and there are 360 total points available. Each question will have three possible choices (A, B, or C).

Any topic can be tested in the morning and/or the afternoon, so you might have an economics item set in the morning and another one in the afternoon. Don't spend a lot of time contemplating which topics might appear in which session.

Save the practice exams for last. Save the practice exams for the last month before the exam. A good strategy would be to take one exam in each of the three weeks leading up to the test. Do your best to mimic actual exam conditions for at least one of the practice exams (e.g., time yourself, have someone turn the heat down and up so that you go from freezing to boiling, hire a construction crew to do some blasting outside your window).

Remember, no matter how challenging we make our practice exams, the actual exam will be different. Also, mainly due to the stress of the exam day, your perception will be that the actual exam was much more difficult than *any* practice exam you have ever seen.

After you have completed an exam, use your results as a diagnostic tool to help you identify areas in which you are weak. One good way to accomplish this is to use your online access to Performance Tracker. This is a tool that will provide you with exam diagnostics to target your study and review effort, and allow you to compare your scores on practice exams to those of other candidates.

Make sure you understand the mistake(s) you made on every question you got wrong (or guessed on). Make a flashcard that illustrates that particular concept, carry it around with you, and quiz yourself until you are confident you have mastered the concept. This "feedback" loop (practice exam, diagnosis of results, identification of concepts yet to be mastered, study of those concepts, and then another practice exam) is a very effective study strategy in the last month before exam day.

Topic Area	Guideline Topic Area Weight
Ethical and Professional Standards	10 to 15%
Quantitative Methods	5 to 10%
Economics	5 to 10%
Financial Reporting and Analysis	15 to 20%
Corporate Finance	5 to 15%
Equity Valuation	15 to 25%
Fixed Income	10 to 20%
Derivatives	5 to 15%
Alternative Investments	5 to 10%
Portfolio Management	5 to 10%
TOTAL	100%

Expect the unexpected. Be prepared for difficult questions on unexpected topics. Only one thing is certain about the exam: you will be surprised by some of the questions.

Guess if you are stumped. It should take you approximately 18 minutes to read the vignette and answer the six questions that make up each item set. Don't fall behind: successful candidates know when to cut their losses by guessing and moving on. If you're stuck, try to eliminate one of the incorrect answers, and then pick one of the remaining choices. If you successfully eliminate one choice you know is wrong, you have a 50/50 chance of selecting the correct answer. There is no penalty for guessing.

Be ready for more than just number-crunching. Your reading comprehension ability is an important component of success on the Level II exam. The vignettes will be long and full of information. Your job is to find the important pieces of information and answer the questions correctly.

There are two approaches to these item sets. You can read the vignette first and then tackle the questions, or you can read the first question and then go back to the vignette to find the data needed to answer it. We recommend the second approach because it saves time and helps you to focus on the details you need. When taking the practice exams, experiment with both techniques and do what works best for you!

My thanks to the Schweser team. I would like to thank all of my colleagues at Schweser for their commitment to quality. Kaplan Schweser would not be the company it is, nor could it provide the products you see, without the help of these content and editing professionals.

You may expect me to end this introduction with a "good luck on the exam." However, you need not be lucky to pass Level II. With your hard work and our assistance, luck will have nothing to do with it. Instead, I'll simply say, "See you next year at Level III."

Best Regards,

Bijesh Tolia

Dr. Bijesh Tolia, CFA, CA
VP of CFA Education and Level II Professor

Kaplan Schweser

Exam 1
Morning Session

Question	Topic	Minutes (Points)
1 to 6	Ethics	18
7 to 12	Corporate Finance	18
13 to 18	Equity	18
19 to 24	Equity	18
25 to 30	Equity	18
31 to 36	Equity	18
37 to 42	Fixed Income	18
43 to 48	Derivatives	18
49 to 54	Derivatives	18
55 to 60	Portfolio Management	18

Test Answers

1.	(A)	(B)	(C)		41.	(A)	(B)	(C)
2.	(A)	(B)	(C)		42.	(A)	(B)	(C)
3.	(A)	(B)	(C)		43.	(A)	(B)	(C)
4.	(A)	(B)	(C)		44.	(A)	(B)	(C)
5.	(A)	(B)	(C)		45.	(A)	(B)	(C)
6.	(A)	(B)	(C)		46.	(A)	(B)	(C)
7.	(A)	(B)	(C)		47.	(A)	(B)	(C)
8.	(A)	(B)	(C)		48.	(A)	(B)	(C)
9.	(A)	(B)	(C)		49.	(A)	(B)	(C)
10.	(A)	(B)	(C)		50.	(A)	(B)	(C)
11.	(A)	(B)	(C)		51.	(A)	(B)	(C)
12.	(A)	(B)	(C)		52.	(A)	(B)	(C)
13.	(A)	(B)	(C)		53.	(A)	(B)	(C)
14.	(A)	(B)	(C)		54.	(A)	(B)	(C)
15.	(A)	(B)	(C)		55.	(A)	(B)	(C)
16.	(A)	(B)	(C)		56.	(A)	(B)	(C)
17.	(A)	(B)	(C)		57.	(A)	(B)	(C)
18.	(A)	(B)	(C)		58.	(A)	(B)	(C)
19.	(A)	(B)	(C)		59.	(A)	(B)	(C)
20.	(A)	(B)	(C)		60.	(A)	(B)	(C)
21.	(A)	(B)	(C)					
22.	(A)	(B)	(C)					
23.	(A)	(B)	(C)					
24.	(A)	(B)	(C)					
25.	(A)	(B)	(C)					
26.	(A)	(B)	(C)					
27.	(A)	(B)	(C)					
28.	(A)	(B)	(C)					
29.	(A)	(B)	(C)					
30.	(A)	(B)	(C)					
31.	(A)	(B)	(C)					
32.	(A)	(B)	(C)					
33.	(A)	(B)	(C)					
34.	(A)	(B)	(C)					
35.	(A)	(B)	(C)					
36.	(A)	(B)	(C)					
37.	(A)	(B)	(C)					
38.	(A)	(B)	(C)					
39.	(A)	(B)	(C)					
40.	(A)	(B)	(C)					

Exam 1
Morning Session

Questions 1–6 relate to Carol Blackwell.

Carol Blackwell, CFA, has been hired into the research department of Blanchard Investments. Blanchard's manager, Thaddeus Baldwin, CFA, has worked in the securities business for more than 50 years. On Blackwell's first day at the office, Baldwin gives her an incomplete research report on Tops Groceries, Inc., to finish up.

Upon researching Tops, information about the financial instability of Tops Groceries' largest customer surfaces. Blackwell revises the research report by lowering the earnings projections. The day the report is to be released, Blackwell learns that Baldwin has replaced the lower, revised earnings projections with his earlier estimates.

Baldwin realizes that many of the firm's practices and policies would benefit from a compliance check. Because Blanchard recently adopted CFA Institute's Research Objectivity Standards, Baldwin wants Blackwell to ensure that the policies and procedures at the firm are in compliance.

During one of his many television interviews, Baldwin was asked about Patel, Inc. Baldwin replied that he had dropped coverage of Patel, but he hadn't had the time to publish a drop coverage note in light of his extensive travel schedule. Since Patel's auditors had announced uncertainty about the firm's ability to remain a going concern five months ago, Baldwin decided to focus on other stocks in the industry instead.

Blanchard's investment banking department recently announced that they were successful in obtaining the account of Teos Toys, Inc. In light of this announcement, Baldwin wants to know whether he can continue to rate Teos' stock favorably.

During a local society luncheon, Blackwell is seated next to CFA candidate Lucas Walters, who has been assigned the task of creating a compliance manual for Borchard & Sons, a small brokerage firm. Walters asks for her advice.

When Walters returns to work, he is apprised of the following situation: Borchard & Sons purchased 25,000 shares of CBX Corp. for equity manager Quintux Quantitative just minutes before the money manager called back and said it meant to buy 25,000 shares of CDX Corp. Borchard then purchased CDX shares for Quintux, but not before shares of CBX Corp. declined by 1.5%. The broker is holding the CBX shares in its own inventory.

Borchard proposes three methods for dealing with the trading error.

Method 1:   Quintux directs additional trades to Borchard worth a dollar value equal to the amount of the trading loss.

Method 2:   Borchard receives investment research from Quintux in exchange for Borchard covering the costs of the trading error.

Method 3:   Borchard transfers the ordered CBX shares in its inventory to Quintux, which allocates them to all of its clients on a pro-rata basis.

1.   Blackwell's *most appropriate* course of action to remain in compliance with the Research Objectivity Standards (ROS) is to:
   A. include a disclosure indicating that lower earnings estimates are available.
   B. follow up the first report with a second report emphasizing lower earnings projections.
   C. remove her name from the report if they release the report with higher earnings estimates.

2.   When updating the proxy-voting policy to conform to CFA Institute recommendations, which of the following recommendations is *least appropriate* for Blanchard to adopt?
   A. Determine the economic impact of non-routine proxy votes.
   B. Follow the same proxy-voting procedures regardless of the nature of the proposal.
   C. If the proxy voter's preference differs from the preference of a client who has delegated his voting powers, go with the client's preference.

3.   According to the Standards of Professional Conduct, Baldwin's *most appropriate* action regarding Teos Toys would be to:
   A. refuse to have any involvement with Teos because of a conflict of interest arising from the firm's other relationships with the company.
   B. complete an independent and objective analysis of Teos and issue a report accordingly.
   C. provide a copy of the research report to analysts at reputable research outfits and ask for some input.

4.   Was Baldwin in compliance with the recommended procedures of the CFA Institute Research Objectivity Standards (ROS) with regard to the timeliness of research reports on Patel, Inc.?
   A. Yes, because he announced that he had dropped coverage in a public appearance on television.
   B. Yes, a negative report from an auditor is sufficient justification for dropping coverage of a stock.
   C. No.

5.   If Walters wants the manual to satisfy the requirements and recommendations of the Code and Standards, which of the following instructions is *least appropriate* to include in the section on fair dealing?

   A. Whenever possible, disseminate investment recommendations to all clients at the same time.

   B. Execute all clients' requested trades promptly and without comment, regardless of the company's opinion on the stock being traded.

   C. Members of the investment-policy committee should not discuss possible changes in investment recommendations with anyone else in the firm until after an official decision has been made.

6.   Which method for dealing with the trading error is *most* consistent with the Code and Standards?

   A. Method 1.

   B. Method 2.

   C. Method 3.

Questions 7–12 relate to Dan Andrews.

Dan Andrews, CFA is the equity analyst for a large pension fund. One of the fund's holdings is Debian Corporation. After a period of rapid growth, Debian has underperformed its peers over the past two years. Debian's management has announced a change in ownership structure for part of its business, or possibly a disposal of part of the business. Several options are under consideration: a spin-off, a carve-out, or an asset sale. Andrews decides to research each of these options to understand the impact on Debian's business and their shareholders. He has read the following comments regarding the various methods:

Statement 1: Involves shares being issued to the general public.

Statement 2: Shareholders have a choice of holding onto the new shares automatically issued to them or disposing of the shares on the open market.

Statement 3: Shareholders will be more easily able to link executive compensation to the performance of the business involved.

Statement 4: The firm separates a portion of its operations from the parent company.

Statement 5: A new independent entity will be created that is completely distinct from the parent; the parent will lose all control of the business.

Debian's management announced in the last conference call that a potential buyer, Fedora, Inc., is interested in buying Ubuntu, one of Debian's divisions. Fedora has offered to pay $90 million cash to buy Ubuntu. Relevant information is provided in Exhibit 1.

Exhibit 1

Value of Ubuntu as a stand-alone business	$78 million
Value of Ubuntu to Debian	$85 million
Value of Fedora (5 million shares, $10 par)	$132 million
Value of Fedora and Ubuntu as a combined entity (post cash acquisition of Ubuntu)	$135 million

Alternatively, Fedora is prepared to offer to buy Ubuntu by directly issuing to the shareholders of Debian a total of 3 million $10 par value shares that will rank equally with its existing shares.

Andrews frequents continuing education seminars offered by his local CFA society. During one of these seminars, Andrews meets Jason Arnold, a corporate governance specialist. Andrews agrees with Arnold that a

©2017 Kaplan, Inc.

comprehensive equity analysis should include an analysis of corporate governance. Andrews, however, is unsure of the core attributes of an effective corporate governance system. Arnold states that he could recall two specific attributes:

Attribute 1: Description of rights and responsibilities of shareholders and other stakeholders.

Attribute 2: Fairness and equitable treatment in all dealings between managers, directors, and shareholders.

Among other companies that Andrews is researching, he has identified a potential acquisition target, Mandriva, Inc. Mandriva has enjoyed good growth over the past few years and is expected to continue to do so in the near future. Andrews wants to value Mandriva using both the comparable company method and the comparable transaction approach. Andrews obtains data on recent acquisitions of similar companies. Exhibit 2 summarizes this data:

Exhibit 2

- The mean price-to-book ratio of comparable firms is estimated to be 2 times, and the mean price-to-earnings ratio of the same comparable firms is 25 times.
- The mean acquisition price-to-book ratio of recent targets is estimated to be 2.80 times, and the mean price-to-earnings ratio of the same firms is 30 times.
- Mandriva's book value per share is $18, and EPS is $1.50.
- The mean takeover premium of recent acquisitions in the same industry as Mandriva is estimated to be 30%.

---

7. Which of the statements correctly reflect aspects of a carve-out?
    A. Statements 1, 4, and 5 only.
    B. Statements 1, 3, and 4 only.
    C. Statements 2, 3, and 4 only.

8. If Fedora pays $90 million cash for the purchase of Ubuntu from Debian, what will be the gain to Debian's and Fedora's shareholders?

	Debian's S/H	Fedora's S/H
A.	$5 million	$3 million
B.	$12 million	$5 million
C.	$12 million	$7 million

9. If Debian shareholders accept the stock offer by Fedora, the economic impact on them would be *closest* to:
    A. a gain of $630,000.
    B. a loss of $630,000.
    C. a loss of $1,612,500.

10. Under Fedora's stock offer, the economic impact on the current shareholders of Fedora is *closest* to:
    A. a loss of $7.5 million.
    B. a gain of $8.6 million.
    C. a gain of $1.6 million.

11. Are Arnold's attributes 1 and 2 of an effective corporate governance system correct?
    A. Both of these attributes are incorrect.
    B. Only one of these attributes is correct.
    C. Both of these attributes are correct.

12. Using the data collected by Andrews, the target takeover price per share of Mandriva under the comparable company analysis and under the comparable transaction analysis is *closest* to:

	Comparable company	Comparable transaction
A.	$24	$48
B.	$24	$50
C.	$48	$48

Questions 13–18 relate to Pacific Computer Components (PCC).

General Investments is considering the purchase of a significant stake in Pacific Computer Components (PCC). Although PCC has stable production output, the company is located in a developing country with an uncertain economic environment. Since the monetary environment is particularly worrisome, General has decided to approach the valuation of PCC from a free cash flow model using real growth rates. In real rate analysis, General uses a modified build-up method for calculating the required real return, specifically:

required real return = country real rate + industry adjustment +
                          company adjustment

Elias Sando, CFA, an analyst with General, estimates the following information for PCC:

Domestic inflation rate	=	8.738%
Nominal growth rate	=	12.000%
Real country return	=	3.000%
Industry adjustment	=	3.000%
Company adjustment	=	2.000%

Additionally, Exhibit 1 reports information from PCC's financial statements for the year just ended (stated in LC).

Exhibit 1: Selected Financial Statement Information for PCC

Investment in fixed capital	LC3,200,000
Investment in working capital	LC400,000
New borrowing	LC2,400,000
Debt repayment	LC2,000,000
Depreciation	LC3,500,000
Interest expense	LC5,000,000
Net income	LC7,000,000
Tax rate	34%
Dividends	LC0

PCC generally maintains relatively constant proportions of equity and debt financing and is expected to do so going forward.

Sando has gathered information on earnings before interest, taxes, depreciation, and amortization (EBITDA) and is contemplating its direct use in another cash flow approach aimed at valuing PCC. Consider the following two statements regarding EBITDA:

Statement 1: EBITDA is not a good proxy for free cash flow to the firm (FCFF) because it does not incorporate the importance of the depreciation tax shield, nor does it reflect the investment in working capital or in fixed capital.

Statement 2: EBITDA is also a poor proxy for FCFE.

13. Free cash flow to equity (FCFE) is *closest* to:
    A. LC7,300,000.
    B. LC8,400,000.
    C. LC10,200,000.

14. Free cash flow to the firm (FCFF) for PCC is *closest* to:
    A. LC7,300,000.
    B. LC8,100,000.
    C. LC10,200,000.

15. The current value of PCC equity using a FCFE model is *closest* to:
    A. LC150,380,000.
    B. LC173,420,000.
    C. LC215,150,000.

16. Suppose that PCC initiates a cash dividend, with a target payout ratio of 25% of net income. What is the *likely* magnitude of the effect of the new cash dividend and the net change in the outstanding debt on future FCFE, all else equal?
    A. The dividend has a large effect, and the debt change has a small effect.
    B. The dividend has a large effect, and the debt change has no effect.
    C. The dividend has no effect, and the debt change has a small effect.

17. Under the assumption that PCC maintains relatively constant proportions of equity and debt financing, the *most appropriate* valuation model is the:
    A. FCFF approach.
    B. FCFE approach.
    C. residual income approach.

18. Are the statements concerning EBITDA correct or incorrect?
    A. Only Statement 1 is correct.
    B. Only Statement 2 is correct.
    C. Both statements are correct.

Questions 19–24 relate to Global Drug World.

Carl Warner, CFA, has been asked to review the financial information of Global Drug World (GDW) in preparation for a possible takeover bid by rival competitor Consolidated Drugstores International (Consolidated). GDW has produced impressive results since going public via an initial public offering in 2008. Through a program of aggressive growth by acquisition, GDW is currently seen as a major player and a threat to Consolidated's own plans for growth and profitability. In preparation for his analysis, Warner has gathered the following financial data from GDW's year-end statements:

GDW Statement of Income for Year ended May 31, 2018

Sales	4,052,173
Expenses	
Cost of goods sold, general and operating expenses	3,735,397
Noncash charges	56,293
Interest on long-term debt	20,265
Other interest	5,223
	3,817,178
Income before income taxes	234,995
Income taxes	70,499
Net income	164,497
Earnings per share	0.72

Partial GDW Balance Sheet on May 31, 2018

Assets	
Current assets (excluding cash)	
Accounts receivable	284,762
Inventories	490,755
Prepaid expenses	23,743
Total current assets (excluding cash)	799,260
Property, plant, and equipment	687,890
Other assets	236,417
Liabilities	
Current liabilities (excluding notes payable)	
Accounts payable and accrued liabilities	296,564
Other	100,039
Total current liabilities (excluding notes payable)	396,603
Long-term debt	262,981
Other liabilities	15,484

Additional Information	
Risk-free rate	4.5%
WACC	7.5%
2018 working capital investment	$7,325
2018 dividends	$82,248
Beta	1.10
Investment in fixed capital in 2018	$143,579
Market risk premium	5%
Total equity May 31, 2017	$1,019,869
Principal repayment of long-term debt in 2018	$33,275
Notes payable issued in 2018	$5,866
2018 change in liabilities	$27,409
Tax rate	30%

As part of his analysis, Warner needs to forecast the free cash flow to the firm (FCFF) for 2019. The best information he has points to an increase in sales of 6%. The earnings before interest and tax (EBIT) margin is not expected to change from the rate of 6.4% achieved in 2018. Additional fixed capital spending is expected to be $36,470. Investment in net working capital is expected to be $24,313. Moreover, Warner notes that the only noncash charge is depreciation, which he estimates will be $60,000.

Warner has been asked to analyze the effect each of the following corporate events, if taken during 2019, would have on GDW's free cash flow to equity (FCFE):

- 20% increase in dividends per share.
- Repurchase of 25% of the firm's outstanding shares using cash.
- New common share offering that would increase shares outstanding by 30%.
- New issue of convertible bonds that are not callable for five years and would increase the level of debt by 10%.

19.   The 2018 free cash flow to the firm (FCFF) for Global Drug World (GDW) in dollars is *closest* to:
      A. $87,728.
      B. $95,374.
      C. $102,378.

20. By how much (in dollars) does GDW's FCFF exceed its free cash flow to equity (FCFE) in 2018?
    A. $9,567.
    B. $45,251.
    C. $52,897.

21. The cost of equity and the sustainable growth rate (using beginning equity) are *closest* to:

	Cost of equity	Sustainable growth rate
A.	6%	16%
B.	10%	8%
C.	10%	16%

22. The 2019 estimate of FCFF is *closest* to:
    A. $191,646.
    B. $210,329.
    C. $215,329.

23. Warner determines that on a per-share basis, the FCFE for GDW in 2018 is $0.19. Further analysis suggests that FCFE per share will grow by $0.02 in each of the next two years before leveling off to a long-term growth rate of 5%. The current value of one share of GDW's equity is *closest* to:
    A. $4.37.
    B. $7.15.
    C. $13.49.

24. Which corporate event that Warner is analyzing is *likely* to have the largest effect on FCFE in 2019?
    A. Share repurchase.
    B. Share offering.
    C. Convertible bond issue.

Questions 25–30 relate to Lee Nguyen Investments.

Marie LeBlanc, CFA, is an analyst at Lee Nguyen Investments, an international equities investment firm. LeBlanc has been asked to value two European cosmetics companies, Schön AG and Hermosa S.A.

The beauty products industry is a mature industry with few competitors. One segment that is growing is luxury skin care; while the cosmetics industry is expected to grow at a steady rate of 3.5%, the luxury skin care segment is expected to grow at 5.5%.

Schön AG, based in Frankfort, Germany, is the largest company in the luxury skin care segment of the cosmetics industry. Schön is considered a very stable company within the cosmetics industry and the luxury skin care segment. Schön's equity beta is 1.00.

LeBlanc collects selected financial information from Schön's income statement and cash flow statement (for the last fiscal year) and from Schön's balance sheet (for the last 2 fiscal year ends). The information is shown in Exhibit 1. Negative numbers are indicated in parentheses. There is no preferred stock, and no long-term asset sales occurred in 20X9.

Exhibit 1: Selected Schön Financial Information (€ millions except for rates and ratios.)

Income Statement	20X9	Balance Sheet	20X8	20X9
Revenue	4,250	Total current assets	2,408	2,577
EBITDA	1,461	Net PPE	3,794	4,150
Operating income	1,169	Notes payable	600	644
Interest expense	150	Long-term debt	2,020	2,070
Income tax rate	30%	Total liabilities	3,210	3,378
Dividends	357	Total equity	2,992	3,349

Other Information	20X9
CF from operations	1,042
CF from investing	(648)
Risk-free rate	2.50%
After-tax cost of debt	4.50%
Cost of equity	8.50%
Target D/E Ratio	1.00

Hermosa S.A., based in Barcelona, Spain, is the third largest company in the luxury skin care segment of the cosmetics industry. Hermosa is considered a growth company within the cosmetics industry and the luxury skin care segment. Hermosa has not issued bonds and all of Hermosa's debt is considered short and intermediate term. For the fiscal year 20X9, FCFF is €143 million and FCFE is €136.23 million. Hermosa pays no dividends. Hermosa's earnings are expected to grow at 14.0% for three years and then at the expected overall rate of growth in the luxury skin care segment. Hermosa's equity beta is 1.20. The risk-free rate is 2.5%. Hermosa's target weight for debt is 25.0%.

LeBlanc gathers additional information on the various companies in luxury skin care industry as shown in Exhibit 2.

Exhibit 2: Luxury Skin Care Stocks

Company	Price per share	Shares outstanding (in millions)	Earnings (trailing twelve months) (in millions)
Schön	€15.42	1,000	€713
Epiderm	€14.95	500	€345
Hermosa	€22.78	200	€193
Radiance	€18.50	100	€75
Bello	€24.78	50	€24

The trailing price-to-earnings ratio for the luxury skin care segment is 22.9X.

Elizabeth Nguyen, one of the partners at Lee Nguyen Investments, approaches LeBlanc about a client interested in buying Hermosa S.A. Nguyen asks LeBlanc about the different methods LeBlanc used to value Hermosa as a buyout possibility.

LeBlanc states that she used three different approaches in her report:

Approach 1: Dividend discount model.

Approach 2: Free cash flow to the firm model.

Approach 3: Trailing price-to-earnings multiples.

25. The free cash flow to equity for Schön AG for 20X9 is *closest* to:
    A. €439 million.
    B. €488 million.
    C. €499 million.

26. Assuming that the growth rate of Schön earnings is equal to the overall cosmetics industry growth rate, the value of the firm is *closest* to:
    A. €17.2 billion.
    B. €33.6 billion.
    C. €49.9 billion.

27. The estimated value of Hermosa stock using FCFE valuation is *closest* to:
    A. €19.70.
    B. €21.40.
    C. €22.10.

28. If the estimated value of Schön's equity based on free cash flow to equity is €17.1 billion, then based on current market price, Schön's stock is:
    A. overvalued.
    B. undervalued.
    C. fairly valued.

29. Using the luxury skin care P/E ratio as the benchmark, Hermosa is *best described* as:
    A. overvalued.
    B. undervalued.
    C. fairly valued.

30. The best approach to valuing Hermosa for a potential acquirer is *most likely*:
    A. Approach #1—Dividend discount model.
    B. Approach #2—Free cash flow to the firm model.
    C. Approach #3—Trailing price-to-earnings multiples.

Questions 31–36 relate to Amie Lear.

Amie Lear, CFA, is a quantitative analyst employed by a brokerage firm. She has been assigned by her supervisor to cover a number of different equity and debt investments. One of the investments is Taylor, Inc. (Taylor), a manufacturer of a wide range of children's toys. Based on her extensive analysis, she determines that her expected return on the stock, given Taylor's risks, is 10%. In applying the capital asset pricing model (CAPM), the result is a 12% rate of return.

For her analysis of the returns of Devon, Inc. (Devon), a manufacturer of high-end sports apparel, Lear intends to use the Fama-French model (FFM). Devon is a small-cap growth stock that has traded at a low market-to-book value in recent years. Lear's analysis has provided a wealth of quantitative information to consider. The return on a value-weighted market index minus the risk-free rate is 5.5%, the small-cap return premium is 3.1%, the value return premium is 2.2%, and the liquidity premium is 3.3%. The risk-free rate is 3.4%. The market, size, relative value, and liquidity betas for Devon are 0.7, –0.3, 1.4, and 1.2, respectively. In estimating the appropriate equity risk premium, Lear has chosen to use the Gordon growth model.

Lear's assistant, Doug Saunders, presents her with a report on macroeconomic multifactor models that includes the following two statements:

Statement 1: Business cycle risk represents the unexpected change in the difference between the return of risky corporate bonds and government bonds.

Statement 2: Confidence risk represents the unexpected change in the level of real business activity.

Lear is also attempting to determine the most appropriate method for determining the required return for Densmore, Inc. (Densmore), a closely held company that is considering a debt issue within the next year. The company has not previously issued debt securities to the public, relying instead on bank financing. She realizes that there are a number of models to consider, including the CAPM, multifactor models, and build-up models.

31.   Based on Lear's analysis, Taylor's stock is *most likely* to be:
      A. correctly valued.
      B. overvalued.
      C. undervalued.

32. According to the FFM, the estimate of the required return for Devon is *closest* to:
    A. 9.4%.
    B. 11.8%.
    C. 13.4%.

33. Lear's choice of the Gordon growth model is an example of which of the following types of estimates of the equity risk premium?
    A. Historical estimate.
    B. Forward-looking estimate.
    C. Macroeconomic model estimate.

34. Which of the following approaches/methods is *most appropriate* for Lear to consider in determining the required return for Densmore?
    A. Build-up method.
    B. Risk premium approach.
    C. Bond-yield plus risk premium method.

35. Are Saunders's statements regarding the macroeconomic multifactor models correct?
    A. Both statements are incorrect.
    B. Only Statement 1 is correct.
    C. Only Statement 2 is correct.

36. Which of the following statements regarding the models used to estimate the required return is *most accurate*?
    A. A strength of the capital asset pricing model (CAPM) is that it usually has high explanatory power.
    B. A strength of multifactor models is their relative simplicity and ease of calculation.
    C. A weakness of build-up models is that they typically use historical values as estimates that may not be relevant to current market conditions.

Questions 37–42 relate to Ranjit Dhami and Paul Stamper.

Ranjit Dhami has just joined Apex Bank NA as an intern in the bond trading department. Sue Jorgenson, Dhami's immediate supervisor, provides him with the current par rate curve for government bonds shown in Exhibit 1.

Exhibit 1: Selected Par Rates

Maturity	Par Rate
1	1.50%
2	2.00%
3	2.25%

A binomial interest rate tree with a 20% volatility assumption is shown in Exhibit 2.

Exhibit 2: Binomial Interest Rate Tree

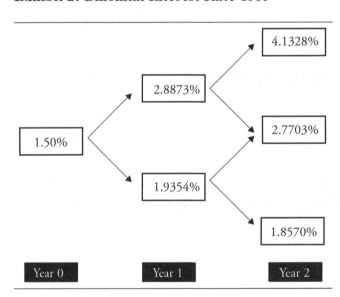

Paul Stamper, one of the bond traders at Apex, shows Dhami information about several trades currently being evaluated. Exhibit 3 shows information on two of the bonds.

Exhibit 3: Selected Information on Potential Trades

Characteristic	Bond A	Bond B
Maturity	3 years	2 years
Option	Callable at par in 1 year	Putable at par in 1 year
Coupon	2%	1.50%
Par Value	$100	$100

Stamper asks Dhami the following questions:

Question 1: Which bond in Exhibit 3 is most likely to exhibit negative convexity?

Question 2: For a given decline in interest rate, which bond is most likely to have lower upside potential?

37. Using the information in Exhibit 1, the three-year spot rate is *closest* to:
A. 2.26%.
B. 2.56%.
C. 2.62%.

38. Using the information in Exhibit 1, the one-year forward rate two years from now is *closest* to:
A. 2.25%.
B. 2.39%.
C. 2.77%.

39. If the three-year forward price of a three-year zero-coupon bond is $0.9151 (per $1 par), the price today of a six-year zero-coupon bond should be *closest* to:
A. $0.7899.
B. $0.8558.
C. $0.9311.

40. The price of bond A in Exhibit 3 is *most accurately* described as being sensitive to shifts in:
A. the one-year par rate only.
B. the three-year par rate only.
C. both the one-year and three-year par rates.

41. The *most accurate* answers to Stamper's questions are:

	Question 1	Question 2
A.	Bond A	Bond A
B.	Bond A	Bond B
C.	Bond B	Bond A

42. Using the rates in Exhibit 2 and the information in Exhibit 3, the value of bond A is *closest* to:
    A. $90.63.
    B. $95.68.
    C. $99.28.

Questions 43–48 relate to Pablo Ramiro, CFA.

Pablo Ramiro, CFA, has just been hired by Alto High Investments (AHI) in its equity portfolios management division. Ramiro has extensive experience in U.S. equity markets, having traded stocks as well as stock options for several years in his previous role.

One reason for the hiring is that AHI's CIO is interested in the use of protective puts to mitigate risk in equity portfolios. Specifically, Ramiro has been asked to demonstrate how a protective put could be used to hedge the risk of AHI's holding in Allavate, Inc. (ALL), a pharmaceutical company that has had a very strong run on the back of several successful anti-allergy drugs.

However, AHI is concerned that ALL's product pipeline has a relatively small number of new drugs, and any downward correction in the general market could have a significant negative impact on ALL's stock price. AHI's analysts have estimated that the stock's price will fall to $38.80 by the expiry of the CBOE contract.

Ramiro has been asked to calculate the expected loss of a protective put strategy using the expected stock price and either Dec 38 or Dec 39 puts as shown in Exhibit 1.

Exhibit 1: ALL Stock and CBOE Option Prices

Current Stock Price:	$41.28
Size Holding:	140,000 shares
Dec 39 Put Price:	$4.20
Dec 38 Put Price:	$3.62

AHI also manages a growth portfolio, currently valued at $10,000,000. The growth portfolio is very similar in composition to the S&P 500 Index, which currently stands at 2,250. Due to an uncertain political climate, AHI is concerned that this portfolio might experience a high degree of volatility over the next 12 months. As a result, the firm is considering using derivatives to hedge the portfolio's exposure.

Ramiro suggests two possible approaches to hedge the risk:

Approach 1

Enter into a one-year total return equity swap, with quarterly settlement dates paying the equity return and receiving 90-day LIBOR. Payments on the swap would be netted, except in the case where the equity reference portfolio falls in value. In this case, AHI would have to pay 90-day LIBOR plus the fall in equity value.

Approach 2

Hedge the risk by selling equity index futures contracts. The number of contracts required is dependent upon the portfolio value and the multiplier in the futures contracts. Using S&P 500 futures contracts with a multiplier of $250, the growth portfolio could be hedged by selling 40,000 contracts.

Although the volatility presents a risk to the portfolio, Ramiro also sees it as an opportunity. He is convinced that the health care sector will indeed experience a high degree of volatility, but the direction of price movement is entirely dependent on the results of an upcoming November election. He believes that the chances of a significant price increase or decrease are almost equal, and, as such, has suggested a volatility trade using December options.

He has researched options prices on Medprods, Inc., a stock AHI has no current holding in. Relevant pricing data along with current stock price is shown in Exhibit 2.

Exhibit 2: Information about Medprods Inc. Stock and Options

Current stock price = $79

Option	Call Price	Call Delta	Put Price	Put Delta
Nov 76	$5.01	0.68	$1.76	−0.32
Nov 78	$3.83	0.58	$2.58	−0.42
Nov 80	$2.85	0.48	$3.58	−0.52
Nov 82	$2.06	0.39	$4.79	−0.61
Dec 76	$5.73	0.66	$2.73	−0.34
Dec 78	$4.60	0.58	$3.22	−0.42
Dec 80	$3.62	0.50	$4.23	−0.50
Dec 82	$2.80	0.42	$5.39	−0.58

Note: *Options expire on the third Friday of each month*

Ramiro believes that by using December call options with a current intrinsic value of $1.00 and appropriate put options, he can set up a long straddle that will guarantee a positive profit as long as the stock price moves in either direction by at least 10%.

Ramiro's colleague, Ruben Hendrix, covers Medprods and is bullish about the company in the very near term. But Hendrix believes that its latest drug is unlikely to pass its final FDA test and the results will be released on December 10. He is, therefore, suggesting a calendar spread strategy, using a November call option with a strike price of 80, and the corresponding December option to take advantage of the anticipated drop in price after the test results are announced.

Finally, Ramiro wants to demonstrate to his supervisor how synthetic options can be created using the underlying asset and another option. As an example, he demonstrates using exhibit 2 that a synthetic call option on Medprods, Inc. could be created using the underlying stock and a put option with the same maturity and strike as the call. To show how the synthetic option he created works, he demonstrates that for a $10.00 increase in the stock price, his synthetic position moves by $4.20, as does the call option.

43. The difference in expected loss from protective put strategies using Dec 38 and Dec 39 puts is *closest* to:
   A. $53,000 and is smaller using Dec 38 puts.
   B. $59,000 and is smaller using Dec 39 puts.
   C. $28,000 and is smaller using Dec 38 puts.

44. Approach 1 to hedging the growth portfolio is *most likely* described:
   A. correctly.
   B. incorrectly as AHI would need to enter as the floating rate receiver.
   C. incorrectly as AHI would receive the floating rate plus the negative equity return.

45. Approach 2 to hedging the growth portfolio is *most likely* described:
   A. correctly.
   B. incorrectly with regard to the direction of the trade.
   C. incorrectly with regard to the number of contracts.

46. Ramiro's comments on his suggested long straddle strategy are *most likely*:
   A. incorrect as a decrease in price of only 10% would lead to a loss.
   B. incorrect as an increase in price of only 10% would lead to a loss.
   C. correct.

47. The strategy suggested by Hendrix is *best* described as:
   A. a long calendar spread with an initial cash outflow of $1.38.
   B. a short calendar spread with an initial cash inflow of $0.77.
   C. a short calendar spread with an initial cash outflow of $6.47.

48. In Ramiro's demonstration of a synthetic call option, he *most likely* combined a long position in the underlying stock with a:
   A. short Nov 78 put.
   B. long Dec 78 put.
   C. long Dec 82 put.

Questions 49–54 relate to Stan Loper.

Stan Loper is unfamiliar with the Black-Scholes-Merton (BSM) option pricing model and plans to use a two-period binomial model to value some call options. The stock of Arbor Industries pays no dividends and currently trades for $45. The up-move factor for the stock is 1.15, while the down factor is 0.87, and the risk-free rate is 4%. He is considering buying two-period European style options on Arbor Industries with a strike price of $40. The delta of these options over the first period is 0.83.

Loper is curious about the effect of time on the value of the calls in the binomial model, so he also calculates the value of a one-period European style call option on Arbor stock with a strike price of 40.

Loper is also interested in using the BSM model to price European and American call and put options. He is concerned, however, whether the assumptions necessary to derive the model are realistic. The assumptions he is particularly concerned about are:

- The volatility of the option value is known and constant.
- Stock prices are lognormally distributed.
- The continuous risk-free rate is known and constant.

Loper would also like to value options on Rapid Repair, Inc., common stock, but Rapid pays dividends, so Loper is uncertain what the effect will be on the value of the options. Loper uses the two-period model to value long positions in the Rapid Repair call and put options without accounting for the fact that Rapid Repair pays common dividends.

49. The value of a two-period 40 call on Arbor Industries stock is *closest* to:
    A. $6.65.
    B. $8.86.
    C. $9.21.

50. The position in calls necessary to hedge a long position in 1,000 shares of stock over the first period is *closest* to:
    A. short 830 calls.
    B. short 1,150 calls.
    C. short 1,205 calls.

51. The value of the one-period 40 call on Arbor stock is *closest* to:
    A. $6.65.
    B. $6.86.
    C. $7.15.

52. The difference in value between the European 40 calls and otherwise identical American 40 calls is *closest* to:
    A. –$1.43.
    B. $0.00.
    C. $1.92.

53. Are the BSM assumptions listed correctly?
    A. No, because stock prices are assumed to be normally distributed.
    B. No, because the expected return on the stock is assumed to be known and constant.
    C. No, because the volatility of the return on the underlying stock is assumed to be known and constant.

54. When Loper failed to account for Rapid Repair dividends, did he *likely* overvalue the calls or the puts?
    A. The calls and the puts are overvalued.
    B. Only the calls are overvalued.
    C. Only the puts are overvalued.

Questions 55–60 relate to Sara Robinson and Marvin Gardner.

Sara Robinson and Marvin Gardner are considering an opportunity to start their own money management firm. Their conversation leads them to a discussion on establishing a portfolio management process and investment policy statements. Robinson makes the following statements:

Statement 1:   Our only real objective as portfolio managers is to maximize the returns to our clients.

Statement 2:   If we are managing only a fraction of a client's total wealth, it is the client's responsibility, not ours, to determine how their investments are allocated among asset classes.

Statement 3:   When developing a client's strategic asset allocation, portfolio managers have to consider capital market expectations.

In response, Gardner makes the following statements:

Statement 4:   While return maximization is important for a given level of risk, we also need to consider the client's tolerance for risk.

Statement 5:   We'll let our clients worry about the tax implications of their investments; our time is better spent on finding undervalued assets.

Statement 6:   Since we expect our investor's objectives to be constantly changing, we will need to evaluate their investment policy statements on an annual basis at a minimum.

Robinson wants to focus on younger clientele with the expectation that the new firm will be able to retain the clients for a long time and create long-term profitable relationships. While Gardner felt it was important to develop long-term relationships, he wants to go after older, high-net-worth clients.

55.   Are Statements 1 and 4 consistent with the appropriate method of developing portfolio objectives?
   A.   Both statements are correct.
   B.   Only Statement 1 is correct.
   C.   Only Statement 4 is correct.

56.   Which one of the following factors is the *least likely* to affect the individual investor's ability to accept risk?
   A.   Required spending needs.
   B.   Financial strength.
   C.   Behavioral factors.

57. Are Statements 2 and 3 correct when considering asset allocation?
    A. Both statements are correct.
    B. Only Statement 2 is correct.
    C. Only Statement 3 is correct.

58. Robinson is uncomfortable with Gardner's position on taxes but she can't specifically identify the source of the discomfort. Which of the following statements *least accurately* reflects proper consideration of tax effects on the investment process?
    A. Because investors are ultimately concerned with after-tax returns, it is important that investors consider their own marginal tax rates and the security's tax status when making any investment decision.
    B. Pensions and endowment funds are typically tax-exempt investors and, therefore, are less concerned with tax considerations.
    C. Investors should rely on accountants or other advisors for tax advice; portfolio managers should focus on finding undervalued investments and not be distracted by tax considerations.

59. The *least* important portfolio constraints for individuals are:
    A. legal and regulatory constraints.
    B. investment horizon constraints.
    C. unique needs.

60. In addition to Statement 6, an appropriately developed investment policy statement is *least likely* to address which of the following elements?
    A. Transportability so as to minimize any disruptions if new managers assume responsibility for the portfolio.
    B. Assurances of minimum returns so clients will be better able to ensure their financial goals are met over the long run.
    C. Barriers to short-term strategy shifts driven by panic or overconfidence stemming from portfolio performance or changes in market environments.

End of Morning Session

Exam 1
Afternoon Session

Question	Topic	Minutes (Points)
61 to 66	Ethics	18
67 to 72	Quantitative Methods	18
73 to 78	Economics	18
79 to 84	Financial Reporting and Analysis	18
85 to 90	Financial Reporting and Analysis	18
91 to 96	Financial Reporting and Analysis	18
97 to 102	Financial Reporting and Analysis	18
103 to 108	Corporate Finance	18
109 to 114	Fixed Income	18
115 to 120	Alternative Investments	18

61.	(A)	(B)	(C)		101.	(A)	(B)	(C)
62.	(A)	(B)	(C)		102.	(A)	(B)	(C)
63.	(A)	(B)	(C)		103.	(A)	(B)	(C)
64.	(A)	(B)	(C)		104.	(A)	(B)	(C)
65.	(A)	(B)	(C)		105.	(A)	(B)	(C)
66.	(A)	(B)	(C)		106.	(A)	(B)	(C)
67.	(A)	(B)	(C)		107.	(A)	(B)	(C)
68.	(A)	(B)	(C)		108.	(A)	(B)	(C)
69.	(A)	(B)	(C)		109.	(A)	(B)	(C)
70.	(A)	(B)	(C)		110.	(A)	(B)	(C)
71.	(A)	(B)	(C)		111.	(A)	(B)	(C)
72.	(A)	(B)	(C)		112.	(A)	(B)	(C)
73.	(A)	(B)	(C)		113.	(A)	(B)	(C)
74.	(A)	(B)	(C)		114.	(A)	(B)	(C)
75.	(A)	(B)	(C)		115.	(A)	(B)	(C)
76.	(A)	(B)	(C)		116.	(A)	(B)	(C)
77.	(A)	(B)	(C)		117.	(A)	(B)	(C)
78.	(A)	(B)	(C)		118.	(A)	(B)	(C)
79.	(A)	(B)	(C)		119.	(A)	(B)	(C)
80.	(A)	(B)	(C)		120.	(A)	(B)	(C)
81.	(A)	(B)	(C)					
82.	(A)	(B)	(C)					
83.	(A)	(B)	(C)					
84.	(A)	(B)	(C)					
85.	(A)	(B)	(C)					
86.	(A)	(B)	(C)					
87.	(A)	(B)	(C)					
88.	(A)	(B)	(C)					
89.	(A)	(B)	(C)					
90.	(A)	(B)	(C)					
91.	(A)	(B)	(C)					
92.	(A)	(B)	(C)					
93.	(A)	(B)	(C)					
94.	(A)	(B)	(C)					
95.	(A)	(B)	(C)					
96.	(A)	(B)	(C)					
97.	(A)	(B)	(C)					
98.	(A)	(B)	(C)					
99.	(A)	(B)	(C)					
100.	(A)	(B)	(C)					

Exam 1
Afternoon Session

Questions 61–66 relate to Connor Burton.

Connor Burton, CFA, is the managing partner for United Partners, a small investment advisory firm that employs three investment professionals and currently has approximately $250 million of assets under management. The client base of United Partners is varied, and accounts range in size from small retirement accounts to a $30 million private school endowment. In addition to Burton's administrative responsibilities as the managing partner at United, he also serves as an investment advisor to several clients. Because United Partners is a small firm, the company does not employ any research analysts but instead obtains its investment research products and services from two national brokerage firms, which in turn execute all client trades for United Partners. The arrangement with the two brokers has enabled United to assure its clients that the firm will always seek the best execution for them by having both brokers competitively bid for United's business.

A prospective client, Harold Crossley, has approached Burton about shifting some of his personal assets under management from MoneyCorp to United Partners. Burton provides Crossley with a packet of marketing information that Burton developed himself. The packet contains five years of historical performance data for a value weighted composite of the firm's discretionary accounts. Burton states that the composite's management style and performance results are representative of the management style and returns that United can be expected to achieve for Crossley. Also included in the information packet are brief bios on each of United's three investment professionals. Crossley notices that all three of United's investment professionals are described as "CFA charterholders," but he is not familiar with the designation. In response to Crossley's inquiry, Burton explains the significance of the program by stating that the designation, which is only awarded after passing three rigorous exams and obtaining the requisite years of work experience, represents a commitment to the highest standards of ethical and professional conduct.

As a condition of moving his account to United Partners, Crossley insists that all of his trades be executed through his brother-in-law, a broker for Security Bank. Security Bank is a large, New York-based broker/dealer but is not one of the two brokerage firms with which United currently does business. Burton contacts Crossley's brother-in-law and determines that Security Bank's trade execution is competitive, but Crossley's account alone would not generate enough volume to warrant any soft dollar arrangement for research materials. However, Crossley's brother-in-law does offer for Security Bank to pay a referral fee to Burton for directing any of United's clients to Security Bank's retail banking division. To bring Crossley on as a client, Burton agrees to the arrangement. Going forward, Burton will use Security Bank to execute all of Crossley's trades.

Several months later, Burton is invited to a road show for an initial public offering (IPO) for SolutionWare, a software company. Security Bank is serving as lead underwriter on SolutionWare's IPO. Burton attends the meeting, which is led by two investment bankers and one software industry research analyst from Security Bank who covers SolutionWare. Burton notes that the bankers from Security Bank have included detailed financial statements for SolutionWare in the offering prospectus and also disclosed that Security Bank provides a warehouse line of credit to SolutionWare. After the meeting, Burton calls Crossley to recommend the purchase of SolutionWare equity. Crossley heeds Burton's advice and tells him to purchase 5,000 shares. Before placing Crossley's order, Burton reads the SolutionWare marketing materials and performs a detailed analysis of expected future earnings and other key factors for the investment decision. Burton determines that the offering would be a suitable investment for his own retirement portfolio. United Partners, being a small firm, has no formal written policy regarding trade allocation, employee participation in equity offerings, or established blackout periods for employee trading. Burton adds his order to Crossley's order and places a purchase order for the combined number of shares with Security Bank. Burton is later notified that the offering was oversubscribed, and United Partners was only able to obtain roughly 75% of the desired number of shares. To be fair, Burton allocates the shares on a pro-rata basis between Crossley's account and his own retirement account. When Burton notifies Crossley of the situation, Crossley is nonetheless pleased to have a position, though smaller than requested, in such a "hot" offering.

61. Did the marketing materials presented to Crossley by Burton violate Standard III(D) Performance Presentation or Standard VII(B) Reference to CFA Institute, the CFA Designation, and the CFA Program?
   A. Standard III(D) only.
   B. Standard VII(B) only.
   C. Both Standard III(D) and Standard VII(B) are violated.

62. According to the CFA Institute Standards of Professional Conduct, the trading arrangement between Burton and Security Bank is *most likely*:
   A. a violation because the practice of directed brokerage violates the member's duty of loyalty to the client.
   B. a violation because although Security Bank's execution is competitive, Burton will not be able to always obtain the best execution for his client.
   C. not a violation because the brokerage is the property of the client.

©2017 Kaplan, Inc.

63. According to CFA Institute Standards of Professional Conduct, which of the following statements *best* describes the circumstances under which Burton may enter into the referral agreement with Security Bank? Burton may enter into the agreement:
   A. under no circumstances.
   B. only after receiving written permission from clients.
   C. only after fully disclosing the referral arrangement to clients and prospective clients.

64. With respect to the road show meeting regarding the initial public offering of SolutionWare, did Security Bank comply with the requirements and recommendations of the CFA Institute Research Objectivity Standards?
   A. No, because it publicly revealed that it also provides corporate finance services for SolutionWare.
   B. No, because it failed to provide Burton with adequate information to make an investment decision.
   C. No, because it allowed an analyst to participate in a marketing road show for a company that he covers.

65. According to CFA Institute Standards of Professional Conduct, Burton's recommendation to Crossley that he purchase shares of the SolutionWare initial public offering is *most likely*:
   A. in violation of Standard III(C) Suitability for not determining the appropriateness of the investment for the portfolio and Standard I(B) Independence and Objectivity for not making the investment recommendation to all of his clients at the same time.
   B. in violation of Standard V(A) Diligence and Reasonable Basis for not thoroughly analyzing the investment before making a recommendation and in violation of Standard III(C) Suitability for not determining the appropriateness of the investment for the portfolio.
   C. in violation of Standard V(A) Diligence and Reasonable Basis for not thoroughly analyzing the investment before making a recommendation and in violation of Standard I(B) Independence and Objectivity for not making the investment recommendation to all of his clients at the same time.

66. According to CFA Institute Standards of Professional Conduct, Burton's participation in the SolutionWare offering *most likely*:
   A. is in violation of the Standards because his actions adversely affected the interests of Crossley.
   B. is in violation of the Standards because he did not disclose his participation in the offering to Security Bank.
   C. is not in violation of the Standards since the shares obtained in the IPO were distributed equitably on a pro-rata basis.

Questions 67–72 relate to Ernie Smith.

Ernie Smith and Jamal Sims are analysts with the firm of Madison Consultants. Madison provides statistical modeling and advice to portfolio managers throughout the United States and Canada.

In an effort to estimate future cash flows and value the Canadian stock market, Smith has been examining the country's aggregate retail sales. He runs two autoregressive regression models in an attempt to determine whether there are any patterns in the data, utilizing nine years of unadjusted monthly retail sales data. One model uses a lag one variable and the other adds a lag twelve variable. The results of both regressions are shown in Exhibits 1 and 2.

Exhibit 1: Canadian Autoregressive Model with Lag 1

Multiple R	0.91
R-Square	0.83
Adjusted R-Square	0.83
Standard Error	17,252.76
Observations	108.00

ANOVA

	df	SS	MS	F	Significance F
Regression	1.00	150,813,197,793	150,813,197,793	506.67	0.00
Residual	106.00	31,551,711,544	297,657,656		
Total	107.00	182,364,909,338			

	Coefficients	Standard Error	T-stat	P-value
Intercept	21,750.16	10,379.77	2.10	0.04
Lag 1	0.92	0.04	22.51	0.00

Exhibit 2: Canadian Autoregressive Model with Lag 1 and Lag 12

Regression Statistics for 2nd Regression	
Multiple R	0.96
R-Square	0.93
Adjusted R-Square	0.92
Standard Error	11,336.27
Observations	108.00

ANOVA

	df	SS	MS	F	Significance F
Regression	2.00	168,871,246,751	84,435,623,375	657.03	<0.01
Residual	105.00	13,493,662,586	128,511,072		
Total	107.00	182,364,909,338			

	Coefficients	Standard Error	T-stat	P-value
Intercept	−24,861.28	7,872.56	−3.16	<0.01
Lag 1	0.30	0.06	5.22	<0.01
Lag 12	0.84	0.07	11.85	<0.01

Sims has been assigned the task of valuing the U.S. stock market and uses data similar to the data that Smith uses for Canada. He decides, however, that the data should be transformed. He takes the natural log of the data and uses it in the following model:

$$\Delta \ln \text{sales}_t = b_0 + b_1 \, \Delta \ln \text{sales}_{t-1}$$

Parameter estimates for the autoregressive model and the actual data for the two most recent months are shown in Exhibit 3.

Exhibit 3: U.S. Autoregressive Model

Intercept	0.052
Lag 1 coefficient	0.684
Actual sales one month ago (−1)	6,270
Actual sales two months ago (−2)	6,184

Smith and Sims are concerned that the data for Canadian retail sales may be more appropriately modeled with an ARCH process. Smith states, that in order to find out, he would take the residuals from the original autoregressive model for Canadian retail sales and then square them.

Sims states that these residuals would then be regressed against the Canadian retail sales data using the following equation: $e_t = b_0 + b_1 X_t$, where e represents the residual terms from the original regression and X represents the Canadian retail sales data. If b_1 is statistically different from zero, then the regression model contains an ARCH process.

Smith also examines the quarterly inflation data for an emerging market over the past nine years. He models the data using an autoregressive model with a lag one independent variable, which he finds is statistically different from zero. He wonders whether he should also include lag two and lag four terms, given the magnitude of the autocorrelations of the residuals shown in Exhibit 4, assuming a 5% significance level. The critical t-values, assuming a 5% significance level and 35 degrees of freedom, are 2.03 for a two-tail test and 1.69 for a one-tail test.

Exhibit 4: Emerging Market Autoregressive Model

Lag	Autocorrelation
1	0.0829
2	0.1293
3	0.0227
4	0.1882

Sims is investigating the performance of 5-year European and British bonds based on the actions of the U.S. Federal Reserve. He uses the U.S. Federal Funds rate. The two regressions he uses are:

$$BY_{E,t} = b_0 + b_1 FF_{US,t}$$

$$BY_{B,t} = b_0 + b_1 FF_{US,t}$$

where: FF is the Federal Funds rate in the United States (US), and BY is the bond yield in the European Union (E) and Great Britain (B).

Before he runs this regression, he investigates the characteristics of the dependent and independent variables. He finds that the Federal Funds rate in the United States and the bond yield in Great Britain have a unit root but that the bond yield in the European Union does not. Furthermore, the Federal Funds rate in the United States and the bond yield in Great Britain are cointegrated, but the Federal Funds rate in the United States and the bond yield in the European Union are not.

67. Which of the following models would be the *best* formulation for the Canadian retail sales data?
    A. $X_t = b_0 + b_1 X_{t-1}$.
    B. $X_t = b_1 X_{t-1} + b_2 X_{t-12}$.
    C. $X_t = b_0 + b_1 X_{t-1} + b_2 X_{t-12}$.

68. The estimate of forecasted sales for the United States this month, using Sims's model, is *closest* to:
    A. $6,329.
    B. $6,453.
    C. $6,667.

69. Are the comments of Smith and Sims on the construction of an ARCH model correct?
    A. Both comments are correct.
    B. Only Smith is correct.
    C. Only Sims is correct.

70. Regarding Smith's emerging market regression, should lag two and lag four terms be included in the regression?
    A. Neither Lag should be included.
    B. Only Lag 2 should be included.
    C. Only Lag 4 should be included.

71. Will Sims's regressions of European and British bond yields on the U.S. Federal Funds rate produce valid results?
    A. Neither Regression is valid.
    B. Only Regression 1 is valid.
    C. Only Regression 2 is valid.

72. Which of the following is the *appropriate* test for cointegration?
    A. Breusch-Pagan.
    B. Durbin-Watson.
    C. Engle-Granger.

Questions 73–78 relate to Frank Hoskins and Paul Lanning.

Frank Hoskins and Paul Lanning are economists for a large U.S. investment advisory firm, Platinum Advisors. Hoskins and Lanning use their independent research on U.S. stocks and international stocks to provide advice for the firm's network of advisors. As the senior economist at Platinum, Hoskins is a partner in the firm and is Lanning's supervisor. Lanning has worked for Platinum for four years. At a lunch meeting, the two economists discuss the usefulness of economic theory, economic data, and the resulting forecasts of the global economic and stock market activity.

Hoskins is investigating the growth prospects of the country of Maldavia. Maldavia is a formerly communist country with a population of 3 million located in Eastern Europe. The Maldavian government had been aggressive in instituting political reform and encouraging the growth of financial markets. However, due to recent increases in stock market volatility, the Maldavian government is considering reigning-in trading volume by imposing a tax on stock market transactions. Hoskins states that this development is not encouraging for future economic growth.

Lanning is examining the country of Petra. Petra is a country of 25 million located in South America and rich with natural resources, including oil. The recently-elected president of Petra, Carlos Basile, has announced that he would like to ensure that the citizens of Petra enjoy the benefits of its natural resources rather than foreign oil companies, and that the government will nationalize these oil companies. Lanning states that these changes would not be beneficial for the future growth of the Petrian economy.

One of the many items they study when examining an economy or stock market is the economic information released by governments and private organizations. Hoskins and Lanning use this information to adjust their economic growth forecasts and to accordingly adjust portfolio allocations to the bond and stock markets. Examining information for Maldavia, Hoskins has learned that the Maldavian private sector has embarked on an ambitious plan to increase labor productivity by purchasing more machinery for its factories. Plotting the productivity curve for Maldavia, Hoskins states that labor productivity should increase because the productivity curve will shift up.

Lanning is examining the historical record of economic growth in Petra. He has gathered the data in Exhibit 1 to determine potential economic growth.

Exhibit 1: Economic Data for Petra from 20X1 to 20X7

Real GDP growth rate	3.9%
Growth rate in capital	1.4%
Growth rate in labor force	1.9%
Labor cost/total factor cost	0.52

Lanning then turns his attention to the countries of Alicia and Felicia. He notes that the GDP growth rate in both countries is comparable. Alicia's capital to labor ratio is USD 5,000 and the output to capital ratio is USD 12,000. Felicia's capital to labor ratio is USD 2,800 while output to capital ratio is USD 10,000. Alicia has a relatively younger labor force and the labor cost represents 35% of total factor cost. Both countries have extensive restrictions on foreign direct investments in their economy.

It has long been Platinum's policy for its economists to use long-term economic growth trends to forecast future economic growth, stock returns, and dividends in a country. Lanning also examines the economy of Tiberia. Tiberia has a population of 11 million and is located in northern Africa. Its economy is diversified, and its main exports are agricultural products and heavy machinery. The country's economy has been growing at an annual rate of 6.2% for the past ten years, in part because of technological advances in the manufacturing of heavy equipment. These advances involve the use of computer-operated welding machines that have made the manufacturing process more efficient. Lanning is worried, however, that the current GDP growth rate may not be sustainable and is considering advising Platinum's portfolio managers to decrease their portfolio allocations to the country. Before doing so, he will consult with Hoskins.

73. Are the statements made by Hoskins and Lanning regarding the future growth of the Maldavian and Petrian economies *most likely* to be correct or incorrect?
    A. Both are correct.
    B. Only Hoskins is correct.
    C. Only Lanning is correct.

74. Hoskins's statement regarding Maldavian labor productivity and its productivity curve is:
    A. incorrect, because labor productivity is not affected in this scenario.
    B. incorrect, because labor productivity will decrease because of the low skill level of the labor force.
    C. incorrect, because although labor productivity will increase, the increase will result from a movement along the productivity curve.

75. Which country will experience a higher growth rate in potential GDP due to capital deepening and due to removal of restrictions on inflow of foreign capital?

	Capital deepening	Removal of restrictions on inflow of capital
A.	Alicia	Felicia
B.	Felicia	Felicia
C.	Felicia	Alicia

76. Petra's GDP growth rate attributable to growth in total factor productivity is *closest* to:
    A. 0.6%.
    B. 1.6%.
    C. 2.24%.

77. The classical growth theory predicts that Tiberia's long-run future GDP per capita is *most likely* to:
    A. decline due to diminishing marginal productivity of capital.
    B. settle at subsistence level due to adjustments in the population.
    C. remain unchanged from the current levels unless the government increases the budget deficit.

78. The endogenous growth theory predicts that the Tiberian GDP growth rate is *most likely* to:
    A. settle at a long-run steady state because of diminishing marginal productivity of capital.
    B. continue to increase because technological advances will be shared by many sectors of the economy.
    C. decline because the current GDP growth rate is not sustainable.

Questions 79–84 relate to Tobin Yoakam.

Tobin Yoakam, CFA, is analyzing the financial performance of Konker Industries, a U.S. company which is publicly traded under the ticker KONK. Yoakam is particularly concerned about the quality of Konker's financial statements and its choices of accounting methodologies.

Below is a summary of Konker's financial statements prepared by Yoakam.

Konker Industries				
Income Statement	**20X8**	**Balance Sheet**		**20X8**
($ in thousands)		*($ in thousands)*		
Gross sales	55,435	Cash and equivalents		457
Sales discounts, returns, and allowances	1,352	Short term marketable securities		927
Net sales	54,083	Accounts receivable (net)		47,740
Cost of goods sold	26,500	Inventories		20,963
SG&A expenses	15,625	PP&E (net of depreciation)		25,371
Depreciation expense	1,082	Total assets		95,458
Earnings before interest and taxes	10,876			
Interest expense	693	Accounts payable		24,994
Earnings before taxes	10,183	Other current liabilities		1,209
Taxes (tax rate 40%)	4,073	Long term debt		21,770
Net income	6,110	Total liabilities		47,973
		Common stock		40,314
Dividends	5,046	Retained earnings		7,171
Net addition to retained earnings	1,064	Total liabilities and shareholders equity		95,458

Konker has an operating lease for several of its large machining tools. The remaining lease term is five years, and the annual lease payments are $2 million. The applicable interest rate on the operating lease is 9%. Yoakam believes that the operating lease should be capitalized and treated as a finance lease. For purposes of adjusting the financial statements, Yoakam believes that the machining tools should be depreciated using straight-line depreciation.

At the beginning of 20X8, Konker formed a qualified special purpose entity (QSPE) and sold a portion of its accounts receivables to the QSPE. Under

U.S. GAAP, QSPE was exempt from consolidation requirements. The total amount of accounts receivables sold to the QSPE was $13.5 million. Yoakam has noted in his research that the Financial Accounting Standards Board (FASB) eliminated qualified special purpose entities.

Konker has three major operating divisions: Konker Industrial, Konker Defense, and Konker Capital. Yoakam has computed the EBIT margin for each division over the last three years, as well as the ratio of the percentage of total capital expenditures to the percentage of total assets for each division.

	EBIT / Assets			CapEx % / Assets %		
	20X8	**20X7**	**20X6**	**20X8**	**20X7**	**20X6**
Konker Industrial	6.2%	7.5%	6.7%	1.5	1.3	1.2
Konker Defense	6.7%	7.2%	6.9%	0.5	0.6	0.7
Konker Capital	10.1%	12.1%	11.1%	0.7	0.6	0.5

Since Yoakam is concerned about the quality of Konker's earnings, he decides to analyze the accrual ratios using the balance sheet approach. The table below contains the last three years of accrual ratios for Konker and the industry average.

Balance Sheet Accrual Ratios	**20X8**	**20X7**	**20X6**
Konker	4.5%	15.0%	7.0%
Industry average	4.8%	4.4%	5.2%

79. With respect to the balance sheet accrual ratio, which of the following, other things equal, would *most likely* lead to an increase in the ratio for a growing company?
     A. Extending the time the firm takes to pay its suppliers.
     B. A significant build-up of cash.
     C. A build-up of inventory.

80. If Yoakam capitalizes Konker's operating lease in his analysis, the Konker's adjusted interest coverage ratio for 20X8 would be *closest* to:
     A. 7.12.
     B. 8.13.
     C. 15.69.

81. When FASB retroactively eliminated the allowance of QSPEs created for the securitization of receivables, the *most likely* impact on Konker's financial statements would have been:
    A. an increase in equity and an increase in interest expense.
    B. no change in assets but an increase in financial leverage ratios.
    C. an increase in financial leverage ratios and a decrease in the interest coverage ratio.

82. An analyst is considering the effects of income reported under the equity method on certain financial ratios. For a firm that reports equity income as non-operating income (not included in EBIT), removing equity income from the financial statements would *most likely* result in:
    A. an increase in the tax burden term in the extended Du Pont decomposition of ROE.
    B. an increase in the asset turnover ratio.
    C. a decrease in the interest coverage ratio.

83. Regarding the three operating divisions of Konker, Yoakam should be *most* concerned that:
    A. Konker is growing the Industrial division over time.
    B. the operating ROA of the Capital division has fallen over the last year.
    C. the ratio of the Capex percent change to the asset percentage is significantly less than one for the Defense division.

84. Based on the balance sheet accruals ratios, Yoakam would *most likely* conclude which of the following regarding the earnings of Konker?
    A. The volatile accruals ratios are indicators that Konker may be manipulating earnings.
    B. Konker's earnings quality was lower than its peer group in 20X8 but higher in 20X6 and 20X7.
    C. Konker's earnings quality worsened from 20X6 to 20X8 but was superior to its peer group over the 3-year period.

Questions 85–90 relate to Galena Petrovich.

Galena Petrovich, CFA, is an analyst in the New York office of TRS Investment Management, Inc. Petrovich is an expert in the industrial electrical equipment sector and is analyzing Fisher Global. Fisher is a global market leader in designing, manufacturing, marketing, and servicing electrical systems and components, including fluid power systems and automotive engine air management systems.

Fisher has generated double-digit growth over the past ten years, primarily as the result of acquisitions, and has reported positive net income in each year. Fisher reports its financial results using International Financial Reporting Standards (IFRS).

Petrovich is particularly interested in a transaction that occurred seven years ago, before the change in accounting standards, in which Fisher used the pooling method to account for a large acquisition of Dartmouth Industries, an industry competitor. She would like to determine the effect of using the purchase method instead of the pooling method on the financial statements of Fisher. Fisher exchanged common stock for all of the outstanding shares of Dartmouth.

Fisher also has a 50% ownership interest in a joint venture with its major distributor, a U.S. company called Hydro Distribution. She determines that Fisher has reported its ownership interest under the equity method, and that the joint venture has been profitable since it was established three years ago. She decides to adjust the financial statements to show how the financial statements would be affected if Fisher had reported its ownership under the acquisition method. Fisher is also considering acquiring 80% to 100% of Brown and Sons Company. Petrovich must consider the effect of such an acquisition on Fisher's financial statements.

Petrovich determines from the financial statement footnotes that Fisher reported an unrealized gain in its most recent income statement related to debt securities that are designated at fair value. Competitor firms following U.S. GAAP classify similar debt securities as available-for-sale.

Finally, Petrovich finds a reference in Fisher's footnotes regarding a special purpose entity (SPE). Fisher has reported its investment in the SPE using the equity method, but Petrovich believes that the consolidation method more accurately reflects Fisher's true financial position, so she makes the appropriate adjustments to the financial statements.

85. Regarding the prior purchase that was accounted for under the pooling of interests method, had Fisher Global reported this purchase under the acquisition method:
    A. the assets and liabilities of the purchased firm would not be included on Fisher's balance sheet.
    B. balance sheet assets and liabilities of the purchased firm would have been reported at fair value.
    C. reported goodwill could be less depending on the fair value of the identifiable assets and liabilities compared to their book values.

86. Had Fisher Global reported its investment in the joint venture under the acquisition method rather than under the equity method, it is *most likely* that:
    A. reported revenue would have been the same.
    B. reported expenses would have been lower.
    C. net income would not have been affected.

87. Regarding any potential goodwill on the acquisition of Brown and Sons being considered by Fisher Global, which of the following statements is *most accurate*? The goodwill will be reported as an asset and:
    A. must be reviewed for impairment at least annually, with different test for impairment under IFRS and U.S. GAAP. Impairment losses can be reversed under U.S. GAAP but not under IFRS.
    B. amortized, and must be reviewed for impairment at least annually, though impairment losses cannot be reversed under either GAAP or IFRS.
    C. must be reviewed for impairment at least annually with different tests for impairment under IFRS and U.S. GAAP. The losses on impairment cannot be reversed under either U.S. GAAP or under IFRS.

88. If Fisher Global decides to purchase only 80% of Brown and Sons, under IFRS they will have the option to:
    A. report the acquisition as either a business combination or as an acquisition.
    B. value the identifiable assets and liabilities of Brown and Sons at their current book values or at fair market value.
    C. report more or less goodwill depending on the accounting method they choose.

89. For comparison purposes, Petrovich decides to reclassify Fisher Global's debt securities as available-for-sale. Ignoring any effect on income taxes, which of the following *best* describes the effects of the necessary adjustments?
    A. Net income is lower and asset turnover is higher.
    B. Return on assets is lower and debt-to-equity is lower.
    C. Return on equity is lower and debt-to-total capital is not affected.

90. What are the *likely* effects on return on assets (ROA) and net profit margin (ignoring any tax effects) of correctly adjusting for Fisher Global's investment in the SPE using the acquisition method?

	ROA	Net profit margin
A.	No change	Decrease
B.	Decrease	No change
C.	Decrease	Decrease

Questions 91–96 relate to Wayward Distributing, Inc.

Jenna Stuart is a financial analyst for Deuce Hardware Company, a U.S. company that reports its results in U.S. dollars. Wayward Distributing, Inc., is a foreign subsidiary of Deuce Hardware, which began operations on January 1, 2017. Wayward is located in a foreign country and reports its results in the local currency called the Rho. Selected balance sheet information for Wayward is shown in the following table.

Selected Balance Sheet Accounts Wayward Distributing Inc. (in Rho)

	12/31/17	12/31/18
Cash and accounts receivable	5,000	5,200
Inventory	3,800	4,900
Net fixed assets	6,200	7,400
Total assets	15,000	17,500
Current liabilities	2,000	2,000
Long-term debt	9,000	9,500
Shareholders' equity	4,000	6,000

Stuart has been asked to analyze how the reported financial results of Wayward will be affected by the choice of the current rate or temporal methods of accounting for foreign operations. She has gathered the following exchange rate information on the $/Rho exchange rate:

- Spot rate on 1/01/18: $0.35 per Rho
- Spot rate on 12/31/18: $0.45 per Rho
- Average spot rate during 2018: $0.42 per Rho

91.   Will the current rate method report a translation gain or loss for 2018, and will that gain or loss be reported on Deuce's income statement or the balance sheet?
     A. Gain on the balance sheet.
     B. Gain on the income statement.
     C. Loss on the balance sheet and a gain on the income statement.

92.   Will the temporal method report a translation gain or loss for 2018, and will that gain or loss be reported on Deuce's income statement or the balance sheet?
     A. Gain on the balance sheet.
     B. Loss on the income statement.
     C. Gain on the balance sheet and a loss on the income statement.

93. Will total asset turnover (calculated using end-of-period balance sheet figures) *likely* be larger when calculated from the Rho financial statements or the financial statements translated into the reporting currency (U.S.$) using the current rate method?
    A. Larger on US$ statements.
    B. Larger on Rho statements.
    C. No difference.

94. Will fixed asset turnover (calculated using end-of-period balance sheet figures) *likely* be lower when calculated using the current rate method or remeasured using the temporal method?
    A. Lower under the temporal method.
    B. Lower under the current rate method.
    C. The same under either method.

95. Suppose for this question only that Stuart has determined that (1) the operating, financing, and investing decisions related to Wayward's operations are typically made by Wayward's local management located in the foreign country; and (2) some of Wayward's accounts receivable are denominated in a different foreign currency called the Del (Dl). Which method is the *most appropriate* to use to translate the Del receivables into Rho, according to U.S. GAAP?
    A. The current rate method.
    B. The temporal method.
    C. Use the current rate for translation with any gains or losses reflected in the income statement.

96. Suppose for this question only that Stuart decides to use the current rate method to translate Wayward's results into U.S. dollars. Is it *likely* that the quick ratio and the interest coverage ratio will be the same or different in Rho before translation and in U.S. dollars after translation?
    A. Neither the quick ratio nor the interest coverage ratio will change.
    B. Only the interest coverage ratio will change.
    C. Only the quick ratio will change.

Questions 97–102 relate to John Baragutti.

John Baragutti, CFA, works in the transaction services arm of HLBB, a large accountancy firm with a substantial advisory business on the east coast of the United States. He is currently advising on a potential M&A transaction between two airlines. Tarpon Airlines, Inc. (Tarpon), which operates out of the east coast of the United States, is the larger of the two companies and its board has entered into discussions with the smaller Clear Air S.A. (Clear). Clear, based in France, would provide Tarpon access to a significant number of landing slots in major European airports.

Baragutti is currently reviewing the income statement of Clear in order to address some concerns raised by Tarpon's board. Merger discussions had initially progressed rapidly after an initial review of Clear's last 5 years' income statements, which revealed an operating profit margin that was in line with that of Tarpon. The board has historically been extremely cautious about acquiring any potential target with a profit margin lower than its own. However, further investigation has revealed concerns regarding the treatment of pension costs in the income statement.

Tarpon runs only a defined contribution pension scheme for its employees and an employee incentive stock option scheme. Clear, however, has a defined benefit scheme that is currently overfunded. Extracts from the pension note included in Clear's annual report are shown in Exhibit 1.

Exhibit 1: Pension Note (Extracts)

Present Value of Defined Benefit Obligations		_Fair Value of Plan Assets_	
	€ million		_€ million_
As at 1 January 2015	8,110	As at 1 January 2015	8,920
Current service cost	170	Return on plan assets	145
Past service cost	15	Employer contributions	306
Interest cost	365	Benefits paid	(202)
Benefits paid	(202)		
Remeasurement (gains)/loss	218		
As at 31 December 2015	8,676	As at 31 December 2015	9,169

Notes:
- Pension benefit obligation has been calculated using the average yield on high-quality corporate bonds with similar durations to the benefits in the scheme, currently 4.5%.
- Due to turbulent economic conditions in the eurozone, return on plan assets was only 1.63%.
- Remeasurement gains at the start of the year totaled €231 million.

Having never accounted for a defined benefit scheme, in its initial review, the board of Tarpon did not consider the impact of the defined benefit plan on the operating margin. As a result, Baragutti has been asked to address three issues.

First, Clear prepares its financial statements using IFRS whereas Tarpon reports under U.S. GAAP. The board wants to gain an understanding of Clear's pension expense for 2015 as computed under U.S. GAAP. Secondly, the disclosure of certain elements of the pension cost has confused the board. Although the notes to the income statement identify that the pension cost has an interest element, this has been included within operating profit.

Finally, the board is concerned about future adjustments that may be required to deal with the amortization of the remeasurement gains that have accumulated in Clear's pension scheme. Baragutti intends to perform the following calculations to deal with each issue independently:

Issue 1

Recalculate pension expense included in the income statement under U.S. GAAP. Baragutti has observed that companies reporting pension expense under U.S. GAAP have used an average of 3% for the expected return on plan assets and he intends to apply this rate where applicable. He does not intend to amortize any of this year's prior service cost.

Issue 2

Assuming IFRS, recalculate the local currency (€) operating margin excluding any pension scheme interest element. The current income statement before Baragutti's adjustments is shown in Exhibit 2.

Issue 3

Baragutti prepares the following note containing two statements to advise the board on the future amortization of actuarial gains and losses:

Statement 1

"Under IFRS, when cumulative remeasurement gains/losses are large enough, they will be amortized through the income statement over the average service life of the employees, reducing net income if net losses are amortized, and increasing net income if net gains are amortized."

Statement 2

"Under U.S. GAAP, the amortization of net actuarial losses will increase leverage (i.e., debt-to-equity ratio), whereas the amortization of net actuarial gains will decrease leverage."

©2017 Kaplan, Inc.

Exhibit 2 – Income Statement (Extracts)

	2015 *€ million*
Revenue	
Passenger	9,321
Cargo	456
Total	**9,777**
Employee costs	3,654
Depreciation, amortization	894
Aircraft operating lease costs	156
Fuel and oil costs	1,853
Engineering and other aircraft costs	542
Landing fees	1,458
Exchange rate losses	221
Ground equipment costs	765
Total Operating Costs	**9,543**
Operating Profit	**234**
Fuel derivative losses	32
Finance costs	193
Finance income	89
Profit before tax	**98**

Note: Employee costs include the defined benefit pension expense for the period.

Baragutti has also been asked to raise any other points he thinks the board should be aware of surrounding this issue. He intends make the following two observations on cash flow calculations and the impact of Tarpon's employee share option scheme.

Cash Flow Calculations

Baragutti noted that the board has used Clear's operating cash flow as a basis for its valuation of the entity. He intends to notify the board that whenever it encounters a company with a defined benefit scheme, in his opinion, it would be advisable to adjust CFO to reflect the fact that employer contributions are not the same as the cost of the scheme.

Employee Share Option Scheme

Although Tarpon does not have a defined benefit pension scheme, it does have an equivalent employee compensation expense in the form of an employee share option scheme. Just as there is a cost to Clear of its defined benefit scheme, the cost of Tarpon's share option scheme will be charged as an expense to the income statement and hence reduce retained earnings and equity.

97. The total periodic pension cost for Clear's defined benefit pension scheme in 2015 is *closest* to:
    A. €405 million.
    B. €421 million.
    C. €623 million.

98. In dealing with issue 1 as outlined, Baragutti is likely to calculate a pension expense *closest* to:
    A. €149 million.
    B. €267 million.
    C. €390 million.

99. Using IFRS and Baragutti's suggested adjustments for issue 2, he is likely to calculate an adjusted operating margin *closest* to:
    A. 1%.
    B. 2%.
    C. 6%.

100. Baragutti is *most likely* to suggest adjusting the cash flow used by the board as a basis of its valuation by:
    A. decreasing it because employer contributions are higher than reported pension expense.
    B. decreasing it because employer contributions are lower than total periodic pension cost.
    C. increasing it.

101. Which of Baragutti's statements on the amortization of actuarial gains and losses in response to issue 3 are *most likely* correct?
    A. Both statements are correct.
    B. Only statement two is correct.
    C. Neither statement is correct.

102. Baragutti's comments regarding Tarpon's employee share option scheme are *most likely*:
    A. correct.
    B. incorrect because the cost of issuing shares under an employee stock option scheme will be taken directly to equity via OCI and hence not reduce retained earnings.
    C. incorrect as the cost of issuing shares under an employee stock option scheme will not reduce equity.

Questions 103–108 relate to Cummings Enterprises, Inc.

Cummings Enterprises, Inc. (CEI), is a U.S. conglomerate that operates in a variety of markets. CEI's marginal tax rate is 40%. One of CEI's divisions manufactures small fiberglass products, such as bird baths and outdoor storage lockers. CEI is currently considering the expansion of its fiberglass product line to include booms and buckets for aerial lift trucks (often called cherry pickers), which are used for applications such as high voltage power line maintenance. The addition of this new product line is expected to increase CEI's sales by $750,000 per year.

Cal Holbrook, CEI's manager of fiberglass operations, is deciding whether to purchase a robotic system to produce cherry picker booms and buckets. The price of the robotic system will be $700,000, plus an additional $100,000 for shipping, site preparation, and installation. The new equipment will require a $50,000 increase in inventory and a $20,000 increase in accounts payable. The company uses MACRS to calculate depreciation for tax purposes and the straight-line method for financial reporting. The project has an expected life of four years, at which time the robot is expected to be sold for $75,000. The project will be funded with the debt/equity mix reflected by the company's current capital structure. CEI's pretax cost of new debt is 7%. Assume a WACC of 8%. Some of the relevant end-of-year cash flows for the robotic project are presented in Exhibit 1.

Exhibit 1: Relevant Cash Flows for Robotics Project

	Year 1	Year 2	Year 3	Year 4
Sales	$750,000	$750,000	$750,000	$750,000
Variable costs	$225,000	$225,000	$225,000	$225,000
Fixed expense	$75,000	$75,000	$75,000	$75,000
Depreciation	$264,000	$360,000	$120,000	$56,000
Earnings before tax (EBT)	$186,000	$90,000	$330,000	$394,000
Total after-tax cash flow	**$375,600**	**$414,000**	**$318,000**	?

Holbrook calculates the NPV of the robotic project and presents his findings to his supervisor, Geoffrey Mans. After reviewing the report, Mans makes the following recommendations:

1. "You forgot to include the $100,000 we have spent so far on consultants and project engineers and who knows what else to evaluate the project's feasibility. Rerun the numbers including that amount and get the revised calculations to me this afternoon."

2. "Rerun the analysis assuming straight-line depreciation for tax purposes. The NPV will be higher, and we'll be more likely to get the project funded."

Cummings has two other projects under consideration that would affect the production of storage lockers. Project 1 relates to changing the production process, and Project 2 relates to expanding the distribution facility. Holbrook estimates the NPV of the expected cash flows for Project 1 at negative $7 million. An additional investment of $3 million would allow management to more rapidly adjust to the demand for a certain type of locker. The value of this flexibility is estimated at $9 million. He estimates that the NPV of the expected cash flows for Project 2 at $3 million. An expansion option would require an additional investment of $2 million. At this time, Cummings does not have any capital rationing restrictions.

Holbrook e-mails the lead analyst for the budgeting group and indicates that he cannot make a decision on Project 2 without knowing the value the expansion option will provide.

Holbrook calls a capital budgeting meeting with CEI's production and quality control manager. Holbrook opens the meeting by stating: "I think we should accept this project based solely on the fact that it provides great operating margins. Nevertheless, I think we should conduct net present value (NPV) analysis to confirm my opinion." Holbrook then receives the following comments:

Comment 1: It is important that interest is included in the cash flows used with NPV analysis because interest is a real and very significant expense.

Comment 2: If applied correctly, the NPV of this project will be higher if we discount economic profits instead of net after-tax operating cash flows in our analysis. I suggest we calculate economic profit as net operating profit after tax minus the dollar cost of capital.

103. Which of the following choices is *closest* to the Year 4 total cash flow for the robotics project in Exhibit 1?
    A. $292,400.
    B. $345,400.
    C. $367,400.

104. Are Mans's recommendations regarding the robotic project correct or incorrect?
    A. Both recommendations are correct.
    B. Only one of the recommendations is correct.
    C. Both recommendations are incorrect.

105. For this question only, assume that the investment in net working capital of $30,000 at the project inception is an inflow and that the amount nets to zero with the outflow that will occur at the end of the project. However, Holbrook does not include a cash flow for net working capital at the beginning or the end of the project. Assuming he correctly analyzes all the other components of the project, has Holbrook correctly estimated the project's net present value?
    A. Yes.
    B. No, he underestimated the project's NPV by approximately $7,950.
    C. No, he underestimated the project's NPV by approximately $2,222.

106. Which of the following choices is *closest* to the overall NPV for Project 1, and is Holbrook correct to wait for more information before deciding on Project 2?
    A. The overall NPV is –$1 million, and Holbrook is correct.
    B. The overall NPV is –$1 million, and Holbrook is incorrect.
    C. The overall NPV is $13 million, and Holbrook is incorrect.

107. The economic income for Year 3 for the robotics project from Exhibit 1 is *closest* to:
    A. $19,400.
    B. $48,700.
    C. $49,400.

108. Are the comments made by the CEI's production and quality assurance manager correct or incorrect?
    A. Both comments are correct.
    B. Only one of the comments is correct.
    C. Both comments are incorrect.

Questions 109–114 relate to Jon Stevenson, CFA.

Jon Stevenson, CFA, is an experienced equity fund manager who has recently taken a position with Lohsi Clearview, a UK-based hedge fund that has combined a wide range of strategies to deliver impressive returns over the last five years. One of the fund's strategies is to invest in high-credit-risk fixed income instruments. The fund has an excellent track record of identifying bonds in this sector that subsequently outperform the market.

Stevenson wishes to familiarize himself with the fund's strategies and has started by looking at some of the techniques used in analyzing fixed income instruments. Exhibit 1 shows the firm's approach to analyzing credit risk.

Exhibit 1: Credit Analysis Tools

Credit Ratings
Before undertaking any level of detailed analysis, the credit rating from the three major agencies should be obtained. Typically an instrument that is investment grade according to all three agencies will not be worthy of further consideration.
Structural Models
An initial analysis using a simple structural model should be undertaken to calculate the present value of the expected loss.
Reduced Form Models
Detailed analysis should be undertaken using the reduced form models used by the fixed income team. This analysis should only be undertaken once the structural model analysis has been completed.

Stevenson is surprised that the fund uses credit ratings to filter out investment grade bonds as not worthy of consideration. In his experience, ratings agencies have often been wrong and he intends to send a note to his supervisor stating the following points arguing that credit ratings should not be relied upon as a filter:

Point 1:   Ratings are volatile over time, which reduces their usefulness as an indication of a debt offering's default probability.

Point 2:   Ratings do not implicitly depend on the business cycle stage, whereas a debt offering's default probability does.

Stevenson has no experience with structural models and is interested in learning more. He finds an analysis that has been completed for a recent bond issue. The results are shown in Exhibit 2.

©2017 Kaplan, Inc.

Exhibit 2: IMC Bond Issue (ID 062014555612) Structural Model Results

Asset value	A_t	1,200
Expected return on assets	μ	0.04
Risk free rate	r	0.02
Face value	K	850
Time to maturity	T–t	1.5
Return volatility	σ	0.28
d_1		1.26452
d_2		0.92159
$N(-d_1)$		0.1030
$N(-d_2)$		0.1784
e_1		1.35200
e_2		1.00907
$N(-e_1)$		0.0882
$N(-e_2)$		0.1565
Expected loss		22.86
PV expected loss		23.51

109. Which of the credit analysis models shown in Exhibit 1 can only be used under the assumption that the issuing company's assets trade in a frictionless market?
    A. Structural models.
    B. Reduced form models.
    C. Both structural models and reduced form models.

110. When using reduced form models, which of the following statements is *most accurate*?
    A. It must be assumed that the riskless rate of interest is constant over time.
    B. The time T value of the company's assets has a lognormal distribution.
    C. For a given state of the economy, whether a company defaults depends only on company-specific considerations.

111. Which of Stevenson's points regarding the reliability of credit ratings is *most accurate*?
    A. Point 1 only.
    B. Point 2 only.
    C. Neither point is correct.

112. According to the structural model shown in Exhibit 2, the maximum amount an investor holding the bond would pay to a third party to remove the risk of default would be:
    A. $0.65.
    B. $22.86.
    C. $23.51.

113. The results shown in Exhibit 2 indicate that the:
    A. time value of money discount exceeds the risk premium for risk of credit loss.
    B. risk premium for risk of credit loss exceeds the time value of money discount.
    C. risk premium for risk of credit loss is $0.65.

114. If the volatility estimate is changed to 30% in the structural model shown in Exhibit 2, the calculated value of IMC Bond would *most likely:*
    A. remain the same.
    B. decrease.
    C. increase.

Questions 115–120 relate to Parkway Terrace.

Rita Larson, CFA, is an investment analyst for Siprah Properties, Inc. A group of wealthy investors, Ken Lundy, Chun Park, and Kareem Shabaz, are interested in purchasing Parkway Terrace, a 120-unit luxury apartment complex in Southeastern Florida. The current owners of Parkway Terrace have agreed to sell the property for $40,000,000.

Siprah represents both the existing owners and the potential new owners and are privy to additional information. Exhibits 1 and 2 show the information Larson has collected during her due diligence.

Exhibit 1: Parkway Terrace Specifics

Parkway Terrace	
Projected first year net operating income	$3.3 million
Location/Condition	Prime/Good
LTV	75.0%
Loan Term	25 years
Loan Interest Rate	4.5%
Monthly Debt Service	$166,750
Square footage	240,000
Expected holding period	10 years

Parkway Terrace	Cost estimates
Effective age of building	10 years
Total economic life	50 years
Estimated value of land	$12,500,000
Replacement cost (p.s.f.)	$175.00
Developer's profit (p.s.f.)	$15.00
Curable deterioration	$5,000,000
Total obsolescence	$4,000,000
Expected selling price in 10 yrs	$60,000,000
Loan balance at end of 10 yrs	$21,797,543

Exhibit 2: Recent Transactions of Luxury Apartment Buildings in Southeastern Florida

Building	Craig Court	Kenton Place	Hester Oasis
Size in square feet	200,000	150,000	300,000
Age in years	7	10	13
Condition	Fair	Good	Good
Location	Prime	Secondary	Secondary
Age of transaction (in months)	9	5	16
Sales price	$32,000,000	$24,000,000	$45,000,000
Projected NOI	$2,560,000	$1,800,000	$3,150,000

Additional information:

- Depreciation is 1.5% per year.
- Condition can be good, fair, or bad. 7.5% is the adjustment needed per classification.
- Location can be prime, secondary, or tertiary. Prime locations are the most sought-after and 7.5% is the adjustment needed per classification.
- Market prices have been increasing at a rate of 0.50% per month.

Lundy states that all returns and ratios must exceed the minimum standards as listed below.

Minimum requirements
Levered required rate of return   20.0%
Debt Service Coverage Ratio   1.50X
Equity Dividend Rate   25.0%

Economic Outlook for Southeast Florida

- Home prices are expected to rise.
- Interest rates are expected to increase.
- Population growth is expected to be higher than in other areas as more wealthy retirees are moving to the region.

The investors make the following statements about how to best approach this investment:

Ken Lundy: "After we buy Parkway Terrace, we should offer shorter leases to take advantage of market conditions."

Chun Park: "I think that after we buy, we should offer long leases to lock-in tenants and maximize profitability."

Kareem Shabaz: "If we buy, we should take advantage of the low interest rates by using as much leverage as possible."

Larson is interested in using a real estate index in her analysis of suitability of real estate as an asset class for several of Siprah's clients. She notes that the firm subscribes to a proprietary index provided by REIQ. The REIQ index is an appraisal-based index that is very popular among real estate professionals. Larson is concerned about appraisal lag in the index and wants to adjust the index to remove this lag.

115. The estimated value of the property using the direct capitalization approach is *closest* to:
    A. $41.3 million.
    B. $42.0 million.
    C. $44.0 million.

116. The estimated value of the property using the sales comparison approach is *closest* to:
    A. $37.6 million.
    B. $42.2 million.
    C. $43.2 million.

117. For this question only, assume that the NOI growth rate is 0%. Based on Lundy's minimum requirements, the Parkway Terrace project is:
    A. not worth pursuing because the equity dividend rate is below the minimum required.
    B. worth pursuing because all three standards are met.
    C. not worth pursuing because the debt service coverage ratio is below the minimum required.

118. The estimated value of the property using the cost approach is *closest* to:
    A. $28.5 million.
    B. $41.0 million.
    C. $45.0 million.

119. Which stated approach is *least likely* to result in an increase in potential returns?
    A. Chun Park's.
    B. Ken Lundy's.
    C. Kareem Shabaz's.

120. To correct for appraisal lag in the REIQ index, which of the following is the *least appropriate* course of action for Larson?
    A. 'Unsmooth' the index.
    B. Use a transaction-based index.
    C. Use more-recent appraisals.

End of Afternoon Session

EXAM 2
MORNING SESSION

Question	Topic	Minutes (Points)
1 to 6	Ethical and Professional Standards	18
7 to 12	Economics	18
13 to 18	Financial Reporting and Analysis	18
19 to 24	Corporate Finance	18
25 to 42	Equity Valuation	54
43 to 48	Fixed Income	18
49 to 54	Derivatives	18
55 to 60	Alternative Investments	18

Test Answers

1. Ⓐ Ⓑ Ⓒ
2. Ⓐ Ⓑ Ⓒ
3. Ⓐ Ⓑ Ⓒ
4. Ⓐ Ⓑ Ⓒ
5. Ⓐ Ⓑ Ⓒ
6. Ⓐ Ⓑ Ⓒ
7. Ⓐ Ⓑ Ⓒ
8. Ⓐ Ⓑ Ⓒ
9. Ⓐ Ⓑ Ⓒ
10. Ⓐ Ⓑ Ⓒ

11. Ⓐ Ⓑ Ⓒ
12. Ⓐ Ⓑ Ⓒ
13. Ⓐ Ⓑ Ⓒ
14. Ⓐ Ⓑ Ⓒ
15. Ⓐ Ⓑ Ⓒ
16. Ⓐ Ⓑ Ⓒ
17. Ⓐ Ⓑ Ⓒ
18. Ⓐ Ⓑ Ⓒ
19. Ⓐ Ⓑ Ⓒ
20. Ⓐ Ⓑ Ⓒ

21. Ⓐ Ⓑ Ⓒ
22. Ⓐ Ⓑ Ⓒ
23. Ⓐ Ⓑ Ⓒ
24. Ⓐ Ⓑ Ⓒ
25. Ⓐ Ⓑ Ⓒ
26. Ⓐ Ⓑ Ⓒ
27. Ⓐ Ⓑ Ⓒ
28. Ⓐ Ⓑ Ⓒ
29. Ⓐ Ⓑ Ⓒ
30. Ⓐ Ⓑ Ⓒ

31. Ⓐ Ⓑ Ⓒ
32. Ⓐ Ⓑ Ⓒ
33. Ⓐ Ⓑ Ⓒ
34. Ⓐ Ⓑ Ⓒ
35. Ⓐ Ⓑ Ⓒ
36. Ⓐ Ⓑ Ⓒ
37. Ⓐ Ⓑ Ⓒ
38. Ⓐ Ⓑ Ⓒ
39. Ⓐ Ⓑ Ⓒ
40. Ⓐ Ⓑ Ⓒ

41. Ⓐ Ⓑ Ⓒ
42. Ⓐ Ⓑ Ⓒ
43. Ⓐ Ⓑ Ⓒ
44. Ⓐ Ⓑ Ⓒ
45. Ⓐ Ⓑ Ⓒ
46. Ⓐ Ⓑ Ⓒ
47. Ⓐ Ⓑ Ⓒ
48. Ⓐ Ⓑ Ⓒ
49. Ⓐ Ⓑ Ⓒ
50. Ⓐ Ⓑ Ⓒ

51. Ⓐ Ⓑ Ⓒ
52. Ⓐ Ⓑ Ⓒ
53. Ⓐ Ⓑ Ⓒ
54. Ⓐ Ⓑ Ⓒ
55. Ⓐ Ⓑ Ⓒ
56. Ⓐ Ⓑ Ⓒ
57. Ⓐ Ⓑ Ⓒ
58. Ⓐ Ⓑ Ⓒ
59. Ⓐ Ⓑ Ⓒ
60. Ⓐ Ⓑ Ⓒ

Exam 2
Morning Session

Use the following information to answer Questions 1 through 6.

Martha Gillis, CFA, trades currencies for Trent, LLC. Trent is one of the largest investment firms in the world, and its foreign currency department trades more currency on a daily basis than any other firm. Gillis specializes in currencies of emerging nations.

Gillis received an invitation from the new finance minister of Binaria, one of the emerging nations included in Gillis's portfolio. The minister has proposed a number of fiscal reforms that he hopes will help support Binaria's weakening currency. He is asking currency specialists from several of the largest foreign exchange banks to visit Binaria for a conference on the planned reforms. Because of its remote location, Binaria will pay all travel expenses of the attendees, as well as lodging in government-owned facilities in the capital city. As a further inducement, attendees will also receive small bags of uncut emeralds (because emeralds are a principal export of Binaria), with an estimated market value of $500.

Gillis has approximately 25 clients that she deals with regularly, most of whom are large financial institutions interested in trading currencies. One of the services Gillis provides to these clients is a weekly summary of important trends in the emerging market currencies she follows. Gillis talks to local government officials and reads research reports prepared by local analysts, which are paid for by Trent. These inputs, along with Gillis's interpretation, form the basis of most of Gillis's weekly reports.

Gillis decided to attend the conference in Binaria. In anticipation of a favorable reception for the proposed reforms, Gillis purchased a long Binaria currency position in her personal account before leaving on the trip. After hearing the finance minister's proposals in person, however, she decides that the reforms are poorly timed and likely to cause the currency to depreciate. She issues a negative recommendation upon her return. Before issuing the recommendation, she liquidates the long position in her personal account but does not take a short position.

Gillis's supervisor, Steve Howlett, CFA, has been reviewing Gillis's personal trading. Howlett has not seen any details of the Binaria currency trade but has found two other instances in the past year where he believes Gillis has violated Trent's written policies regarding trading in personal accounts.

One of the currency trading strategies employed by Trent is based on interest rate parity. Trent monitors spot exchange rates, forward rates, and short-term government interest rates. On the rare occasions when the forward rates do not accurately reflect the interest differential between two countries, Trent places trades to take advantage of the riskless arbitrage opportunity. Because Trent is such a large player in the exchange markets, its transactions costs are very low, and Trent is often able to take advantage of mispricings that are too small for others to capitalize on. In describing these trading opportunities to clients, Trent suggests that "clients willing to participate in this type of arbitrage strategy are guaranteed riskless profits until the market pricing returns to equilibrium."

1. According to CFA Institute Standards of Professional Conduct, Gillis may accept the invitation to attend the conference in Binaria without violating the Standards:
    A. so long as she pays her own travel expenses and refuses the gift of emeralds.
    B. so long as she refuses the gift of emeralds.
    C. because she would be the guest of a sovereign government.

2. Given that Gillis's weekly reports to clients are market summaries rather than specific investment recommendations, what are her record-keeping obligations according to CFA Institute Standards of Professional Conduct? Gillis must:
    A. maintain records of her conversations with local government officials and also keep copies of the research reports prepared by local analysts.
    B. only maintain records of her conversations with local government officials and her own summaries of the research reports prepared by local analysts.
    C. keep her own summaries of the research reports prepared by local analysts, but she has no obligation to maintain records of her conversations with local government officials.

3. Regarding Gillis's transactions in the Binaria currency, she has violated the Standards by:
    A. taking the long position and by selling the position before issuing a recommendation to clients.
    B. selling the position before issuing the recommendation to clients, although taking the long position was not a violation.
    C. not disclosing the trades in her report because the trades are acceptable as long as they are disclosed.

4. According to CFA Institute Standards of Professional Conduct, Howlett's best course of action with regard to the suspected violations by Gillis would be to:
   A. meet with Gillis in person, explain the nature of the violations, and seek assurances that such violations will not recur.
   B. warn Gillis to cease the trading activities and report the violation to Howlett's supervisor immediately.
   C. place limits on Gillis's personal trading and increase monitoring of Gillis's personal trades.

5. Based on the information given, and according to CFA Institute Standards, which of the following statements *best* describes Trent's compliance procedures relating to personal trading in foreign currencies? The compliance procedures:
   A. appear adequate because Howlett was able to identify potential violations.
   B. appear adequate, but Howlett's monitoring of Gillis's trades indicates poor supervisory responsibility.
   C. should include both duplicate confirmations of transactions and preclearance procedures for personal trades.

6. Trent's arbitrage trading based on interest rate parity is successful mostly due to Trent's large size, which provides it with an advantage relative to smaller, competing currency trading firms. Has Trent violated CFA Institute Standards of Professional Conduct with respect to its trading strategy or its guarantee of results?
   A. The trading strategy and guarantee of results are both violations of CFA Institute Standards.
   B. The trading strategy is legitimate and does not violate CFA Institute Standards, but the guarantee of investment return is a violation of Standards.
   C. Both the trading strategy and guarantee statement comply with CFA Institute Standards.

Use the following information to answer Questions 7 through 12.

Jill Surratt, CFA, and Elizabeth Castillo, CFA, are analysts for Summit Consulting. Summit provides investment advice to hedge funds and actively managed investment funds throughout the United States and Canada.

Surratt and Castillo have a client, Tom Carr, who is interested in increasing his returns from foreign currency positions. Carr currently has a position in Japanese yen (¥) that he wishes to convert to Taiwanese dollars (NT$) because he thinks the Taiwanese currency will appreciate in the near term. He does not have a quote for yen in terms of the NT$ but has received quotes for both currencies in terms of the U.S. dollar. The quotes are $0.008852-56 for the yen and $0.02874-6 for the Taiwanese dollar. He would like to purchase NT$10 million.

In discussing these quotes, Surratt notes that the bid-ask spread is affected by many factors. She states that if an economic crisis were expected in the Asian markets, then the bid-ask spread of the currency quotes should widen. Castillo states that if a dealer wished to unload an excess inventory of yen, the typical response would be to lower her ask for the yen, thereby narrowing the bid-ask spread.

In regards to changes in currency values, Surratt states that under the Mundell-Fleming model, if the U.S. Federal Reserve restricts the growth of the money supply and foreign interest rates remain constant, then the interest rate differential (U.S. interest rate minus counter currency interest rate) should increase, thereby increasing the value of the dollar.

In addition to using monetary policy, Summit Consulting uses anticipated changes in fiscal policy to forecast exchange rates and the balance of payments for a country. Castillo states that, under the Mundell-Fleming model, if the U.S. Congress were to unexpectedly reduce the budget deficit, then this should have a positive impact on the value of the dollar in the short run because foreigners would have more confidence in the U.S. economy.

Another of Summit's clients is Jack Ponder. Ponder would like to investigate the possibility of using covered interest arbitrage to earn risk-free profits over the next three months, assuming initial capital of $1 million. He asks Surratt to gather information on the inflation rates, interest rates, spot rates, and forward rates for the U.S. dollar and the Swiss franc (SF). Surratt has also used technical analysis to obtain a projection of the future spot rate for the two countries' currencies. The information is presented below:

Spot rate	$0.85 / SF
Three-month forward rate (as of today) for SF	$0.80 / SF
Expected spot rate three months from now	$0.60 / SF
Three-month inflation rate in Switzerland (annualized)	2.0%
Three-month inflation rate in the U.S. (annualized)	6.0%
Three-month interest rate for SF (annualized)	12.0%
Three-month interest rate for U.S. dollars (annualized)	18.0%

Ponder has a carry trade open involving the Bun (the currency of Bundovia). Ponder notices that Bundovia has a current account deficit and asks Surrat about the impact of such a deficit on the value of the Bun. Surrat states that the impact on the Bun depends on three factors:

Factor 1: The expected size of the current account deficit in the future.
Factor 2: The influence of exchange rates on domestic prices.
Factor 3: The response of import and export demand to changes in import and export prices.

7.   The yen cost to Carr of buying NT$10 million is *closest* to:
      A. ¥3,077,000.
      B. ¥32,453,000.
      C. ¥32,490,000.

8.   Are Surratt and Castillo correct with regard to their statements concerning the currency bid-ask spreads?
      A. Only Surratt is correct.
      B. Only Castillo is correct.
      C. Both Surratt and Castillo are correct.

9.   Evaluate Surratt's statements concerning the impact of monetary policy on currency values. Surratt is:
      A. correct.
      B. incorrect, because restrictive monetary policy in the United States would lead to a lower value of the dollar.
      C. incorrect, because restrictive U.S. monetary policy would be matched by foreign governments.

10.   Regarding Castillo's statements concerning the effect of fiscal policy on currency values, Castillo is:
      A. correct.
      B. incorrect, because under the Mundell-Fleming model, restrictive U.S. fiscal policies lead to a short-run devaluation of the dollar.
      C. incorrect, because under the Mundell-Fleming model, restrictive U.S. fiscal policies lead to an increase in the value of the dollar in the long run.

11.   Which of the following *best* describes the covered interest arbitrage that Ponder should execute? Borrow in:
      A. Swiss francs to make an arbitrage profit of $80,313.
      B. U.S. dollars to make an arbitrage profit of $80,313.
      C. Swiss francs to make an arbitrage profit of $75,588.

12.   How many of the factors identified by Surrat regarding Bundovia's current account deficit are accurate?
      A. One factor only.
      B. Two factors only.
      C. All three factors.

Use the following information to answer Questions 13 through 18.

Lauren Jacobs, CFA, is an equity analyst for DF Investments. She is evaluating Iron Parts Inc. Iron Parts is a manufacturer of interior systems and components for automobiles. The company is the world's second-largest original equipment auto parts supplier, with a market capitalization of $1.8 billion. Based on Iron Parts's low price-to-book value ratio of 0.9× and low price-to-sales ratio of 0.15×, Jacobs believes the stock could be an interesting investment. However, she wants to review the disclosures found in the company's financial statements. In particular, Jacobs is concerned about Iron Parts's defined benefit pension plan. The following information for 20X7 and 20X8 is provided.

In millions, December 31	20X8	20X7
Projected benefit obligation (PBO)	$635	$500
Current service cost	37	33
Actual return on plan assets	37	32
Benefits paid	22	15
Past service cost	80	45
Fair market value of plan assets	395	327
Discount rate	6.0%	5.5%
Expected return on plan assets	8.2%	7.5%
Rate of compensation increase	4.0%	4.0%

Iron Parts reports under U.S. GAAP.

Jacobs wants to fully understand the impact of changing pension assumptions on Iron Parts's balance sheet and income statement. In addition, she would like to compute Iron Parts's true pension expense.

13. As of December 31, 20X8, the pension plan would be reflected on Iron Parts's balance sheet as a:
    A. $175 million liability.
    B. $240 million liability.
    C. $183 million asset.

14. Which of the following *best* describes the effects of the change in Iron Parts's discount rate for 20X8, all else being equal?
    A. Service cost decreased and the pension plan appeared more funded.
    B. Pension expense decreased and the PBO increased.
    C. Interest cost increased and retained earnings decreased.

15.   How much did Iron Parts contribute to its pension plan during 20X8?
      A. $31 million.
      B. $36 million.
      C. $53 million.

16.   Which of the following *best* describes the effect(s) of the change in Iron Parts's expected return on the plan assets, all else being equal?
      A. Pension expense decreased and the PBO increased.
      B. Retained earnings increased and the pension plan appeared more funded.
      C. Net income increased.

17.   For this question only, assume that Iron Parts reports under IFRS. The amount of periodic pension cost reported on the 20X8 P&L would be *closest* to:
      A. $48 million.
      B. $69 million.
      C. $127 million.

18.   For the year ended December 31, 20X8, Iron Parts's total periodic pension cost is *closest* to:
      A. $67 million.
      B. $120 million.
      C. $157 million.

Use the following information to answer Questions 19 through 24.

Donnie Nelson, CFA, has just taken over as chief financial officer of MavsHD, a high-tech company that delivers high-definition technology to a broad-based group of sports enthusiasts. MavsHD has 40% debt and 60% equity in its capital structure. For the year just ended, net income and dividends for MavsHD were $145 million and $21.75 million, respectively. The consensus estimate for net income at the end of the current year is $153 million. The company's current book value is $550 million. MavsHD's stock is currently trading on the NYSE for a price of $50 per share and has been steadily decreasing for the past 12 months.

MavsHD has gone through its pioneer and growth phases and is now settling in to the early stages of maturity. The business model is starting to shift from relying almost exclusively on new customers to retaining and satisfying existing customers. The previously experienced very high growth rate has slowed considerably. Nelson believes that shareholder composition has changed over time as well, favoring shareholders who have a greater interest in dividend stability than in explosive growth. In the past, however, the firm has favored a low dividend rate due to the availability of attractive internal investment opportunities.

Nelson wants to develop an optimal dividend policy for MavsHD that will create the most value for the shareholders and at the same time protect corporate assets. He is concerned, however, that there is sometimes a disconnect between an optimal dividend policy and how actual dividend rates are perceived in the marketplace.

Nelson is preparing a recommendation to senior management and the board of directors regarding the firm's dividend policy going forward. Nelson is considering recommending that MavsHD engage in a stock repurchase plan and repurchase 1.5 million shares of the 12.75 million shares outstanding. This repurchase would eliminate any need to increase the cash dividend payout. Other managers at the firm, besides Nelson, believe MavsHD should increase its dividend and gravitate toward what they perceive to be the target payout ratio over the next eight years. Thus, at the end of the current year, the firm would increase the dividend payment by $250,000 over the dividend in the prior year.

During the board meeting, two of the directors raised concerns over Nelson's proposed repurchase plan. The directors' comments follow:

Director 1: I support the repurchase plan, especially relative to varying our dividend. Firms should not vary dividends—this lowers investors' confidence and can adversely impact the firm's cost of equity and its share price.

Director 2:   A share repurchase does not take away the uncertainty associated with future stock value. According to the bird-in-the-hand theory, investors prefer higher dividends because capital gains are uncertain. The theory states that if we increase our dividend payout, the value of MavsHD equity will increase. Thus, I propose a dividend increase rather than a repurchase.

One of the board members, Jason Neely, proposed an alternative dividend policy plan one week after the meeting at which Nelson presented his plan. Neely's proposal involves utilizing a residual dividend model. Neely rationalizes his plan by claiming that relative to a stable dividend policy, his proposal would increase the volatility of dollar dividends paid to shareholders but would simultaneously increase the firm's ability to exploit value additive investment projects using internally generated funds. Because of this enhanced access to value additive projects, MavsHD's cost of equity capital will experience a marginal decrease, which will further increase the overall value of the firm.

19.   Using the target payout ratio adjustment model approach to estimate dividend increases, determine which of the following is *closest* to the target payout ratio estimated by MavsHD's managers.
    A. 15%.
    B. 20%.
    C. 25%.

20.   If the board proceeds with Nelson's proposed stock repurchase plan as suggested, which of the following is *least likely* to be true? MavsHD:
    A. would be increasing financial leverage.
    B. is trying to signal the market that despite the declining share price, future prospects for the company are good.
    C. will reduce the wealth of all shareholders, including those who tender their shares for repurchase if the repurchase price is at a premium to the current stock price.

21.   For this question only, assume that MavsHD's marginal investor is in a 39.6% tax bracket for capital gains and a 15% tax bracket for dividends. If MavsHD declares a dividend of $2.25 per share, the change in MavsHD's stock price when the stock goes ex-dividend will be *closest* to:
    A. 1.36.
    B. 1.91.
    C. 3.17.

22. In light of the fact that several different groups of investors hold shares in MavsHD, evaluate the directors' comments regarding Nelson's proposed stock repurchase plan.
    A. Only Director 1 is correct.
    B. Only Director 2 is correct.
    C. Both Director 1 and Director 2 are correct.

23. If MavsHD plans to make $160 million in net investments in the current year, what will be the company's dividend payout ratio using the residual dividend model?
    A. 37.3%.
    B. 58.2%.
    C. 62.8%.

24. Evaluate Neely's comments about his proposed residual dividend plan. Neely's comments are:
    A. correct.
    B. incorrect, because the equity cost of capital would not decrease under the proposed plan.
    C. incorrect, because the firm would not have greater access to internal funds for investment.

Use the following information to answer Questions 25 through 30.

Jared Rojas, CFA, is an analyst at Van Westmoreland Investments, an international equities investment firm. Rojas has been assigned to value three U.S. companies in the paper products industry. The long-term growth rate for this industry is expected to be 3.4%.

Basil Montreux Company (BMC) is the largest company in the paper products industry. BMC is considered to be a stable and mature company. The equity beta of BMC based on a single factor capital asset pricing model is 0.90.

Exhibit 1 shows selected information from BMC's financial statements for the fiscal year ending 20X2.

Exhibit 1: Selected Financial Information for BMC

Income Statement	20X2
Revenue	$20,000.0 million
EBITDA	$3,750.0 million
Operating income	$3,290.0 million
Interest expense	$600.0 million
Income tax rate	30.0%
Payout ratio	72.0%
Total assets	$31,997.0 million

Exhibit 2: Additional Information

Risk-free rate	4.0%
Market risk premium	5.0%
Size premium	2.0%
Value premium	4.0%
Liquidity premium	4.5%

Marcel Schultz Company (MSC) is another company in the paper products industry; MSC focuses on the specialty products niche. MSC is expected to enjoy a growth rate of 25% over the next three years, after which the growth rate is expected to match the overall industry growth rate. Last year's reported dividend was $278.0 million and reported earnings were $505.4 million.

MSC's market model regression beta is 1.12. Due to beta drift, this beta needs to be adjusted.

Sunil Gurpreet Company (SGC) is a small company focusing on new high-density paper, which has found application in the aerospace industry. SGC's earnings and revenues are expected to grow at 30% for eight years, after which time the technology will lose patent protection and SGC's growth rate will revert to the industry's overall growth rate. Last year's reported earnings were $160 million but these earnings are believed to be of poor quality. SGC has never paid dividends. SGC's earnings can be volatile, but cash flows have been positive and stable. Rojas obtains inputs to estimate SGC's cost of equity as shown in Exhibit 3.

Exhibit 3: SGC's Cost of Equity Factor Exposures

SGC	β Market	β Size	β Value	β Liquidity
Factor sensitivities	1.20	0.50	−0.20	0.20

Rojas additionally gathers the following market data regarding the three companies:

Exhibit 4: Current Market Price and Shares Outstanding

Company	Market Price	Shares outstanding (millions)
BMC	$26.50	1,000
MSC	$34.25	250
SGC	$28.45	100

25. Using an appropriate valuation model, the estimated value per share of BMC is *closest* to:
 A. $16.50.
 B. $26.50.
 C. $27.60.

26. Using an appropriate valuation model, the estimated value per share of MSC is *closest* to:
 A. $ 33.00.
 B. $ 33.80.
 C. $ 34.50.

27. The *most appropriate* model to use in estimating the value of SGC is the:
    A. residual income model.
    B. dividend discount model.
    C. free cash flow model.

28. The fraction of SGC's market price that is attributable to the value of growth is *closest* to:
    A. 21%.
    B. 34%.
    C. 50%.

29. If the justified leading P/E for BMC stock is 14.1X, then BMC stock is *best* described as:
    A. overvalued.
    B. undervalued.
    C. fairly valued.

30. For this question only, assume that SGC's cost of equity is 12% and that the firm pays a regular dividend, most recently $0.80. If the initial growth rate is expected to decrease linearly over the coming eight years to the long-term industry growth rate, the estimated value of SGC stock is *closest* to:
    A. $20.
    B. $26.
    C. $30.

Use the following information to answer Questions 31 through 36.

Arnaud Aims is assisting with the analysis of several firms in the retail department store industry. Because one of the industry members, Flavia Stores, has negative earnings for the current year, Aims wishes to normalize earnings to establish more meaningful P/E ratios. For the current year (2016) and six previous years, selected financial data are given below. All data are in euros.

Exhibit 1: Selected Financial Data for Flavia Stores, 2010–2016

	2016	2015	2014	2013	2012	2011	2010
Earnings per share	(1.05)	1.90	1.65	0.99	1.35	0.77	1.04
Book value per share	9.11	10.66	9.26	8.11	7.62	6.77	6.50
Return on equity	(0.115)	0.178	0.178	0.122	0.177	0.114	0.160

Aims wishes to estimate normalized EPS for 2016 using two different methods, the method of historical average EPS and the method of average rate of return on equity. He will leave 2016 EPS and ROI out of his estimates. Based on his normalized EPS estimates, he will compute a trailing P/E for 2016. The stock price for Flavia Stores is €26.50.

Aims is also looking at price-to-book ratios as an alternative to price-to-earnings ratios. Three of the advantages of P/B ratios that Aims recalls are as follows:

Advantage 1: Because book value is a cumulative balance sheet account encompassing several years, book value is more likely than EPS to be positive.

Advantage 2: For many companies, especially service companies, human capital is more important than physical capital as an operating asset.

Advantage 3: Book value represents the historical purchase cost of assets, as well as accumulated accounting depreciation expenses. Inflation and technological changes can drive a wedge between the book value and market value of assets.

Aims used a constant growth DDM to establish a justified P/E ratio based on forecasted fundamentals. One of his associates asked Aims whether he could easily establish a justified price-to-sales (P/S) ratio and price-to-book (P/B) ratio from his justified P/E ratio. Aims replied, "I could do this fairly easily.

If I multiply the trailing P/E ratio times the net profit margin, the ratio of net income to sales, the result will be the P/S ratio. If I multiply the leading P/E ratio times the return on equity, the ratio of net income to beginning book value of equity, the result will be the P/B ratio."

Aims's associate likes to use the price-earnings-to-growth (PEG) ratio because it appears to address the effect of growth on the P/E ratio. For example, if a firm's P/E ratio is 20 and its forecasted 5-year growth rate is 10%, the PEG ratio is 2.0. The associate likes to invest in firms that have an above-industry-average PEG ratio. The associate also says that he likes to invest in firms whose leading P/E is greater than its trailing P/E. Aims tells the associate that he would like to further investigate these two investment criteria.

Finally, Aims makes two comments to his associate about valuation ratios based on EBITDA and on dividends.

Comment 1:   EBITDA is a pre-interest-expense figure, so I prefer a ratio of total equity value to EBITDA over a ratio of enterprise value to EBITDA.

Comment 2:   Dividend yields are useful information because they are one component of total return. However, they can be an incomplete measure of return, because investors trade off future earnings growth to receive higher current dividends.

31.   Using the information in Exhibit 1, estimate the P/E ratio for Flavia Stores using EPS estimated with the method of historical average EPS. The P/E ratio is *closest* to:
A. 18.4.
B. 20.6.
C. 27.9.

32.   Using the information in Exhibit 1, estimate the P/E ratio for Flavia Stores using EPS estimated with the method of average return on equity. The P/E ratio is *closest* to:
A. 16.0.
B. 18.8.
C. 25.0.

33.   Which one of the three advantages recalled by Aims *most likely* represents a good reason to consider using a P/B ratio?
A. Advantage 1.
B. Advantage 2.
C. Advantage 3.

34. Is Aims correct in describing how we could transform a justified P/E ratio into a P/S ratio or a P/B ratio?
    A. Yes.
    B. No. He is correct about the P/S ratio but incorrect about the P/B ratio.
    C. No. He is correct about the P/B ratio but incorrect about the P/S ratio.

35. When Aims further investigates the two investment criteria (the PEG ratio and the comparison between the trailing and leading P/E ratio), should he find his colleague's use of them to be appropriate?
    A. No.
    B. The PEG ratio criterion is appropriate, but the P/E ratio criterion is not.
    C. The P/E ratio criterion is appropriate, but the PEG ratio criterion is not.

36. Are Aims's two comments about the dividend yield and EBITDA ratios correct?
    A. Yes.
    B. No. The comment about EBITDA ratios is correct, but the comment about dividend yields is incorrect.
    C. No. The comment about dividend yields is correct, but the comment about EBITDA ratios is incorrect.

Use the following information to answer Questions 37 through 42.

Marsha McDonnell and Frank Lutge are analysts for the private equity firm Thorngate Ventures. Their primary responsibility is to value the equity of private firms in developed global economies. Thorngate's clients consist of wealthy individuals and institutional investors. The firm invests in and subsequently actively manages its portfolio of private firms.

During a discussion with junior analysts at the firm, McDonnell compares the characteristics of private firms with those of public firms and makes the following statements:

Statement 1: Private firms typically have higher risk premiums and required returns than public firms because private firms are usually smaller and thus thought to be riskier. Furthermore, the lack of access to liquid public equity markets can limit a private firm's growth.

Statement 2: Because of their higher risk, private firms may not be able to attract as many qualified applicants for top positions as public firms. Due to the higher risk, the managers they do attract tend to have a shorter-term view of the firm and their tenure at the firm, compared to public firm managers. As a result, the private firm may neglect profitable long-term projects.

Due to its considerable success, Thorngate has recently attracted a substantial inflow of capital from investors. To deploy that capital, McDonnell and Lutge are considering the purchase of Albion Biotechnology. Albion is using advances in biotechnology for application in the pharmaceutical field. The analysts are primarily interested in Albion because the firm's research team is developing a drug that Thorngate's current pharmaceutical firm is also working on. McDonnell estimates that combining research teams would result in advances that no pharmaceutical competitor could match for at least two years. The firm is currently owned by its founders, who are familiar to Lutge through previous social contacts. Lutge hopes to avoid a competitive bidding process for the firm, because its founders have not publicly advertised the firm's sale.

McDonnell is also examining the prospects of Balanced Metals, a metal fabrication firm. Thorngate currently does not have any manufacturing firms in its portfolio, and Balanced would provide needed exposure. The growth in sales at Balanced has been impressive recently, but it is expected to slow considerably in the years ahead due to increased competition from overseas firms. The firm's most valuable assets are its equipment and factory, located in a prime industrial area.

Balanced was previously considered for possible purchase by a competitor in the metal fabrication industry. Although the sale was not consummated, McDonnell has learned that the firm estimated that costs could be reduced at Balanced by eliminating redundant overhead expenses. McDonnell has obtained the following financial figures from the Balanced Metals CFO, as well as the previously estimated synergistic savings from cost reductions. Capital expenditures will equal depreciation plus approximately 4% of the firm's incremental revenues. McDonnell wants to forecast Balanced's free cash flow to the firm (FCFF) for the next year.

Current revenues	$22,000,000
Revenue growth	7%
Gross profit margin	25%
Depreciation expense as a percent of sales	1%
Working capital as a percent of sales	15%
SG&A expenses	$5,400,000
Synergistic cost savings	$1,200,000
Tax rate	30%

Lutge is valuing a noncontrolling equity interest in Jensen Gear, a small outdoors equipment retailer. Jensen has experienced healthy growth in earnings over the past three years. However, given its size and private status, Lutge does not expect that Jensen can be easily sold. To obtain the appropriate price multiple for the Jensen valuation, he has prepared a database of price multiples from the sale of entire public and private companies over the past ten years, organized by industry classification. Using historical data, Lutge estimates a control premium of 18.7% and discount for lack of marketability of 24%.

To obtain the cost of capital for Jensen, Lutge uses a cost of capital database that includes public company betas, cost of equity, weighted average cost of capital, and other financial statistics by industry. Given Jensen's small size, Lutge obtains a size premium using the smallest-firm-size decile of the database. McDonnell examines Lutge's cost of capital calculations and makes the following statements.

Statement 1: I am concerned about the use of this database. The estimate of the size premium may result in an undervaluation of the Jensen equity interest.

Statement 2: The use of betas and the CAPM from the database may be inappropriate. If so, Lutge should consider using the build-up method whereby an industry risk premium is used instead of beta.

37. Regarding the statements made by McDonnell on the comparison of private firms and public firms, are both statements correct?
   A. Yes.
   B. No, both statements are incorrect.
   C. No, one statement is correct, but the other statement is incorrect.

38. Which of the following *best* describes the standard of value that McDonnell and Lutge will apply to Albion Biotechnology?
   A. Market value.
   B. Intrinsic value.
   C. Investment value.

39. Which of the following is *closest* to the FCFF that McDonnell should estimate for Balanced Metals?
   A. –$117,800.
   B. $344,120.
   C. $722,120.

40. Which of the following income approaches would be *most* appropriate for valuing Balanced Metals?
   A. The free cash flow method.
   B. The excess earnings method.
   C. The capitalized cash flow method.

41. Which of the following is *closest* to the total adjustment for control and marketability that would be applied to the Jensen valuation?
   A. A discount of 5.3% would be applied.
   B. A discount of 36.0% would be applied.
   C. A discount of 42.7% would be applied.

42. Regarding the statements made by McDonnell on Lutge's cost of capital calculations for Jensen, are both statements correct?
   A. Yes.
   B. No, both statements are incorrect.
   C. No, one statement is correct, but the other statement is incorrect.

Use the following information to answer Questions 43 through 48.

Youri Wabush, CFA, works as an analyst for Solsbury Peak, a small investment house based in the United States. Wabush focuses primarily on fixed-income investment opportunities in the United States.

Every Monday, Wabush attends a morning briefing along with John Rafita, the firm's leading economist. Rafita presents his macroeconomic forecasts with a heavy focus on likely interest rate moves. Of particular interest to Wabush is Rafita's update on forward rates, which he provides on the first Monday of every month. Rafita provides an interpolated U.S. Treasuries spot rate curve along with current forward rate curves and a commentary on whether or not he believes the curves will remain stable in the short, medium. and long term.

The most recent U.S. Treasuries spot curve presented by Rafita is shown in Exhibit 1.

Exhibit 1: U.S. Treasuries Spot Curve

Maturity (years)	1	2	3	5	7	10	20	30
Spot Rate (%)	0.13	0.29	0.65	1.29	2.05	2.70	3.42	3.76

Rafita also presents his view on the likely progression of the spot rate curve over the next year and a description of fixed-income strategies that should be successful if these changes are realized. His notes are presented below in Exhibit 2.

Exhibit 2: Rafita Yield Curve Notes

U.S. Treasury Spot Curve Progression

The central bank has announced its intention to keep target rates constant for at least the next 15 months. This unprecedented level of transparency should allow fixed-income managers to forecast rates with a high degree of accuracy for the next year. As a result, I anticipate that the spot curve at this time next year will be almost identical to the no-arbitrage forward curve we're seeing now.

Minority Strategy

My estimate is that there is a sizeable minority, perhaps 20–25%, of fixed income portfolio managers who will continue to ride the yield curve as they have since 2008. With an upward-sloping curve such as the one we currently face, managers have historically been slow to move away from these strategies.

Wabush is not convinced that the central bank will follow through on their commitment to keep rates constant. He has heard rumors that the bank will announce next month that the policy will be reviewed, with the potential for almost immediate changes in target rates. Wabush is concerned that this will introduce significant volatility into the term structure of interest rates.

Wabush intends to test the impact on one of his fixed-income portfolios of the three theoretical yield curve shifts shown in Exhibit 3.

Exhibit 3: Theoretical Yield Curve Shifts

Theoretical Shift A	
Short term (2 yr.)	+70bps
Medium term (5 yr.)	+0bps
Long term (15 yr.)	+50bps

Theoretical Shift B	
Short term (2 yr.)	+30bps
Medium term (5 yr.)	+30bps
Long term (15 yr.)	+30bps

Theoretical Shift C	
Short term (2 yr.)	−10bps
Medium term (5 yr.)	+40bps
Long term (15 yr.)	+50bps

Wabush has estimated that the key rate durations of his portfolio are as shown in Exhibit 4.

Exhibit 4: Key Rate Durations

Maturity	Key Rate Duration
2 year	0.50
5 year	1.20
15 year	0.80

43. Based on information in Exhibit 1, which of the following statements is *least accurate*?
    A. Any U.S. Treasuries' forward curve will be upward sloping.
    B. Any U.S. Treasuries' forward curve will lie below the spot curve.
    C. A U.S. Treasuries' forward curve can be implied from the spot curve.

44. Using the spot rate curve given in Exhibit 1, the one-year forward rate one year from today is *closest* to:
    A. 0.27%.
    B. 0.35%.
    C. 0.45%.

45. If Rafita's comments on the U.S. Treasury spot curve progression in Exhibit 2 prove to be correct, it is *most likely* that:
    A. the one-year holding period return on a two-year, zero-coupon U.S. Treasury starting today would be 0.13%.
    B. the one-year holding period return on a two-year, zero-coupon U.S. Treasury starting today would be 0.16%.
    C. the one-year holding period return on a two-year, zero-coupon U.S. Treasury starting today would be 0.29%.

46. Fixed-income managers using the minority strategy described by Rafita in Exhibit 2 are *most likely* to:
    A. invest in bonds with a maturity longer than their investment horizon.
    B. match the maturity of the bond portfolio with their investment horizon.
    C. invest in bonds with a maturity shorter than their investment horizon.

47. If the rumors Wabush has heard regarding the central bank announcement are true, the uncertainty would *most likely* increase volatility:
    A. in short-term rates more than in long-term rates.
    B. in long-term rates more than in short-term rates.
    C. equally in long-term and short-term rates.

48. Given the information in Exhibits 3 and 4, which of the theoretical yield curve movements is *most likely* to result in a large percentage change in the value of Wabush's portfolio?
    A. Theoretical shift A.
    B. Theoretical shift B.
    C. Theoretical shift C.

Use the following information to answer Questions 49 through 54.

Paul Durham, CFA, is a senior manager in the structured bond department within Newton Capital Partners (NCP), an investment banking firm located in the United States. Durham has just returned from an international marketing campaign for NCP's latest structured note offering, a series of equity-linked fixed-income securities or ELFS. The bonds will offer a 4.5% coupon paid annually along with the annual return on the S&P 500 Index and will have a maturity of five years. The total face value of the ELFS series is expected to be $200 million.

Susan Jacobs, a fixed-income portfolio manager and principal with Smith & Associates, has decided to include $10 million worth of ELFS in her fixed-income portfolio. At the end of the first year, however, the S&P 500 Index value is 1,054, significantly lower than the initial value of 1,112 set by NCP at the time of the ELFS offering. Jacobs is concerned that the four remaining years of the ELFS life could have similar results and is considering her alternatives to offset the equity exposure of the ELFS position without selling the bonds. Jacobs decides to offset her portfolio's exposure to the ELFS by entering into an equity-swap contract. The LIBOR term structure is shown below in Exhibit 1.

Exhibit 1: LIBOR Term Structure

	LIBOR	Discount Factor
1-Year	3.2%	0.9690
2-Year	4.1%	0.9242
3-Year	4.9%	0.8718
4-Year	5.3%	0.8251

To gain further understanding of different derivative contracts, Jacobs met with Jonathan Widby, senior analyst with Smith and Associates. Widby made the following statements:

Statement 1: $N(d_2)$ in the BSM is interpreted as the risk-neutral probability that a put option will expire in the money.

Statement 2: A call option on a dividend-paying stock can be valued using the BSM if we reduce the current stock price by the present value of dividends expected over the life of the option.

Statement 3: For options on currencies, the carry benefit is not a dividend but rather interest earned on a deposit of the foreign currency.

Statement 4: Under the Black model, a call option on futures is modeled as a portfolio containing a long bond position and a short futures position.

To offset any credit risk associated with the equity swap, Widby recommends using an index trade strategy by entering into a credit default swap (CDS) as a protection buyer. Widby's strategy would involve purchasing credit protection on an index comprising largely the same issuers (companies) included in the equity index underlying the swap. Widby suggests the CDS should have a maturity equal to that of the swap to provide maximum credit protection.

49. Which of the following strategies would be *most* appropriate given Jacobs's situation and desire to offset the equity exposure of the ELFS position in her portfolio? Establish an equity swap as the:
    A. floating-rate payer and S&P 500 Index return receiver.
    B. fixed-rate receiver and S&P 500 Index return payer.
    C. fixed-rate payer and S&P 500 Index return receiver.

50. Based on the strategy appropriate for Jacobs's portfolio, determine the contract rate on the swap strategy.
    A. 4.5%.
    B. 3.6%.
    C. 4.9%.

51. If Jacobs enters into a $10 million 4-year 4.50% annual-pay fixed-rate equity swap as the equity return payer, what is the value to Jacob of the swap after one year (immediately after settlement) if the index has increased from 1,054 to 1,103, the LIBOR term structure is as given below, and the 3-year annual-pay swap fixed rate is currently 5.0%?

    LIBOR
    1-year: 4.10%
    2-year: 4.70%
    3-year: 5.29%

    A. –$136,885
    B. –$464,982
    C. –$602,555

52. Regarding statements 1 and 2 made by Widby:
    A. both statements are correct.
    B. only statement 1 is correct.
    C. only statement 2 is correct.

53. Regarding statements 3 and 4 made by Widby:
    A. both statements are correct.
    B. only statement 3 is correct.
    C. only statement 4 is correct.

54. Which of the following *best* evaluates Widby's suggested use of credit default swaps to offset the credit risk of the equity swap? Widby's recommended strategy is:
    A. correct.
    B. incorrect, because the maturity of the CDS is not properly specified.
    C. incorrect, because the CDS does not reference the proper credit risk.

Use the following information to answer Questions 55 through 60.

Julian Fuentes, CFA, analyzes real estate investments for AI Partners (AIP), a private equity real estate investment firm. Although AIP has primarily invested in nonresidential commercial property, they are considering a multi-family residential investment along with nonresidential commercial properties. Fuentes has been asked to prepare selected data on three potential investment properties. Fuente's results are presented in Exhibit 1.

Exhibit 1: Selected Property Data

Property type	Property #1 Multi-family	Property #2 Office building	Property #3 Retail Center
Occupancy	93%	92%	95%
Square feet or # units	325 (u)	125,000 (sf)	315,000 (sf)
Gross potential rent	$3,900,000	$4,312,500	$2,765,850
Other income	$ 25,000	$ 440,000	$ 780,000
Potential gross income	$3,925,000	$4,752,500	$3,545,850
Vacancy loss	$ 273,000	$ 425,000	$ 138,293
Effective gross income	$3,652,000	$4,327,500	$3,407,557
Property management fees	$ 145,000	$ 172,500	$ 138,288
Other operating expenses	$1,800,500	$2,163,750	$1,703,800
Net operating income (NOI)	$1,706,500	$ 1,991,250	$1,565,469

Other information:

1. Each property except Property #3 is located in an active market.

2. Property #2 is an older office building with architectural features characteristic of the period in which it was constructed.

3. Property #2 is located in an area that is undergoing extensive renovation.

Radna Margulies, AIP's Chief Investment Officer, asks Fuentes to focus on the multi-family opportunity presented as Property #1. This request is based on her forecast of pent-up demand in the housing market. Fuentes forecasts net operating income for Property #1 for the first five years as presented in Exhibit 2. A list of discounted cash flow valuation assumptions for an equity-only transaction is presented in Exhibit 3.

Exhibit 2: Property #1: Net Operating Income Forecast

	Year 1	Year 2	Year 3	Year 4	Year 5
NOI	$1,706,500	$1,774,760	$1,845,750	$1,919,580	$1,996,364

Exhibit 3: Property #1: DCF Assumptions

Investment holding period	5 years
Going-in capitalization rate	8.25%
Terminal capitalization rate	7.50%
Discount rate	9.50%
Income/value growth rate	Constant

After reviewing valuation data for the three properties, Margulies requests that Fuentes discuss funding terms with Amiable Life Insurance Company (ALIC) for Property #1. Fuentes is offered a rate of 5.5%, interest only, on a 5-year term loan. ALIC stipulates a maximum loan-to-value (LTV) of 70% and minimum debt service coverage ratio of 1.5x.

Fuentes receives an appraisal of $30 million for the value for Property #1.

55. Which property valuations are *most likely* to be heavily affected by their unique characteristics?
    A. Property #1 and Property #2.
    B. Property #1 and Property #3.
    C. Property #2 and Property #3.

56. Which property is likely to have the greatest operational risk resulting from management expenses?
    A. Property #1.
    B Property #2.
    C. Property #3.

57. Which approach would an appraiser *most likely* use for valuing Property #2?
    A. Cost approach.
    B. Income approach.
    C. Sales comparison approach.

58. Based on Exhibits 2 and 3, the valuation for Property #1 based on the discounted cash flow approach will be *closest* to:
   A. $22,798,000.
   B. $24,295,000.
   C. $24,633,000.

59. Based on the appraised value, Amiable Life Insurance Company would be willing to loan a maximum amount *closest* to:
   A. $20.7 million.
   B. $21.0 million.
   C. $21.7 million.

60. AIP's estimated return on equity on Property #1 using leverage as compared to return on equity without using any leverage will *most likely* be:
   A. lower.
   B. greater.
   C. the same.

End of Morning Session

EXAM 2
AFTERNOON SESSION

Question	Topic	Minutes (Points)
61 to 66	Ethical and Professional Standards	18
67 to 72	Quantitative Analysis	18
73 to 78	Financial Reporting and Analysis	18
79 to 84	Corporate Finance	18
85 to 96	Equity Valuation	36
97 to 108	Fixed Income	36
109 to 114	Derivatives	18
115 to 120	Portfolio Management	18

61.	(A)	(B)	(C)		101.	(A)	(B)	(C)
62.	(A)	(B)	(C)		102.	(A)	(B)	(C)
63.	(A)	(B)	(C)		103.	(A)	(B)	(C)
64.	(A)	(B)	(C)		104.	(A)	(B)	(C)
65.	(A)	(B)	(C)		105.	(A)	(B)	(C)
66.	(A)	(B)	(C)		106.	(A)	(B)	(C)
67.	(A)	(B)	(C)		107.	(A)	(B)	(C)
68.	(A)	(B)	(C)		108.	(A)	(B)	(C)
69.	(A)	(B)	(C)		109.	(A)	(B)	(C)
70.	(A)	(B)	(C)		110.	(A)	(B)	(C)
71.	(A)	(B)	(C)		111.	(A)	(B)	(C)
72.	(A)	(B)	(C)		112.	(A)	(B)	(C)
73.	(A)	(B)	(C)		113.	(A)	(B)	(C)
74.	(A)	(B)	(C)		114.	(A)	(B)	(C)
75.	(A)	(B)	(C)		115.	(A)	(B)	(C)
76.	(A)	(B)	(C)		116.	(A)	(B)	(C)
77.	(A)	(B)	(C)		117.	(A)	(B)	(C)
78.	(A)	(B)	(C)		118.	(A)	(B)	(C)
79.	(A)	(B)	(C)		119.	(A)	(B)	(C)
80.	(A)	(B)	(C)		120.	(A)	(B)	(C)
81.	(A)	(B)	(C)					
82.	(A)	(B)	(C)					
83.	(A)	(B)	(C)					
84.	(A)	(B)	(C)					
85.	(A)	(B)	(C)					
86.	(A)	(B)	(C)					
87.	(A)	(B)	(C)					
88.	(A)	(B)	(C)					
89.	(A)	(B)	(C)					
90.	(A)	(B)	(C)					
91.	(A)	(B)	(C)					
92.	(A)	(B)	(C)					
93.	(A)	(B)	(C)					
94.	(A)	(B)	(C)					
95.	(A)	(B)	(C)					
96.	(A)	(B)	(C)					
97.	(A)	(B)	(C)					
98.	(A)	(B)	(C)					
99.	(A)	(B)	(C)					
100.	(A)	(B)	(C)					

Exam 2
Afternoon Session

Use the following information to answer Questions 61 through 66.

Mikale Natschavin, CFA is the managing director of Blue Lotus LP, a boutique investment bank specializing in M&A consulting in the professional services arena. Blue Lotus also manages a fund (Xeta fund) for several institutional clients. The fund was run by a team of four managers. During the recent downturn, commensurate with the decline in the size of the fund, Blue Lotus downsized the firm.

Paul Vakil, CFA, one of the managers of Xeta, was laid off by Blue Lotus. During his exit interview Natschavin wished Vakil well and, on behalf of the firm, gave him permission to use Xeta fund's past performance when seeking new employment opportunities. Vakil included the performance of the fund to demonstrate his success but did not give any indication of a team approach. Vakil also did not mention to Natschavin or the personnel manager that he was still in possession of the company-issued laptop. Vakil had stored several models the team had developed in pursuing investment strategies on that laptop's hard disk.

Within a few months, Vakil joined the equity research department of Patarsby and Singly, a brokerage firm. Vakil, with the help of a quant specialist at Patarsby, improved the models and started using them in his new role. Things turned out very well for Vakil at Patarsby, and clients waited eagerly for release of his monthly recommendations. During a society event, Vakil ran into Alia Dutt, one of the other team managers of Xeta fund. Dutt congratulated Vakil. Later in the evening, Vakil spoke to Dutt about one of the companies he is following—Sandhirst Inc. Vakil stated that his preliminary research indicates that the short-term outlook for Sandhirst is very promising. Dutt also met Neil Savin, Frapco Inc.'s controller at the event. Frapco is a national grocery chain and a long-time client of Blue Lotus. Savin informed Dutt that the new layout in the stores has been a hit, and that he expects revenues and earnings for the current quarter to be well above consensus forecast.

The next day, Dutt placed a large order for Sandhirst stock for the Xeta fund. Dutt also placed a large order for a retail ETF. Dutt is a member of an online forum where she discusses investments under a pseudonym. Dutt has formed a very loyal following over time as others realized that her posts were very articulate and, therefore, the work of a professional. Dutt recommended

Frapco stock in the forum but attributed the recommendation to a general uptick in grocery store margins nationwide—a known fact based on recent earnings announcements of other grocers.

The following week at a charity golf tournament, Vakil met with Bob Snead, his college roommate. Snead was a very successful hedge fund manager. Both of the funds run by Smead were currently closed to new investment, though Snead was considering reopening the investments in the near future. At Vakil's insistence, Snead agreed to allow new investments into the two funds using a newly started intermediary fund as long as Vakil is the fund's manager. Vakil quickly convinced his bosses at Patarsby to open an intermediary fund and marketed the fund to existing Patarsby clients as a way into Snead hedge funds. Not knowing how long the deal with Snead would hold up, and wanting to quickly ramp up assets under management, Vakil accepted deposits from all Patarsby clients, even some that were relatively new accounts.

61. Regarding Vakil's reference to Xeta fund's performance in his resume, which of the following is *most accurate* regarding compliance with the Code and Standards? Vakil violated:
A. Standard III(D) – Performance Presentation.
B. Standard IV(A) –Duties to Employer: Loyalty.
C. Standard IIID – Performance Presentation as well as Standard IV(A) – Duties to Employer: Loyalty.

62. Vakil's use of the Blue Lotus models at Patarsby is *least likely* to be a violation under:
A. Standard I(C) – Professionalism: Misrepresentation.
B. Standard II(A) – Integrity of Capital Markets: Material Nonpublic Information.
C. Standard IV(A) – Duties to Employer: Loyalty.

63. Vakil's conversation with Dutt regarding Sandhirst stock is *most likely* a violation of:
A. Standard IV(A) – Duties to Employer: Loyalty.
B. Standard II(A) – Integrity of Capital Markets: Material Nonpublic Information.
C. Standard III(C) – Duties to Clients: Suitability.

64. With regards to investments in Sandhirst stock and retail ETF, Dutt *most likely* violated:
A. Standard II(A) – Material and Nonpublic Information by investing in Sandhirst stock but not by investing in the retail ETF.
B. Standard II(A) – Material and Nonpublic Information by investing in the retail ETF but not by investing in Sandhirst stock.
C. Standard II(A) – Material and Nonpublic Information in both instances.

65. Dutt's recommendation of Frapco stock in the online forum is *most likely*:
     A. a violation of Standard II(A) – Material and Nonpublic Information even though she attributed the recommendation to publicly available information.
     B. not a violation under Standard II(A) – Material and Nonpublic Information.
     C. violation of Standard III(E): Preservation of Confidentiality.

66. Vakil's conduct regarding the intermediary fund to channel investments into Snead funds is *most likely* a violation under:
     A. Standard II(B) Integrity of Capital Markets: Market Manipulation.
     B. Standard III(D) Duties to Clients: Suitability.
     C. Standard III(D) Duties to Clients: Fair Dealing.

Use the following information to answer Questions 67 through 72.

Research associate Kate Sawyer is responsible for identifying the determinants of performance for her firm's Progressive Fund (PF). All tests performed at Sawyer's firm are examined at the 0.05 level of significance. Sawyer examines the following regressions using monthly data observed for a 36 month period:

(1) $R_{PF,t} = b_0 + b_1 R_{M,t} + b_2 VMG_t + e_{PF,t}$

(2) $\hat{e}_{PF,t}^2 = a_0 + a_1 R_{M,t} + a_2 VMG_t + u_{PF,t}$

> where:
> $R_{PF,t}$ = the return on the Progressive Fund in month t
> $R_{M,t}$ = the return on the Wilshire 5000 stock market index in month t
> VMG_t = the return on value stocks minus the return on growth stocks in month t
> $\hat{e}_{PF,t}^2$ = the estimated squared regression errors derived from equation (1)

Exhibit 1: Equation (1) Regression Results

Variable	Coefficient	p-values
Constant	−0.005	0.030
R_M	1.250	0.001
VMG	0.200	0.980

The R^2 from equation (1) equals 0.80. A colleague, Jack Lockhart, makes two recommendations to Sawyer:

Recommendation 1: My research indicates that inflation-rate changes are highly correlated with the Wilshire 5000 stock index returns. Therefore, I recommend adding the inflation change variable to your regression.

Recommendation 2: My research indicates that the slope coefficients of your regression changed significantly after the passage of Regulation Fair Disclosure, which took place in the middle of your 3-year sample period. Your regression pools across two distinct sample periods. Therefore, I recommend correcting your current regression equation (1) for model misspecification.

In her conversation with Lockhart, Sawyer explains that she is concerned that her regression equation (1) may ignore other important determinants

©2017 Kaplan, Inc.

of performance for the Progressive Fund. Sawyer explains that she is aware that the omission of important independent variables affects the quality of the parameter estimates of the regression. She makes the following claims, assuming the omitted variables are correlated with the included variables:

Claim 1: The parameter estimates of equation (1) are unbiased.

Claim 2: The parameter estimates of equation (1) are inconsistent.

67. Of the slopes for the two independent variables, R_M and VMG, determine which are statistically significant at the 0.05 level?
    A. Both slopes are statistically significant.
    B. Only the slope for R_M is statistically significant.
    C. Only the slope for VMG is statistically significant.

68. The R^2 derived for equation (1) indicates which of the following for equation (1)?
    A. Regression sum of squares exceeds the error sum of squares.
    B. Regression sum of squares exceeds the total sum of squares.
    C. Mean regression sum of squares is less than the mean total sum of squares.

69. Sawyer decides to test regression equation (1) for the existence of conditional heteroskedasticity. Sawyer is likely to conclude that her regression does not exhibit conditional heteroskedasticity if the R^2 from equation (2) is:
    A. close to 0.
    B. close to 1.
    C. close to 0.80.

70. Regarding Lockhart's Recommendation 1, the econometric problem that is *most likely* to be introduced by including the inflation change variable in regression equation (1) is:
    A. model misspecification.
    B. serial correlation.
    C. multicollinearity.

71. Regarding Lockhart's Recommendation 2, the *most likely* form of model misspecification to which he refers is:
    A. stationarity model misspecification.
    B. time-series model misspecification.
    C. functional form model misspecification.

72. Regarding Claim 1 and Claim 2 made by Sawyer about the effects of omitted variables, which claims are correct?
    A. Claim 1 only.
    B. Claim 2 only.
    C. Both Claim 1 and Claim 2.

Use the following information to answer Questions 73 through 78.

Gary Smith, CFA, has been hired to analyze a specialty tool and machinery manufacturer, Whitmore Corporation (WMC). WMC is a leading producer of specialty machinery in the United States. At the end of 2014, WMC purchased York Tool Company (YTC), an Australian firm in a similar line of business. YTC has partially integrated its marketing functions within WMC but still maintains control of its operations and secures its own financing. Following is a summary of the income statement and balance sheet for YTC (in millions of Australian dollars – AUD) for the past three years as well as exchange rate data over the same period.

Income Statement (AUD millions)	2014	2015	2016
Revenues	765	820	870
COGS	484	520	580
SG&A	171	183	200
Depreciation expense	50	50	50
Interest expense	18	17	16
Income before tax	42	50	24
Taxes	21	25	12
Net income	**21**	**25**	**12**

Balance Sheet (AUD millions)

	2014	2015	2016		2014	2015	2016
Cash	22	25	20	Current liabilities	616	593	584
Accounts receivable	400	422	460	Long-term debt	180	170	160
Inventories	20	25	30				
Prepaid expenses	8	20	25	Common stock	50	50	50
Net Fixed assets	500	450	400	Retained earnings	104	129	141
Total assets	950	942	935	Total liabilities & equity	950	942	935

Exchange rates (AUD / USD)	2014	2015	2016
Average exchange rate	1.40	1.30	1.45
Year-end exchange rate	1.20	1.40	1.50
Historical exchange rate	1.20	1.20	1.20

Smith has discovered that WMC has a small subsidiary in Ukraine. The subsidiary follows IAS accounting rules and uses FIFO inventory accounting. The Ukrainian subsidiary was acquired ten years ago and has been fully integrated into WMC's operations. WMC obtains funding for the subsidiary whenever the company finds profitable investments within Ukraine or surrounding countries. According to forecasts from economists, the Ukrainian currency is expected to depreciate relative to the U.S. dollar over the next few years. Local currency prices are forecasted to remain stable, however.

One of the managers at WMC asks Smith to analyze a third subsidiary located in India. The manager has explained that real interest rates in India over the past three years have been 2.00%, 2.50%, and 3.00%, respectively, while nominal interest rates have been 34.64%, 29.15%, and 25.66%, respectively. Smith requests more time to analyze the Indian subsidiary.

73. Calculate the percent change in YTC net income shown on the WMC financial statements from 2015 to 2016.
    A. −52.0%.
    B. −55.2%.
    C. −56.9%.

74. If WMC uses the temporal method, YTC's net monetary liabilities leave WMC exposed to loss in the event of:
    A. currency (AUD) depreciation.
    B. currency (AUD) appreciation.
    C. either currency depreciation or currency appreciation.

75. Determine whether the translated total asset turnover for YTC for 2016 would be higher under the current rate method or under the temporal method.
    A. Temporal method.
    B. Current rate method.
    C. No difference between temporal and current rate methods.

76. For the period 2014–2016, WMC's annual USD revenue growth rate attributable to its Australian subsidiary is *most likely*:
    A. 1.85% lower than the local currency revenue growth rate.
    B. 3.62% higher than the local currency revenue growth rate.
    C. 3.45% lower than the local currency revenue growth rate.

77. Which of the following statements regarding the consolidation of WMC's Ukrainian subsidiary for the next year is *least likely* correct? Compared to the temporal method, the Ukrainian subsidiary's translated:
    A. net income before translation gains or losses would be higher using the current rate method.
    B. debt-to-equity ratio would be higher using the current rate method.
    C. gross profit margin would be lower using the current rate method.

78. Which of the following statements related to the consolidation of WMC's Indian subsidiary is *least likely* correct?
    A. The Indian economic environment meets the criteria to be classified as a hyperinflationary economy.
    B. IFRS would allow WMC to translate the inflation-indexed value of nonmonetary assets of the Indian subsidiary at the current exchange rate.
    C. WMC can reduce potential translation losses from the Indian subsidiary by issuing debt denominated in U.S. currency and purchasing fixed assets for the subsidiary.

Use the following information to answer Questions 79 through 84.

Voyager Inc., a primarily Internet-based media company, is buying The Daily, a media company with exposure to newspapers, television, and the Internet.

Company Descriptions
Voyager Inc. is organized into two segments: Internet and newspaper publishing. The Internet segment operates Web sites that offer news, entertainment, and advertising content in text and video format. The Internet segment represents 75% of the company's total revenues. The newspaper publishing segment publishes 10 daily newspapers. The newspaper publishing segment represents 25% of the company's total revenues.
The Daily is organized into three segments: newspaper publishing (60% of revenues), broadcasting (35% of revenues), and Internet (5% of revenues). The newspaper publishing segment publishes 101 daily newspapers. The broadcasting segment owns and operates 25 television stations. The Internet segment consists of an Internet advertising service. The Daily's newspaper publishing and broadcasting segments cover the 20 largest markets in the United States.

Voyager's acquisition of The Daily is the company's second major acquisition in its history. The previous acquisition was at the height of the merger boom in the year 2000. Voyager purchased the Dragon Company at a premium-to-net-asset value, thereby doubling the company's size. Voyager used the pooling method to account for the acquisition of Dragon; however, because of FASB changes to the Business Combination Standard, Voyager will use the acquisition method to account for the Daily acquisition.

(in millions except per share data)	Voyager Inc. *(before merger)*	The Daily *(before merger)*
Revenues	$1,800	$7,600
Operating income	$415	$998
Earnings	$200	$650
Assets	$1,900	$14,700
Debt	$200	$2,500
Equity	$1,100	$7,600
Number of shares	117.6 million	213.1 million
Stock price per share	$68	$35
Earnings per share	$1.70	$3.05
PE ratio	40.0x	11.5x

Voyager has made an all-cash offer of $45 per share to acquire The Daily. Wall Street is skeptical about the merger. While Voyager has been growing its revenues by 40% per year, The Daily's revenue growth has been less than 2% per year. Michael Renner, the CFO of Voyager, defends the acquisition by stating that The Daily has accumulated a large amount of tax losses and that the combined company can benefit by immediately increasing net income after the merger. In addition, Renner states that the new Voyager will eliminate the inefficiencies of its Internet operations and thereby boost future earnings. Renner believes that the merged companies will have a value of $17.5 billion.

In the past, The Daily's management has publicly stated its opposition to merging with any company, a position management still maintains. As a result of this situation, Voyager submitted its merger proposal directly to The Daily's board of directors, while the firm's CEO was on vacation. Upon returning from vacation, The Daily's CEO issued a public statement claiming that the proposed merger was unacceptable under any circumstances.

79. Voyager used the pooling of interests method when accounting for the 2000 acquisition of Dragon, rather than the acquisition method it would use today. Which of the following is *least likely* a feature of the pooling of interests method?
   A. Operating results for prior periods are restated as though the two firms were always combined.
   B. The pooling of interests method combines historic book values and fair values.
   C. The pooling of interests method combines historic book values.

80. Based on Renner's comments defending Voyager's acquisition of The Daily, indicate whether his comments about net income and elimination of inefficiencies are *most likely* correct.
   A. Only Renner's comment that unused tax losses will immediately translate into higher net income is correct.
   B. Only Renner's comment that the elimination of inefficiencies within the Internet operations will create additional value is correct.
   C. Both comments are correct.

81. Assuming that Renner's estimate of the value of the merged companies is correct, calculate the acquirer's gain from the merger.
   A. $7,910.5 million.
   B. $9,503.2 million.
   C. $11,634.2 million.

82. Assume that Voyager offers 63 million shares of its stock, rather than cash, to acquire The Daily. The share price of the combined company is *closest* to:
    A. $145 per share.
    B. $150 per share.
    C. $155 per share.

83. The management of The Daily is not pleased with the $45 per share offering price. Which of the following is the *most likely* takeover defense The Daily would consider in an effort to stop the acquisition?
    A. Immediately amend The Daily bylaws to establish a staggered board.
    B. File suit against Voyager for antitrust violations.
    C. Restrict the voting rights of shareholders owning more than 10% of The Daily stock.

84. Which of the following *best* characterizes Voyager's proposal to merge with The Daily?
    A. Bear hug.
    B. Proxy fight.
    C. White knight.

Use the following information to answer Questions 85 through 90.

Zi Wang is a senior buy-side equity analyst with Shandong Securities. Wang must review the work of several junior colleagues before investment recommendations go to the Shandong portfolio managers. One recommendation from a junior analyst is given in Exhibit 1.

Exhibit 1

Summary of investment characteristics for Aussie Shipping Company	
Current dividend	AUD 2.20 (AUD is Australian dollar)
Dividend growth rate	5%, perpetual
Equity beta	1.20
Risk-free rate	5.2%
Equity risk premium	4.5%
Current stock price	AUD 33.50
Estimated intrinsic value	AUD 41.25
Investment recommendation	Buy

This same junior analyst e-mailed Wang, saying "I'm in a meeting and hate to bother you. I don't have my calculator or computer with me. We have a British stock with a current £4.00 dividend that is expected to grow at 40% per year for two years and then forever after at 6%. If we assume a required return of 12%, what is the value of this stock?"

In a few minutes, Wang e-mails him back: "The British stock is worth £110.42."

The junior analyst sends back a second e-mail. "Thanks. If we can buy this stock for £90, what rate of return would we get? Assume the same dividend pattern as in my first e-mail."

Wang replies to the second e-mail: "I used trial and error and found an expected rate of return for the British stock of 12%."

One of Shandong's portfolio managers asks Wang to clarify the PVGO (present value of growth opportunities) concept for him. Wang tells him, "PVGO is the part of a stock's total value that comes from future growth opportunities. PVGO is conventionally estimated as the market value per share minus the book value per share."

The Shandong portfolio manager quickly follows up with two more requests. He says, "I need a couple of favors. First, could you describe the sustainable growth rate concept for us? We've been arguing about it among ourselves. And, second, could you review some highlighted phrases from a research report we received from one of our investment bankers? We aren't sure that

©2017 Kaplan, Inc.

the analyst who wrote this report is very competent." The highlighted phrases are:

Phrase 1: When calculating the justified P/E ratios based on a constant growth model like the Gordon model, the forward P/E should be greater than the trailing P/E.

Phrase 2: A free cash flow approach might be preferable when the company's cash flows differ substantially from dividends or when the investor takes a control perspective.

Phrase 3: When the required rate of return increases, the value of a share of stock should decrease even if the stock's dividend has a negative growth rate.

85.   Upon review, should Wang accept the estimated intrinsic value and investment recommendation for Aussie Shipping?
A. Yes.
B. No. The intrinsic value is AUD 39.29, although the recommendation is still a "buy."
C. No. The intrinsic value is AUD 31.67, and the recommendation should be "do not buy."

86.   Is Wang's estimate of the British stock price correct?
A. Yes.
B. No. The value is £86.90.
C. No. The value is £121.67.

87.   Is Wang's estimate of the expected rate of return for the British stock approximately correct?
A. Yes.
B. No. The rate of return is closer to 13%.
C. No. The rate of return is closer to 14%.

88.   Is Wang's description of PVGO *most likely* correct?
A. Yes.
B. No. PVGO is the difference between the price and the value of assets in place. The value of assets in place is estimated by dividing dividends per share by the required rate of return.
C. No. PVGO is the difference between the price and the value of assets in place. The value of assets in place is estimated by dividing earnings per share by the required rate of return.

89.   How should Wang describe sustainable growth? "The sustainable growth rate is the rate of dividend and earnings growth that can be sustained for a given return on equity, assuming that:
       A. no additional external capital is raised."
       B. additional debt capital may be raised, keeping the capital structure constant."
       C. additional equity capital may be raised proportional to the amount of earnings retained."

90.   Which of the three phrases in the investment banker's report is *least likely* to be correct?
       A. Phrase 1.
       B. Phrase 2.
       C. Phrase 3.

©2017 Kaplan, Inc.

Use the following information to answer Questions 91 through 96.

Yummy Doughnuts (YD) sells a variety of doughnuts and other related items through both company-owned locations and franchise locations. YD has experienced significant growth over the past five years. However, barriers to entry are low and competition is increasing.

Linda Haas, CFA, follows YD for Gibraltar Capital. Gibraltar Capital prides itself on its thorough fundamental analysis of investment opportunities. The company uses a bottom-up approach to the investment process. Haas's security selection process utilizes residual income models to determine a stock's intrinsic value. Haas obtains YD's 2018 financial statements shown in Exhibit 1. In addition, Haas provides supporting information about YD's financials and other related material found in Exhibit 2.

Exhibit 1: Yummy Doughnuts's 2018 Income Statement and Balance Sheet

In millions, except for per share items	2018
Revenue	$300
Cost of goods sold	$205
SG&A	$40
Depreciation expense	$6
Income from operations	$49
Interest expense	$1
Pretax income	$48
Income tax (40% tax rate)	$19
Net income	$29
Shares outstanding	18.6
EPS	$1.56

In millions	2018		2018
Assets		**Liabilities and equity**	
Cash	$15	Accounts payable	$12
Accounts receivable	$27	Accrued expenses	$26
Inventory	$16	Current liabilities	$38
Current assets	$58		
Property and equipment	$113	Total long-term debt (7% coupon, at par value)	$12
Long-term investments	$10	Equity	$131
Total assets	**$181**	**Total liabilities & equity**	**$181**

Exhibit 2: Additional Information

- YD uses the FIFO method of inventory valuation.
- 2018 cash operating taxes equal $15 million. This amount includes all appropriate tax adjustments. 2018 NOPAT was estimated to be $42 million.
- Haas believes that YD will have a 17% ROE and a 10% long-term growth rate over the foreseeable future.
- Haas estimates YD's cost of equity to be 15.0%
- YD expects annual capital expenditures to remain at about $37 million.
- YD's stock currently trades at $15.50 per share.
- YD's bonds are currently trading at par value.
- YD's total adjusted capital base was $200 million at the end of 2017.

Haas makes the following statements during her YD presentation to the investment committee:

Statement 1: Based on ROE mean reversion, YD's continuing residual income is assumed to decline to zero over time.

Statement 2: The residual income model states that if YD's ROE equals its equity cost of capital, then YD's intrinsic value will equal its book value per share.

91. For this question only, a careful evaluation of YD's financial statement reveals that the decrease in value of available-for-sale securities has been reported in the other comprehensive income (OCI) section of stockholder's equity. The *most likely* impact on the computation of residual income due to accounting for available-for-sale securities would be:
    A. a reduction in residual income due to lower ROE.
    B. a reduction in residual income due to lower ROE and book value.
    C. an increase in residual income due to higher ROE.

92. Based on Exhibits 1 and 2, YD's weighted average cost of capital (WACC) is *closest* to:
    A. 12%.
    B. 13%.
    C. 15%.

93. For this question only, assume a weighted average cost of capital (WACC) of 12.0%. YD's economic value added (EVA) during the year 2018 is *closest* to:
    A. $6 million.
    B. $18 million.
    C. $24 million.

94. Based on Exhibit 1, Exhibit 2, and the single-stage residual income model, YD's intrinsic value is *closest* to:
    A. $8.00 per share.
    B. $10.00 per share.
    C. $12.00 per share.

95. Haas notes that the multi-stage residual equity income model captures more detail in calculating YD's intrinsic value. An assumption of the model is that ROE fades to the cost of equity over time, which is known as a persistence factor (varying from 0 to 1). Identify which characteristic indicates a higher persistence of abnormal earnings.
    A. Low dividend payout.
    B. Low price-to-earnings ratio.
    C. High dividend yield.

96. Haas makes a statement about an assumption concerning residual income (Statement 1) and the residual income model (Statement 2). Which of the statements is correct?
    A. Only Statement 1 is correct.
    B. Only Statement 2 is correct.
    C. Both Statements 1 and 2 are correct.

Use the following information to answer Questions 97 through 102.

Michael Thomas, CFA, is a fixed-income portfolio manager for TFC Investments. As part of his portfolio strategy for the Prosperity Fund, Thomas seeks out bonds that he expects to be upgraded or downgraded. Potential upgrades that Thomas identifies are added to the portfolio (or, if already in the portfolio, are increased in proportion to other holdings). Potential downgrades are sold from the portfolio. Thomas's portfolio's current holdings include several bonds issued by companies in the oil and gas exploration and refining industries. Year-end rating updates are expected to occur in a few days, and Thomas is preparing to adjust his portfolio in advance of expected changes in credit ratings.

Thomas has been discussing his fixed-income strategies with fellow portfolio manager Shawna Reese. Reese suggests that while Thomas's general approach is suitable, the overall credit-analysis strategy could be improved. Reese recommends using the present value of expected loss as a metric in credit analysis.

Reese makes the following statement to Thomas:

Reese's Statement: "The present value of expected loss is a credit measure that makes two modifications to the expected loss metric. The first adjustment relates to risk premium, and the second is related to the time value of money."

Reese provides information about 2-year, 4% Pistar Inc. bonds as shown in Exhibit 1. The coupon on the bonds is paid semiannually.

Exhibit 1: Term Structure of Credit Spreads on Pistar bonds

Time to Cash Flow	Risk-Free Spot Rate	Credit Spread (%)
0.5	1.50%	0.20%
1	1.75%	0.25%
1.5	2.00%	0.30%
2	2.25%	0.35%

As part of his portfolio analysis, Thomas also compares credit metrics suitable for ABS to those that are suitable for sovereign debt.

Thomas concludes his analysis by comparing the swap rate curve to a government bond yield curve.

©2017 Kaplan, Inc.

97. The risk premium mentioned in Reese's statement is *most likely* referring to the:
    A. difference in yield between a risky security and a treasury security.
    B. additional premium for risky securities that have embedded options.
    C. adjustment to the probabilities to account for risk of the cash flows.

98. Under the option analogy of the structural model, owning a company's debt is economically equivalent to owning a riskless bond and simultaneously:
    A. buying an American put option on the assets of the company.
    B. selling a European put option on the assets of the company.
    C. buying a European put option on the assets of the company.

99. Which of the following statements *least accurately* describes an assumption made under the structural form models of credit analysis?
    A. The company's assets trade in frictionless markets.
    B. The risk-free interest rate is constant.
    C. The value of the company's assets at maturity of the debt has a normal distribution.

100. The present value of expected loss on $1,000 face-value Pistar bonds is *closest* to:
    A. $6.96.
    B. $18.27.
    C. $43.44.

101. Do the credit risk measures probability of default and probability of loss *most closely* relate to asset-backed securities (ABS) or sovereign bonds?

Probability of default	Probability of loss
A. ABS	ABS
B. ABS	Sovereign bond
C. Sovereign bond	ABS

102. Which of the following statements regarding the choice between government bond yield curves and swap-rate curves as a benchmark interest rate curve is *most accurate*?
    A. The swap-rate curve is preferred because swap curves are comparable across countries since they reflect similar levels of credit risk.
    B. Government bond yield curves are preferred because they are based on a more complete set of market yields.
    C. Government bond yield curves are preferred because the lack of a liquid secondary market can distort swap yields compared with government bond yields.

Use the following information to answer Questions 103 through 108.

MediSoft Inc. develops and distributes high-tech medical software used in hospitals and clinics across the United States and Canada. The firm's software provides an integrated solution to monitoring, analyzing, and managing output from a variety of diagnostic medical equipment including MRIs, CT scans, and EKG machines. MediSoft has grown rapidly since its inception ten years ago, averaging 25% growth in sales over the past decade. The company went public three years ago. Twelve months after its IPO, MediSoft made two bond offerings, the first of which was a convertible bond.

At the time of issuance, the convertible bond had a coupon rate of 7.25%, a par value of $1,000, a conversion price of $55.56, and ten years until maturity. Two years after issuance, the bond became callable at 102% of par value. Soon after the issuance of the convertible bond, the company issued another series of bonds, which were putable but contained no conversion or call features. The putable bonds were issued with a coupon of 8.0%, a par value of $1,000, and 15 years until maturity. The putable bond has a European-style option exercisable 10 years after issuance at par. The bonds were issued three years ago.

MediSoft's convertible bonds are now trading in the market for a price of $947 with an estimated straight value of $917. The company's putable bonds are trading at a price of $1,052. Volatility in the price of MediSoft's common stock has been relatively high over the past few months. Currently, the stock is priced at $50 on the New York Stock Exchange and is expected to continue its annual dividend in the amount of $1.80 per share.

High-tech industry analysts for Brown & Associates, a money management firm specializing in fixed-income investments, have been closely following MediSoft ever since it went public three years ago. In general, portfolio managers at Brown & Associates do not participate in initial offerings of debt investments, preferring instead to see how the issue trades before considering taking a position in the issue. Because MediSoft's bonds have had ample time to trade in the marketplace, analysts and portfolio managers have taken an interest in the company's bonds. At a meeting to discuss the merits of MediSoft's bonds, the following comments were made by various portfolio managers and analysts at Brown & Associates:

> "Choosing to invest in MediSoft's convertible bond would benefit our portfolios in many ways, but the primary benefit is the limited downside risk associated with the bond. Because the straight value will provide a floor for the value of the convertible bond, downside risk is limited to the difference between the market price of the bond and the straight value."

©2017 Kaplan, Inc.

"Decreasing volatility in the price of MediSoft's common stock as well as increasing volatility in the level of interest rates are expected in the near future. The combined effects of these changes in volatility will be a decrease in the price of MediSoft's putable bonds and an increase in the price of the convertible bonds. Therefore, only the convertible bonds would be a suitable purchase."

103. Calculate the market conversion premium per share for MediSoft's convertible bonds.
    A. $2.61.
    B. $2.95.
    C. $5.56.

104. The minimum value of the convertible bond today is *closest* to:
    A. $900.
    B. $917.
    C. $947.

105. Suppose that MediSoft wants to issue new bonds but wants to issue the bonds at-or-above par value. Which of the following bonds would *most closely* match their criteria?
    A. 7-year, 7.25% convertible bond with a conversion price of $56.
    B. 7-year, 7.25% callable bond, callable in two years at 102% of par.
    C. 7-year, 8% coupon bond extendible for five years at the same coupon rate.

106. Under what circumstances will the analyst's comments regarding the limited downside risk of MediSoft's convertible bonds be accurate?
    A. Short-term and long-term interest rates are expected to remain the same.
    B. The Federal Reserve Bank decides to pursue a restrictive monetary policy.
    C. The convertible bond is trading in the market as a common stock equivalent.

107. If the OAS on Medisoft's straight bond was estimated to be 48bps, which of the following statements is *most accurate*?
    A. The OAS of callable bond will be greater than 48bps, and the OAS of the convertible bond will be less than 48bps.
    B. The OAS of the convertible bond will be less than 48bps, while the OAS of the putable bond will be greater than 48bps.
    C. The OAS of the callable, putable and convertible bond should be equal to 48bps.

108. Evaluate the portfolio managers' comments regarding the changes in the values of MediSoft's bonds resulting from changes in the volatility of the company's common stock and the volatility of interest rates. The managers were:
    A. correct only with regard to the convertible bonds.
    B. correct only with regard to the putable bonds.
    C. incorrect with regard to both securities.

Use the following information to answer Questions 109 through 114.

James Walker is the chief financial officer for Lothar Corporation, a U.S. mining company that specializes in worldwide exploration for and excavation of precious metals. Lothar Corporation generally tries to maintain a debt-to-capital ratio of approximately 45% and has successfully done so for the past seven years. Due to the time lag between the discovery of an extractable vein of metal and the eventual sale of the excavated material, the company frequently must issue short-term debt to fund its operations. Issuing these one- to six-month notes sometimes pushes Lothar's debt-to-capital ratio above its long-term target, but the cash provided from the short-term financing is necessary to complete the majority of the company's mining projects.

Walker has estimated that extraction of silver deposits in southern Australia has eight months until project completion. However, funding for the project will run out in approximately six months. In order to cover the funding gap, Walker will have to issue short-term notes with a principal value of $1,275,000 at an unknown future interest rate. To mitigate the interest rate uncertainty, Walker has decided to enter into a forward rate agreement (FRA) based on LIBOR which currently has a term structure as shown in Exhibit 1.

Exhibit 1

LIBOR Rates (t = 0)	
	LIBOR
90-day	4.28%
180-day	4.52%
240-day	5.11%
360-day	5.92%

Exhibit 2

LIBOR Rates (t = 90)	
	LIBOR
90-day	5.12%
150-day	5.96%
210-day	6.03%
300-day	6.41%

Three months after establishing the position in the forward rate agreement, LIBOR interest rates have shifted, causing the value of Lothar's FRA position to change as well. The new LIBOR term structure is shown in Exhibit 2.

While Walker is estimating the change in the value of the original FRA position, he receives a memo from the chief operating officer of Lothar, Maria Steiner, informing him of a major delay in one of the company's South African mining projects. In the memo, Steiner states the following:

"As usual, the project delay will require a short-term loan to cover the funding shortage that will accompany the extra time until project completion. I have estimated that in 210 days, we will require a 90-day project loan in the amount of $2,350,000. I would like you to establish another FRA position, this time with a contract rate of 6.95%."

Walker discusses some of these strategies with Pete Barka, partner at the brokerage firm that clears derivatives trades for Lothar. Barka suggests options on the Nasdaq 100 index futures as a use for Lothar's excess cash. September futures price on the Nasdaq 100 index is currently at 4243. Three-month calls and puts with a strike price of 4200 are available. Exhibit 3 shows information about the options.

Exhibit 3: Three-Month Options on Nasdaq 100

Strike price (for both calls and puts)	$4200
Call premium	$243
Put premium	$196
Implied volatility	26%
Continuously compounded risk-free rate	0.35%
$N(d_1)$	0.5597
$N(d_2)$	0.5080

109. Given data in Exhibit 1, which of the following was *closest* to the price of the FRA on the date of the contract's inception?
    A. 4.7%.
    B. 6.8%.
    C. 7.2%.

110. Which of the following is *closest* to the value of the forward rate agreement three months after the inception of the contract (from Walker's perspective)? For this question only, assume that the interest rate at inception was 6.0%.
    A. $2,340.
    B. −$3,266.
    C. $3,266.

111. Using the Black model, the call option on the index futures is *best* valued as:
    A. the present value of the difference between the strike rate multiplied by 0.5597 and the current futures price multiplied by 0.508.
    B. the present value of the difference between the current futures price times 0.5597 and the exercise price multiplied by 0.508.
    C. the future value of the difference between the current spot price multiplied by 0.5597 and the exercise price multiplied by 0.508.

112. When the silver is removed from the mine, it will be sold to an Australian subsidiary before being exported. Walker is concerned that the price of silver and the Australian dollar will both depreciate over the next eight months. Which of the following strategies will be *most* appropriate given Walker's expectations? Establish a:
    A. short position in a silver forward contract and a short position in a U.S. dollar currency forward contract.
    B. long position in a silver forward contract and a short position in an Australian dollar currency forward contract.
    C. short position in a silver forward contract and a long position in a U.S. dollar currency forward contract.

113. Which of the following is the *most accurate* way to replicate a payer swap?
    A. A zero-cost portfolio consisting of a long cap and a short floor with the same strike rate.
    B. A short cap and long floor with strike rate equal to the swap fixed rate.
    C. A long FRA with maturity equal to the swap tenor.

114. Which of the following transactions should Walker initiate in order to comply with Steiner's request regarding the funding shortage at the South African gold mine? Establish a:
    A. long position in an off-market FRA by making a payment to the short position.
    B. short position in an off-market FRA by receiving a payment from the long position.
    C. long position in an off-market FRA by receiving a payment from the short position.

Use the following information to answer Questions 115 through 120.

Hong Zhou, Jianguo Yeung, and Jm Leor Joeng work for Pearl Asset Management, a large private wealth advisory firm. During lunch they discuss various unique client situations they face and how they plan to resolve them.

Yeung mentions that yesterday he prepared an IPS for one of his clients. Some of the constraints in the IPS included:

Constraint 1:   The client requires a minimum return of 8.2% per year.

Constraint 2:   The client needs $50,000 to repay a major loan in six months' time.

Constraint 3:   The client plans to retire in 12 years' time, at which point the portfolio will need to be sufficient to support the client's ongoing lifestyle.

Zhou, Yeung, and Joeng are all developing multifactor models to attempt to explain asset price returns. Zhou has built his model based on standardized sensitivities of asset returns to intrinsic valuation model inputs. When Zhou asks Yeung about factors that his model uses to explain the differences in returns of different asset classes, Yeung replies that he can't define exactly what the factors are but insists that his model uses statistical relationships that have been proven to hold over time. Joeng discounts both Zhou and Yeung's approaches and instead insists that surprises cause stock prices to move. Hence, he has built his model based on surprises rather than sensitivities to absolute factors.

Zhou wishes to combine the actively managed Lincoln investment fund with a passively managed fund that tracks the Russell 2000 (which is the benchmark for the Lincoln fund). Expected risk and return data is as follows:

	Lincoln Fund	Russell 2000
Expected annual return	7.6%	6.5%
Return standard deviation	19.0%	11.0%
Active risk	5.0%	0.0%
The risk-free rate is 3.0%		

Joeng asks Zhou about risk premium on an asset. Specifically, Joeng wants to know the impact on the risk premium if an asset's future value is negatively correlated with investors' utility from future consumption. Joeng also wants to know the relationship between a country's growth rate and the real risk-free rate.

115. How many of Yeung's constraints would be accurately regarded as a constraint in an investment policy statement?
    A. One.
    B. Two.
    C. Three.

116. Regarding the use of multifactor models, which of the following statements is *most likely* to be correct?
    A. Zhou is using a macroeconomic model, Yeung is using a fundamental factor model, and Joeng is using principal component analysis.
    B. Zhou is using a fundamental factor model, Yeung is using principal component analysis, and Joeng is using a macroeconomic model.
    C. Zhou is using principal component analysis, Yeung is using a macroeconomic model, and Joeng is using a fundamental factor model.

117. To achieve the optimal level of active risk, what proportion of funds would Zhou allocate to the Lincoln fund?
    A. 53%.
    B. 82%.
    C. 151%.

118. The highest Sharpe ratio that Zhou can achieve by combining the Lincoln fund and the Rusell 2000 is *closest* to:
    A. 0.39.
    B. 0.42.
    C. 1.12.

119. With regard to Joeng's question, Zhou would *most appropriately* reply that the risk premium would be:
    A. lower.
    B. higher.
    C. unaffected by the correlation.

120. For countries with high expected economic growth, it is *least likely* that:
    A. real risk-free rates will be high.
    B. inter-temporal rate of substitution will be high.
    C. investors will save less.

End of Afternoon Session

Exam 3
Morning Session

Question	Topic	Minutes (Points)
1 to 6	Ethics	18
7 to 12	Ethics	18
13 to 18	Economics	18
19 to 24	Financial Reporting and Analysis	18
25 to 30	Financial Reporting and Analysis	18
31 to 36	Equity	18
37 to 42	Equity	18
43 to 48	Equity	18
49 to 54	Fixed Income	18
55 to 60	Fixed Income	18

Test Answers

1. Ⓐ Ⓑ Ⓒ
2. Ⓐ Ⓑ Ⓒ
3. Ⓐ Ⓑ Ⓒ
4. Ⓐ Ⓑ Ⓒ
5. Ⓐ Ⓑ Ⓒ
6. Ⓐ Ⓑ Ⓒ
7. Ⓐ Ⓑ Ⓒ
8. Ⓐ Ⓑ Ⓒ
9. Ⓐ Ⓑ Ⓒ
10. Ⓐ Ⓑ Ⓒ

11. Ⓐ Ⓑ Ⓒ
12. Ⓐ Ⓑ Ⓒ
13. Ⓐ Ⓑ Ⓒ
14. Ⓐ Ⓑ Ⓒ
15. Ⓐ Ⓑ Ⓒ
16. Ⓐ Ⓑ Ⓒ
17. Ⓐ Ⓑ Ⓒ
18. Ⓐ Ⓑ Ⓒ
19. Ⓐ Ⓑ Ⓒ
20. Ⓐ Ⓑ Ⓒ

21. Ⓐ Ⓑ Ⓒ
22. Ⓐ Ⓑ Ⓒ
23. Ⓐ Ⓑ Ⓒ
24. Ⓐ Ⓑ Ⓒ
25. Ⓐ Ⓑ Ⓒ
26. Ⓐ Ⓑ Ⓒ
27. Ⓐ Ⓑ Ⓒ
28. Ⓐ Ⓑ Ⓒ
29. Ⓐ Ⓑ Ⓒ
30. Ⓐ Ⓑ Ⓒ

31. Ⓐ Ⓑ Ⓒ
32. Ⓐ Ⓑ Ⓒ
33. Ⓐ Ⓑ Ⓒ
34. Ⓐ Ⓑ Ⓒ
35. Ⓐ Ⓑ Ⓒ
36. Ⓐ Ⓑ Ⓒ
37. Ⓐ Ⓑ Ⓒ
38. Ⓐ Ⓑ Ⓒ
39. Ⓐ Ⓑ Ⓒ
40. Ⓐ Ⓑ Ⓒ

41. Ⓐ Ⓑ Ⓒ
42. Ⓐ Ⓑ Ⓒ
43. Ⓐ Ⓑ Ⓒ
44. Ⓐ Ⓑ Ⓒ
45. Ⓐ Ⓑ Ⓒ
46. Ⓐ Ⓑ Ⓒ
47. Ⓐ Ⓑ Ⓒ
48. Ⓐ Ⓑ Ⓒ
49. Ⓐ Ⓑ Ⓒ
50. Ⓐ Ⓑ Ⓒ

51. Ⓐ Ⓑ Ⓒ
52. Ⓐ Ⓑ Ⓒ
53. Ⓐ Ⓑ Ⓒ
54. Ⓐ Ⓑ Ⓒ
55. Ⓐ Ⓑ Ⓒ
56. Ⓐ Ⓑ Ⓒ
57. Ⓐ Ⓑ Ⓒ
58. Ⓐ Ⓑ Ⓒ
59. Ⓐ Ⓑ Ⓒ
60. Ⓐ Ⓑ Ⓒ

Exam 3
Morning Session

Questions 1–6 relate to Glenda Garvey.

Glenda Garvey is interning at Samson Financial in the summer to earn money for her last semester of MBA studies. She took the Level III CFA® exam in June but has not yet received her results. Garvey's work involves preparing research reports on small companies.

Garvey is at lunch with a group of co-workers. She listens to their conversation about various stocks and takes note of a comment from Tony Topel, a veteran analyst. Topel is talking about Vallo Engineering, a small stock he has tried repeatedly to convince the investment director to add to the monitored list. While the investment director does not like Vallo, Topel has faith in the company and has gradually accumulated 5,000 shares for his own account. Another analyst, Mary Kennedy, tells the group about Koral Koatings, a paint and sealant manufacturer. Kennedy has spent most of the last week at the office doing research on Koral. She has concluded that the stock is undervalued and consensus earnings estimates are conservative. However, she has not filed a report for Samson, nor does she intend to. She said she has purchased the stock for herself and advises her colleagues to do the same. After she gets back to the office, Garvey purchases 25 shares of Vallo and 50 shares of Koral for herself.

Samson pays its interns very little, and Garvey works as a waitress at a diner in the financial district to supplement her income. The dinner crowd includes many analysts and brokers who work at nearby businesses. While waiting tables that night, Garvey hears two employees of a major brokerage house discussing Metrona, a nanotechnology company. The restaurant patrons say that the broker's star analyst has issued a report with a buy rating on Metrona that morning. The diners plan to buy the stock the next morning. After Garvey finishes her shift, restaurant manager Mandy Jones, a longtime Samson client, asks to speak with her. Jones commends Garvey for her hard work at the restaurant, praising her punctuality and positive attitude, and offers her two tickets to a Yankees game as a bonus.

The next morning, Garvey buys 40 shares of Metrona for her own account at the market open. Soon afterward, she receives a call from Harold Koons, one of Samson's largest money-management clients. Koons says he got Garvey's name from Bertha Witt, who manages the Koons's account. Koons wanted to reward the analyst who discovered Anvil Hammers, a machine-tool company whose stock soared soon after it was added to his portfolio. Garvey prepared the original report on Anvil Hammers. Koons offers Garvey two free round-trip tickets to the city of her choice. Garvey thanks Koons, then asks her immediate supervisor, Karl May, about the gift from Koons but does not mention the gift from Jones. May approves the Koons' gift.

After talking with May, Garvey starts a research project on Zenith Enterprises, a frozen-juice maker. Garvey's gathers quarterly data on the company's sales and profits over the past two years. Garvey uses a simple linear regression to estimate the relationship between GDP growth and Zenith's sales growth. Next she uses a consensus GDP estimate from a well-known economic data reporting service and her regression model to extrapolate growth rates for the next three years.

Garvey is not working at the diner that night, so she goes home to work on her biography for an online placement service. In it she makes the following two statements:

Statement 1: I'm a Level III CFA candidate, and I expect to receive my charter this fall. The CFA program is a grueling, 3-part, graduate-level course, and passage requires an expertise in a variety of financial instruments, as well as knowledge of the forces that drive our economy and financial markets.

Statement 2: I expect to graduate with my MBA from Braxton College at the end of the fall semester. As both an MBA and a CFA, I'll be in high demand. Hire me now while you still have the chance.

Akshay Nagoree, CFA, is a portfolio manager for several pension funds at Samson. His wife is treasurer and 15% shareholder of Gatedon Electric. The market value of Mrs. Nagoree's Gatedon shares is now $2 million. Samson's research department is recommending the stock to its trust officers and pension fund portfolio managers. Samson has adopted CFA Institute's Research Objectivity Standards.

1. During the lunch conversation, which CFA Institute Standard of Professional Conduct was *most likely* violated?
    A. III(B) Fair Dealing.
    B. IV(A) Loyalty.
    C. V(A) Reasonable Basis.

2. Does Garvey's acceptance of the gifts from Koons and Jones violate Standard I(B) Independence and Objectivity?
    A. Accepting Koons' gift was a violation.
    B. Accepting Jones' gift was a violation.
    C. Neither gift would result in a violation.

3. Did Garvey violate Standard II(A) Material Nonpublic Information when she purchased Vallo and Metrona?
   A. Buying Vallo was a violation.
   B. Buying Metrona was a violation.
   C. Neither purchase was a violation.

4. In her estimation of Zenith's future growth rate, what standard did Garvey violate?
   A. Standard I(C) Misrepresentation regarding plagiarism.
   B. Standard V(A) Diligence and Reasonable Basis.
   C. Both I(C) and V(A).

5. Did the two statements in Garvey's biography violate Standard VII(B) Reference to CFA Institute, the CFA designation, and the CFA program?
   A. Statement 1 is a violation.
   B. Statement 2 is a violation.
   C. Both statements are violations.

6. Based on the Research Objectivity Standards, which of the following is Nagoree's *most appropriate* course of action for the accounts under his management?
   A. Nagoree is permitted to buy Gatedon stock without stipulation because it is his wife, not he, who is a shareholder in Gatedon.
   B. Nagoree is permitted to buy the stock after disclosing his wife's ownership to his supervisor and to the trustees of all the pension funds he manages.
   C. Nagoree is prohibited from buying the stock because of his inability to render an unbiased and objective investment opinion given his wife's affiliation with the company.

Questions 7–12 relate to Maria Harris.

Maria Harris is a CFA® Level III candidate and portfolio manager for Islandwide Hedge Fund. Harris is commonly involved in complex trading strategies on behalf of Islandwide and maintains a significant relationship with Quadrangle Brokers, which provides portfolio analysis tools to Harris. Recent market volatility has led Islandwide to incur record-high trading volume and commissions with Quadrangle for the quarter. In appreciation of Islandwide's business, Quadrangle offers Harris an all-expenses-paid week of golf at Pebble Beach for her and her husband. Harris discloses the offer to her supervisor and compliance officer and, based on their approval, accepts the trip.

Harris has lunch that day with C. K. Swamy, CFA, her old college roommate and future sister-in-law. While Harris is sitting in the restaurant waiting for Swamy to arrive, Harris overhears a conversation between the president and chief financial officer (CFO) of Progressive Industries. The president informs the CFO that Progressive's board of directors has just approved dropping the company's cash dividend, despite its record of paying dividends for the past 46 quarters. The company plans to announce this information in about a week. Harris owns Progressive's common stock and immediately calls her broker to sell her shares in anticipation of a price decline.

Swamy recently joined Dillon Associates, an investment advisory firm as an equity analyst. Swamy plans to continue serving on the board of directors of Landmark Enterprises, a private company specializing in online gaming owned by her brother-in-law, for which she receives $2,000 annually. Swamy also serves as an unpaid advisor to the local symphony on investing their large endowment and receives four season tickets to the symphony performances.

After lunch, Alice Adams, a client, offers Harris a 1-week cruise as a reward for the great performance of her account over the previous quarter. Bert Baker, also a client, has offered Harris two airplane tickets to Hawaii if his account beats its benchmark by more than 2% over the following year.

Juliann Clark, a CFA candidate, is an analyst at Dillon Associates and a colleague of Swamy's. Clark participates in a conference call for several analysts in which the chief executive officer at Dex says his company's board of directors has just accepted a tender offer from Monolith Chemicals to buy Dex at a 40% premium over the market price. Clark contacts a friend and relates the information about Dex and Monolith. The friend promptly contacts her broker and buys 2,000 shares of Dex's stock.

Ed Michaels, CFA, is director of trading at Quadrangle Brokers. Michaels has recently implemented a buy program for a client. This buy program has driven up the price of a small-cap stock, in which Islandwide owns shares, by approximately 5% because the orders were large in relation to the average daily trading volume of the stock. Michaels's firm is about to bring shares of an OTC firm to market in an

©2017 Kaplan, Inc.

IPO. Michaels has publicly announced that, as a market maker in the shares, his trading desk will create additional liquidity in the stock over its first 90 days of trading by committing to minimum bids and offers of 5,000 shares and to a maximum spread of one-eighth.

Carl Park, CFA, is a retail broker with Quadrangle and has been allocated 5,000 shares of an oversubscribed IPO. One of his clients has been complaining about the execution price of a trade Park made for her last month, but Park knows from researching it that the trade received the best possible execution. In order to calm the client down, Park increases her allocation of shares in the IPO above what it would be if he allocated them to all suitable client accounts based on account size. He allocates a pro-rata portion of the remaining shares to a trust account held at his firm for which his brother-in-law is the primary beneficiary.

7. By accepting the trip from Quadrangle, has Harris complied with the CFA Institute Code and Standards?
   A. Harris may accept the trip because she maintains a significant relationship with Quadrangle that contributes to the performance of client accounts.
   B. Harris may accept the trip because she disclosed the trip to her supervisor and compliance officer and accepted based on their approval.
   C. Harris may not accept the trip because the offer from Quadrangle could impede her ability to make objective investment decisions on behalf of the client.

8. Has either Harris or Clark violated Standard II(A) Integrity of Capital Markets: Material Nonpublic Information?
   A. Harris is in violation.
   B. Clark is in violation.
   C. Both are in violation.

9. According to the Standards of Practice, with respect to the two offers from Adams and Baker, Harris:
   A. may accept both offers if she discloses them to her employer.
   B. may accept both gifts only if she discloses them to her employer and receives permission.
   C. must disclose the offer from Adams to her employer if she accepts it but must receive her employer's permission to accept the offer from Baker.

10. Has Michaels violated Standard II(B) Integrity of Capital Markets: Market Manipulation with respect to any of the following?
    A. The buy program is a violation.
    B. The liquidity activity is a violation.
    C. There is no violation.

11. According to Standard IV Duties to Employers, which of the following is *most likely* required of Swamy? Swamy must:
    A. secure written permission from her employer before performing services for the symphony.
    B. inform her immediate supervisor at Dillon in writing that she (Swamy) must comply with the Code and Standards.
    C. disclose to her employer any additional compensation she receives from Landmark Enterprises and secure written permission to serve on the board.

12. Which action by Park violated Standard III(B) Duties to Clients: Fair Dealing?
    A. Increasing allocation to the problem client.
    B. Decreased allocation to the brother-in-law and other firm clients.
    C. Both actions are violations.

Questions 13–18 relate to Barton Wilson.

Barton Wilson, a junior analyst, is a new hire at a money center bank. He has been assigned to help Juanita Chevas, CFA, in the currency trading department. Together, Wilson and Chevas are working on the development of new trading software designed to detect profitable opportunities in the foreign exchange market. Obviously, they are interested in risk-free arbitrage opportunities. However, they have also been instructed to investigate the possibility of longer-term currency exposures that are not necessarily risk-free. To test the logic of their new software, Wilson gathers the following market data:

- Spot JPY/USD exchange rate = 120.
- Spot EUR/USD exchange rate = 0.7224.
- U.S. risk-free interest rate = 7%.
- Eurozone risk-free rate = 9.08%.
- Japanese risk-free rate = 3.88%.
- Yield curves in all three currencies are flat.

In addition to in-house currency transactions, the new software program is also intended to provide insight into currency exposure and hedging needs for the bank's major customers. These customers typically include large multinational firms. Essentially, the bank wants to provide consulting services to its clients concerning which currency exposures offer the most lucrative opportunities. In this process, the bank will rely on deviations from international parity conditions as an indicator of long-term currency movements. Several bank customers have engaged in a carry trade with Bundovian Bunco (BU) as the investment currency and the USD as the funding currency. The bank will provide risk management advice to customers as it pertains to their FX carry trades.

Wilson obtains the following data from the econometrics department:

- JPY/USD spot rate one year ago = 116.
- EUR/USD spot rate one year ago = 0.7200.
- Anticipated and historical U.S. annual inflation = 3%.
- Anticipated and historical Japanese annual inflation = 0%.
- Anticipated and historical Eurozone annual inflation = 5%.

One of the bank's major customers has significant business interests in Japan and in the Eurozone and has long exposure to both currencies. The customer has traditionally hedged all currency risk. However, the customer's new risk manager has decided to leave some currency exposure unhedged in an attempt to profit from long-term currency exposure.

13. According to relative purchasing power parity, the expected JPY/EUR spot rate two years from now is *closest* to:
   A. 149.92.
   B. 157.70.
   C. 183.14.

14. Are the Japanese and Eurozone inflation forecasts provided by the econometrics department consistent with the inflation rates implied by the international Fisher relation, given a U.S. inflation rate of 3%?
   A. Both forecasts are consistent.
   B. Neither forecast is consistent.
   C. One forecast is consistent and the other is not.

15. According to the uncovered interest rate parity, in 12 months, the JPY/USD exchange rate would *most likely* be:
   A. 116.50.
   B. 123.74.
   C. 117.96.

16. For this question only, suppose that the Japanese government wants to fix the JPY/USD exchange rate at 100. Under the Mundell-Fleming model, the Japanese government's ability to follow an expansionary monetary policy would be limited by:
   A. its fiscal policy.
   B. the price sensitivity of its exports to the United States.
   C. its USD reserves.

17. Based on the assumption that international parity conditions will hold in the long run, should the JPY and Euro currency exposures of the bank's major customer be left unhedged?
   A. Both currencies should be left unhedged.
   B. Neither currency should be left unhedged.
   C. One currency should be left unhedged and the other should not.

18. When advising customers pursuing carry trade, the bank could *most accurately* describe the strategy's return distribution as:
   A. negatively skewed, with fat tails.
   B. either positively or negatively skewed, with skinny tails.
   C. positively skewed, with normal tails.

Questions 19–24 relate to Snowboards and Skateboards, Inc.

Ota L'Abbe, a supervisor at an investment research firm, has asked one of the junior analysts, Andreas Hally, to draft a research report dealing with various accounting issues.

Excerpts from the request are as follows:

- "There's an exciting company that we're starting to follow these days. It's called Snowboards and Skateboards, Inc. They are a multinational company with operations and a head office based in the resort town of Whistler in western Canada. However, they also have a significant subsidiary located in the United States."
- "Look at the subsidiary and deal with some foreign currency issues, including the specific differences between the temporal and current rate methods of translation, as well as the effect on financial ratios."
- "The attached file contains the September 30, 2018, financial statements of the U.S. subsidiary. Translate the financial statements into Canadian dollars in a manner consistent with U.S. GAAP."

The following are statements from the research report subsequently written by Hally:

Statement 1:   Subsidiaries whose operations are well-integrated with the parent will use the current rate method of translation.

Statement 2:   Self-contained, independent subsidiaries whose operating, investing, and financing activities are primarily located in the local market will use the temporal method of translation.

Snowboards and Skateboards, Inc. (U.S.)	(U.S. dollars)
Balance Sheet as of 9/30/2018	
Cash and accounts receivable	775,000
Inventory	600,000
Property, plant, and equipment (PP&E) – net	730,000
Total assets	2,105,000
Accounts payable	125,000
Long-term debt	400,000
Common stock	535,000
Retained earnings	1,045,000
Total liabilities and shareholders' equity	2,105,000

Income Statement for the Year ended 9/30/2018	
Sales	1,352,000
Cost of goods sold	(1,205,000)
Depreciation	(140,000)
Net income	7,000

Other information to be considered:

- *Exchange rates (CAD/USD)*

Fiscal 2017 (average)	1.44
Fiscal 2018 (average)	1.35
October 1, 2014	1.50
September 30, 2017	1.48
June 30, 2018	1.37
September 30, 2018	1.32

- Beginning inventory for fiscal 2018 had been purchased evenly throughout fiscal 2017. The company uses the FIFO inventory value method.

- Dividends of USD 25,000 were declared on June 30, 2018.

- All of the remaining inventory at the end of fiscal 2018 was purchased evenly throughout fiscal 2018.

- All of the PP&E was purchased, and all of the common equity was issued at the inception of the company on October 1, 2014. No new PP&E has been acquired, and no additional common stock has been issued since then. However, they plan to purchase new PP&E starting in fiscal 2019.

- The beginning retained earnings balance for fiscal 2018 was CAD 1,550,000.

- The accounts payable on the fiscal 2018 balance sheet were all incurred on June 30, 2018.

- The U.S. subsidiary's operations are highly integrated with the main operations in Canada.

- The remeasured inventory for 2018 using the temporal method is CAD 810,000.

- Costs of goods sold under the temporal method in 2018 is CAD 1,667,250.

19. Are Hally's statements regarding foreign currency translation correct?

	Statement 1	Statement 2
A.	Yes	Yes
B.	Yes	No
C.	No	No

20. Which of the following *best* describes the effect on the parent's fiscal 2018 sales when translated to Canadian dollars? Sales, relative to what it would have been if the CAD/USD exchange rate had not changed, will be:
    A. lower because the U.S. dollar depreciated during fiscal 2018.
    B. higher because the average value of the Canadian dollar depreciated during fiscal 2018.
    C. lower because the U.S. dollar appreciated during fiscal 2018.

21. As compared to the temporal method, which of the following financial statement elements of the parent are lower under the current rate method?
    A. Cash and accounts receivable.
    B. Depreciation expense and cost of goods sold.
    C. Common stock and dividends paid.

22. Using the appropriate translation method, which of the following *best* describes the effect of changing exchange rates on the parent's fiscal 2018 financial statements?
    A. An accumulated loss of CAD 242,100 is reported in the shareholders' equity.
    B. A loss of CAD 31,200 is recognized in the income statement.
    C. A gain of CAD 27,400 is recognized in the income statement.

23. As compared to the temporal method, the parent's fixed asset turnover for fiscal 2018 using the current rate method is:
    A. higher.
    B. lower.
    C. the same.

24. Suppose the parent uses the current rate method to translate the subsidiary for fiscal 2018. Will return on assets and net profit margin in U.S. dollars before translation be the same as, or different than, the translated Canadian dollar ratios?

Return on assets	Net profit margin
A. Same	Different
B. Different	Different
C. Different	Same

Questions 25–30 relate to Wayland, Inc., and Optimax.

Kevin Rathbun, CFA, is a financial analyst at a major brokerage firm. His supervisor, Elizabeth Mao, CFA, asks him to analyze the financial position of Wayland, Inc. (Wayland), a manufacturer of components for high quality optic transmission systems. Mao also inquires about the impact of any unconsolidated investments.

On December 31, 2017, Wayland purchased a 35% ownership interest in a strategic new firm called Optimax for $300,000 cash. The pre-acquisition balance sheets of both firms are found in Exhibit 1.

Exhibit 1: Pre-Acquisition Balance Sheets for Wayland and Optimax

Balance sheets as of Dec. 31, 2017 *in thousands*	Wayland	Optimax
Assets		
Cash	$710	$100
Marketable securities	2,550	–
Inventory	2,000	400
Accounts receivable	3,000	500
Property, plant, and equipment	2,450	1,000
Total assets	**$10,710**	**$2,000**
Liabilities		
Accounts payable	$3,310	400
Long-term debt	5,000	1,000
Equity	2,400	600
Total liabilities and equity	**$10,710**	**$2,000**

On the acquisition date, all of Optimax's assets and liabilities were stated on its balance sheet at their fair values except for its property, plant, and equipment (PP&E), which had a fair value of $1.2 million. The remaining useful life of the PP&E is 10 years with no salvage value. Both firms use the straight-line depreciation method.

For the year ended 2018, Optimax reported net income of $250,000 and paid dividends of $100,000.

During the first quarter of 2019, Optimax sold goods to Wayland and recognized $15,000 of profit from the sale. At the end of the quarter, half of the goods purchased from Optimax remained in Wayland's inventory.

Wayland currently uses the equity method to account for its investment in Optimax.

Rathbun also notes that Wayland owns shares in Vanry, Inc. (Vanry). Rathbun gathers the data in Exhibit 2 from Wayland's financial statements. The year-end portfolio value is the market value of all Vanry shares held on December 31. All security transactions occurred on July 1, and the transaction price is the price that Wayland actually paid for the shares acquired. Vanry pays a cash dividend of $1 per share at the end of each year. Wayland expects to sell its investment in Vanry in the near term and accounts for it as *held-for-trading*.

Exhibit 2: Share Transaction Data, Vanry, Inc.

Year	Year-End Portfolio Value	Year-End Shares Held	Year-End Share Price	Transaction Price (July 1)
2017	$1,875,000	25,000[a]	$75	$85
2018	$2,280,000	30,000	76	78

[a] Purchased on July 1, 2017.

Wayland owns some publicly traded bonds of the Rotor Corporation that it reports as held-to-maturity securities.

25. The amount of goodwill as a result of Wayland's acquisition of Optimax is *closest* to:
    A. $0.
    B. $20,000.
    C. $50,000.

26. What amount should Wayland report in its balance sheet as a result of its investment in Optimax at the end of 2018?
    A. $352,000.
    B. $345,500.
    C. $380,500.

27. Which of the following *best* describes Wayland's treatment of the intercompany sales transaction for the quarter ended March 31, 2019? Wayland should reduce its equity income by:
    A. $2,625.
    B. $7,500.
    C. $15,000.

28. Which of the following statements is *least accurate* under the new IFRS standards (IFRS 9)?
    A. Equity investments held for trading must be measured at fair value through profit or loss.
    B. Equity investments once measured as fair value through OCI cannot be reclassified to be measured as fair value through profit or loss.
    C. Debt securities that meet the business model test and the cash flow characteristic test must be measured at amortized cost.

29. Regarding the Rotor Corporation bonds, under the current standards, Wayland would have the option to reclassify them as designated at fair value from held-to-maturity under:
    A. U.S. GAAP only.
    B. IFRS only.
    C. both IFRS and U.S. GAAP.

30. As a result of its investment in Vanry, what amount should Wayland recognize in its income statement for the year ended 2018?
    A. $35,000 profit.
    B. $45,000 profit.
    C. $55,000 profit.

Questions 31–36 relate to Lorenz Kummert.

Lorenz Kummert is a junior equity analyst who is following Schubert, Inc. (Schubert), a small publicly traded company in the United States. His supervisor, Markus Alter, CFA, has advised him to use the residual income model to analyze Schubert.

In his preliminary report to Alter, Kummert makes the following statements:

Statement 1: Residual income models are appropriate when expected free cash flows are negative for the foreseeable future.

Statement 2: Residual income models are not applicable when dividends are volatile.

Kummert has determined Schubert's cost of equity, cost of debt, and weighted average cost of capital (WACC) to be 12.8%, 8.4%, and 11.9%, respectively. Book value of long-term debt and equity was $6,200,000 and $3,281,000 respectively on January 1, 2018. The stock price on December 31, 2018, is $36 per share and there are 130,000 shares outstanding. The relevant tax rate is 30%, and return on equity (ROE) is expected to be 14%.

Summarized financial information about Schubert for 2018 is provided in Exhibits 1 and 2.

Exhibit 1: Schubert, Inc., Balance Sheet on December 31, 2018

Cash	$ 125,000	Accounts payable	$ 426,000
Accounts receivable	975,000	Accrued liabilities	774,000
Inventory	1,215,000	Long-term debt	6,211,000
Fixed assets (net)	9,277,000		
		Common shares	2,100,000
		Retained earnings	2,081,000
Total assets	$11,592,000	Total liabilities and equity	$11,592,000

Exhibit 2: Schubert, Inc., Income Statement for the year ended December 31, 2018

Sales	$9,423,000
Cost of sales	4,580,000
Selling, general, and administrative	1,230,000
Depreciation	1,745,000
Interest expense	522,000
Income tax expense	403,800
Net income	$942,200

Based on his analysis of several years of financial statements, Kummert notes that 2018 was an exceptionally profitable year for Schubert, and that its dividend payouts are usually low because the funds are mainly reinvested in the firm to promote growth. Furthermore, there are very few nonrecurring items on the income statement. Upon review of Kummert's preliminary report, Alter concurs with his analysis of the financial statements but reminds him that Schubert's long-term debt is currently trading at 95% of its book value. He also cautions Kummert that violations of the clean surplus relation can bias the results of the residual income model.

The consensus annual EPS estimate for 2019 is $4.50, and the dividend payout ratio for 2019 is estimated at 5%.

31. Are Kummert's statements regarding the residual income model correct?
    A. Both statements are incorrect.
    B. Only Statement 1 is correct.
    C. Only Statement 2 is correct.

32. Assuming that Kummert and Alter are correct with their conclusions regarding Schubert's financial statements, which of the following levels would *best* describe the strength of the persistence factor with respect to Schubert's residual income?
    A. Low persistence factor.
    B. Medium persistence factor.
    C. High persistence factor.

33. Which of the following amounts is *closest* to the forecast of Schubert's book value per share and residual income, respectively, for 2019?

	Book value per share	Residual income
A.	$36.43	$0.38
B.	$38.00	$2.32
C.	$36.40	$2.32

34. Which of the following amounts are *closest* to Schubert's economic value added (EVA) for fiscal year 2018 and market value added (MVA) as of fiscal year-end 2018, respectively?

	EVA	MVA
A.	$179,361	$188,450
B.	$23,455	$369,500
C.	($70,900)	$369,500

35. Which of the following amounts is *closest* to Schubert's implied growth rate in residual income?
    A. 0.34%.
    B. 2.75%.
    C. 12.63%.

36. Regarding Alter's caution about violations of the clean surplus relationship, examples of items that can violate this relationship include:
    A. foreign currency gains and losses under the current rate method.
    B. changes in the market value of debt and equity held as trading securities.
    C. changes in net working capital.

Questions 37–42 relate to Ferguson Department Stores, Inc.

Matthew Emery, CFA, is responsible for analyzing companies in the retail industry. He is currently reviewing the status of Ferguson Department Stores, Inc. (FDS). FDS has recently gone through extensive restructuring in the wake of a slowdown in the economy that has made retailing particularly challenging. As part of his analysis, Emery has gathered information from a number of sources.

Ferguson Department Stores, Inc.

FDS went public in 1979 following a major acquisition, and the Ferguson name quickly became one of the most recognized in retailing. Ferguson had been successful through most of its first 30 years in business and has prided itself on being the one-stop shopping destination for consumers living on the West Coast of the United States. Recently, FDS began to experience both top and bottom line difficulties due to increased competition from specialty retailers who could operate more efficiently and offer a wider range of products in a focused retailing sector. When the company's main bank reduced FDS's line of credit, a serious working capital crisis ensued, and the company was forced to issue additional equity in an effort to overcome the problem. FDS has a cost of capital of 10% and a required rate of return on equity of 12%. Dividends are growing at a rate of 8%, but the growth rate is expected to decline linearly over the next six years to a long-term growth rate of 4%. The company recently paid an annual dividend of $1.

At the end of 2018, FDS announced that it would be expanding its retail operations, moving to a warehouse concept, and opening new stores around the country. FDS also announced it would close some existing stores, write-down assets, and take a large restructuring charge. Upon reviewing the prospects of the firm, Emery issued an earnings-per-share forecast for 2019 of $0.90. He set a 12-month share price target of $22.50. Immediately following the expansion announcement, the share price of FDS jumped from $14 to $18.

Exhibit 1: Summary Income Statement, Ferguson Department Stores, Inc.
(U.S. $ millions, except per share data and shares outstanding)

	2018	2017
Sales	$6,435.9	$6,322.7
Cost of goods sold, operating, administrative, and selling expenses	6,007.9	5,875.9
Depreciation and amortization	148.7	146.6
Interest expense	59.8	59.5
Unusual items—expense	189.1	5.0
Earnings before tax	30.4	235.7
Income taxes—current	49.3	7.5
Income taxes—future	(71.1)	93.5
	(21.8)	101.0
Net earnings for the year	$52.2	$134.7
Earnings per share: Basic	$0.49	$1.26
Fully diluted	$0.49	$1.26
Weighted average shares outstanding	106,530,610	106,530,610

In 2018, FDS also reported an unusual expense of $189.1 million related to restructuring costs and asset write downs.

Exhibit 2: Selected Industry Information for 2018

Estimated earnings growth rate	0.10
Mean trailing price/earnings (P/E) ratio	22.50
Mean price/sales (P/S) ratio	0.50

In response to questions from a colleague, Emery makes the following statements regarding the merits of earnings yield compared to the P/E ratio:

Statement 1: For ranking purposes, earnings yield may be useful whenever earnings are either negative or close to zero.

Statement 2: A high E/P implies the security is overpriced.

37. The value of one share of FDS using the H-model is *closest* to:
    A. $14.50.
    B. $16.50.
    C. $19.33.

38. Given Emery's dividend forecast for FDS, is the H-model the appropriate valuation model to use to value FDS?
    A. Yes.
    B. No, the H-model is appropriate when the dividend growth rate declines at a linear rate for a short period of time during stage one, followed by a 1-year suspension in dividends before the previous dividend is reinstated, and then dividends grow at a long-term constant rate.
    C. No, the H-model is appropriate when the dividend growth rate grows during the first stage followed by a period of stable growth in dividends in stage two, followed by a dividend growth rate that declines linearly in perpetuity.

39. Assuming that the cost of equity for FDS does not change, the present value of growth opportunities in the share price following the announcement that the company would be expanding its retail operations, using Emery's 2019 earnings forecast, is *closest* to:
    A. $9.00.
    B. $10.50.
    C. $12.50.

40. Are Emery's statements regarding the earnings yield and E/P ratio correct?
    A. One statement is correct and the other statement is incorrect.
    B. Both statements are correct.
    C. Both statements are incorrect.

41. Assuming a tax rate of 34%, the underlying earnings per share (EPS) for FDS in 2018 is *closest* to:
    A. $1.26.
    B. $1.36.
    C. $2.27.

42. According to FDS's price-to-sales ratio for 2018, based on the post-expansion announcement stock price, FDS is:
    A. underpriced relative to the industry.
    B. overpriced relative to the industry.
    C. properly priced relative to the industry.

Questions 43–48 relate to Universal Home Supplies, Inc.

Michael Robbins, CFA, is analyzing Universal Home Supplies, Inc. (UHS), which has recently gone through some extensive restructuring.

Universal Home Supplies, Inc.

UHS operates nearly 200 department stores and 78 specialty stores in over 30 states. The company offers a wide range of products, including women's, men's, and children's clothing and accessories, as well as home furnishings, electronics, and other consumer goods. The company is considering cutting back on or eliminating its electronics business entirely. UHS manufactures many of its own apparel products domestically in a large factory located in Kentucky. This central location permits shipping to distribution points around the country at reasonable costs. The company operates primarily in suburban shopping malls and offers mid- to high-end merchandise mainly under its own private label. At present, more than 70% of the company's customers live within a 10-minute drive of one of the company's stores. Web site activity measured in dollar sales volume has increased by over 18% in the past year. Shares of UHS stock are currently priced at $25. Dividends are expected to grow at a rate of 6% over the next eight years and then continue to grow at that same rate indefinitely. The company has a cost of capital of 10.2%, a beta of 0.8, and just paid an annual dividend of $1.25.

UHS has faced serious cash flow problems in recent years as a consequence of its strategy to pursue an upscale clientele in the face of increased competition from several "niche retailers." The firm has been able to issue new debt recently and has also managed to extend its line of credit. The two financing agreements required a pledge of additional assets and a promise to install a super-efficient inventory tracking system in time to meet holiday shopping demand.

Exhibit 1: Summary Income Statement for Universal Home Supplies, Inc. (U.S. $ millions, except per share data and shares outstanding)

	2018	2017
Sales	$7,400.1	$7,383.8
Cost of goods sold, operating, administrative, and selling expenses	7,081.3	7,028.9
Depreciation and amortization	157.7	155.6
Earnings before interest expense and income taxes	161.1	199.3
Interest expense	42.6	45.4
Earnings before tax	118.5	153.9
Income taxes—current	40.3	52.3
Net earnings for the year	$78.2	$101.6
Earnings per share: Basic	$0.82	$1.40
Fully diluted	$0.82	$1.34
Weighted average shares outstanding	95,366,000	72,572,000

Exhibit 2: Book Value per Share (BVPS in $) and Return on Equity (ROE), Universal Home Supplies, Inc.

Year	2018	2017	2016	2015
BVPS	$25.58	$33.62	$37.54	$32.26
ROE	3.2%	4.0%	4.5%	3.9%

Exhibit 3: 2018 Selected Industry Information

Estimated earnings growth rate	0.10
Mean trailing price/earnings (P/E) ratio	22.50
Mean price/sales (P/S) ratio	0.50

Robbins is asked by his supervisor to carefully consider the advantages and drawbacks of using the price-to-sales ratio (P/S) and to determine the appropriate valuation metrics to use when returns follow patterns of persistence or reversals.

Robbins also estimates a cross-sectional model to predict UHS's P/E:

$$\text{predicted P/E} = 5 - (10 \times \text{beta}) + [3 \times \text{4-year average ROE(\%)}]$$
$$+ [2 \times \text{8-year dividend growth forecast(\%)}]$$

where ROE and growth forecast are in percentages (i.e., 10 instead of 0.10 for 10%).

43. Based on the H-model, the implied expected rate of return for UHS is *closest* to:
    A. 8.8%.
    B. 10.2%.
    C. 11.3%.

44. Robbins should conclude that a key drawback to using the price-to-sales (P/S) ratio in the investment process is that P/S is:
    A. positive even when earnings per share is negative.
    B. not appropriate for valuing the equity of mature companies.
    C. susceptible to manipulation with respect to revenue recognition.

45. Is UHS stock, at the end of 2018, *best* described as overvalued or undervalued according to the:

	Trailing PEG ratio?	P/S ratio?
A.	Undervalued	Undervalued
B.	Overvalued	Undervalued
C.	Undervalued	Overvalued

46.   Based on the method of average return on equity (ROE), the normalized
      EPS for UHS is *closest* to:
      A. $0.94.
      B. $1.00.
      C. $1.26.

47.   The predicted P/E for UHS using Robbins's model is *closest* to:
      A. 20.7.
      B. 23.6.
      C. 30.5.

48.   Robbins should conclude that patterns of persistence or reversals in returns
      provide the *most appropriate* rationale for valuation using:
      A. unexpected earnings.
      B. relative-strength indicators.
      C. standardized unexpected earnings.

Questions 49–54 relate to William Rogers.

William Rogers, a fixed-income portfolio manager, needs to eliminate a large cash position in his portfolio. He would like to purchase some corporate bonds. Two bonds that he is evaluating are shown in Exhibit 1. These two bonds are from the same issuer, and the current call price for the callable bond is 100. Assume that the issuer will call if the bond price exceeds the call price.

Rogers is also concerned about increases in interest rates and is considering the purchase of a putable bond. He wants to determine how assumed increases or decreases in interest rate volatility affect the value of the straight bonds and bonds with embedded options. After Rogers performs some analysis, he and his supervisor, Sigourney Walters, discuss the relative price movement between the two bonds in Exhibit 1 when interest rates change significantly.

During the discussions, Rogers makes the following statements:

Statement 1: If the volatility of interest rates decreases, the value of the callable bond will increase.

Statement 2: The noncallable bond will not be affected by a change in the volatility or level of interest rates.

Statement 3: When interest rates decrease, the value of the noncallable bond increases by more than the callable bond.

Statement 4: If the volatility of interest rates increases, the value of the putable bond will increase.

Walters mentors Rogers on bond concepts and then asks him to consider the pricing of a third bond. The third bond has five years to maturity, a 6% annual coupon, and pays interest semiannually. The bond is both callable and putable at 100 at any time. Walters indicates that the holders of the bond's embedded options will exercise if the option is in-the-money.

Exhibit 1: Bond Descriptions

	Noncallable Bond	Callable Bond
Price	99.77	98.21
Time to maturity (years)	5	5
Time to first call date (years)	n/a	4
Annual coupon	6.00%	6.00%
Interest payment	Semiannual	Semiannual
Yield to maturity	6.0542%	6.4227%

©2017 Kaplan, Inc.

Rogers obtained the prices shown in Exhibit 1 using software that generates an interest rate lattice. He uses his software to generate the interest rate lattice shown in Exhibit 2.

Exhibit 2: Interest Rate Lattice (Annualized Interest Rates)

	0.5	1.0	1.5	2.0	2.5	3.0	3.5	4.0	4.5
									15.44%
								14.10%	
							12.69%		12.46%
						11.85%		11.38%	
					9.75%		10.25%		10.05%
				8.95%		9.57%		9.19%	
			7.91%		7.88%		8.28%		8.11%
		7.35%		7.23%		7.74%		7.42%	
	6.62%		6.40%		6.37%		6.69%		6.54%
6.05%		5.95%		5.85%		6.25%		5.99%	
	5.36%		5.17%		5.15%		5.40%		5.28%
		4.81%		4.73%		5.05%		4.83%	
			4.18%		4.16%		4.36%		4.26%
				3.82%		4.08%		3.90%	
					3.37%		3.52%		3.44%
						3.30%		3.15%	
							2.84%		2.77%
								2.54%	
									2.24%

Years: 0.5 1.0 1.5 2.0 2.5 3.0 3.5 4.0 4.5

49. Evaluate Rogers's statements 1 and 3.
    A. Only Statement 1 is correct.
    B. Only Statement 3 is correct.
    C. Both statements are correct.

50. Evaluate Rogers's statements 2 and 4.
    A. Only Statement 2 is correct.
    B. Only Statement 4 is correct.
    C. Both statements are correct.

51. The market value of the embedded call option in Exhibit 1 is *closest* to:
    A. 1.56.
    B. 1.65.
    C. 1.79.

52. For this question only, ignore the information from Exhibit 1 and any other calculations in other questions. Rather, assume that the interest rate lattice provided in Exhibit 2 is constructed to be arbitrage-free. However, when Rogers calculates the price of the callable bond using the interest rates in the lattice, he gets a value higher than the market price of the bond.

    Is the price of the third callable and putable bond *likely* to be less than, equal to, or greater than 100%, and is the option-adjusted spread (OAS) on the callable bond *likely* to be zero, positive, or negative?

	Price of third bond	OAS of callable bond
A.	Less than 100%	Zero
B.	Equal to 100%	Positive
C.	Greater than 100%	Negative

53. Using the information in the question and the following relevant portion of the interest rate and pricing trees, Rogers calculates the value of the noncallable bond at node A.

    Corresponding portion of the interest rate tree (given as bond-equivalent yields):

    8.95%

    7.91%

    7.23%

Years	1.5	2.0

    Corresponding portion of the binomial price tree:

    91.73%

    A ----▶

    96.17%

Years	1.5	2.0

    The price of the noncallable bond at node A is *closest* to:
    A. 89.84% of par.
    B. 93.26% of par.
    C. 96.14% of par.

54. Using the information in the question and the following relevant portion of the interest rate and pricing trees, Rogers calculates the value of the callable bond at node B.

Corresponding portion of the interest rate tree (given as bond-equivalent yields):

$$3.44\%$$

$$3.15\%$$

$$2.77\%$$

Years	4.0	4.5

Corresponding portion of the callable bond price tree:

$$\$100.00$$

B ----➤

$$\$100.00$$

Years	4.0	4.5

The price of the callable bond at node B is *closest* to:
A. 100.0% of par.
B. 101.4% of par.
C. 102.5% of par.

Questions 55–60 relate to Ted Thompson.

Ted Thompson, CIO for Aplius Insurance company, is evaluating the credit risk management models for the company's fixed income portfolio. Thompson meets with Nambi Musa, who is the head of Aplius's credit risk analysis department. Musa assures Thompson that his team has updated the credit risk analysis models over recent years and that these updated models have performed well over the past 12 months. Thompson, however, is not pleased with the losses incurred on Aplius's municipal bond holdings in the last quarter.

Musa mentions that while the credit risk analysis department continues to use credit ratings, they are also evaluating other analytical tools including structural models. He specifically mentions present value of expected loss as one credit risk measure currently being used. Musa makes the following statements:

Statement 1: "One of the strengths of credit ratings is that they tend to be stable over time and hence reduce the price volatility in debt markets."

Statement 2: "The present value of expected loss on a bond is the maximum amount an investor would be willing to pay to an insurer to bear the credit risk of that security."

Statement 3: "One of the assumptions of the structural models of credit analysis is that the default risk changes over a business cycle."

Statement 4: "In case of an ABS, credit analysis focuses on the probability of loss instead of the probability of default."

Musa further discusses the credit analysis metrics that are newly developed. As an example, he illustrates the valuation conducted on 1-year, 5% Zeta Corp. senior unsecured bonds. Exhibit 1 shows the report. Rates are continuously compounded.

Exhibit 1: Valuation of 1-year, 5% Zeta Corp. Bond

Time to Cash Flow	Cash Flow	Risk-Free Spot Rate (%)	Credit Spread (%)
0.5	25	0.23	0.8
1	1025	0.25	0.85

Thompson then tells Musa that the credit analysis department should focus on reduced form models. Thompson states that, "reduced form models perform better than structural models as they tend to impose assumptions on the outputs of the structural model. However, reduced form models require a specification of the company's balance sheet composition."

©2017 Kaplan, Inc.

55. Musa's statement 1 is *most likely*:
    A. correct.
    B. incorrect because credit ratings are unstable over time.
    C. incorrect because of the implied relation to price volatility in debt markets.

56. Musa's statement 2 is *most likely*:
    A. correct.
    B. incorrect as the statement only considers credit risk.
    C. incorrect as the statement should refer to expected loss and not to present value of expected loss.

57. Musa's statement 3 is *most likely*:
    A. correct.
    B. incorrect as structural models assume that default risk is constant over a business cycle.
    C. incorrect as structural models assume that default risk is constant over the life of the bond.

58. Musa's statement 4 is *most likely*:
    A. correct.
    B. incorrect as credit analysis of ABS focuses on the probability of default instead of the probability of loss.
    C. incorrect as credit analysis of ABS focuses on probability of tranche default instead of probability of default.

59. Using information in Exhibit 1, the present value of expected loss for the Zeta Corp. bond is *closest* to:
    A. $7.74.
    B. $8.25.
    C. $8.76.

60. Thompson's statement about reduced form models relative to structural model is *most likely*:
    A. correct.
    B. incorrect regarding assumptions imposed.
    C. incorrect regarding specification of balance sheet composition being required.

End of Morning Session

Exam 3
Afternoon Session

Question	Topic	Minutes (Points)
61 to 66	Quantitative Methods	18
67 to 72	Financial Reporting and Analysis	18
73 to 78	Financial Reporting and Analysis	18
79 to 84	Corporate Finance	18
85 to 90	Corporate Finance	18
91 to 96	Equity	18
97 to 102	Derivatives	18
103 to 108	Derivatives	18
109 to 114	Alternative Investments	18
115 to 120	Portfolio Management	18

61.	(A)	(B)	(C)		101.	(A)	(B)	(C)
62.	(A)	(B)	(C)		102.	(A)	(B)	(C)
63.	(A)	(B)	(C)		103.	(A)	(B)	(C)
64.	(A)	(B)	(C)		104.	(A)	(B)	(C)
65.	(A)	(B)	(C)		105.	(A)	(B)	(C)
66.	(A)	(B)	(C)		106.	(A)	(B)	(C)
67.	(A)	(B)	(C)		107.	(A)	(B)	(C)
68.	(A)	(B)	(C)		108.	(A)	(B)	(C)
69.	(A)	(B)	(C)		109.	(A)	(B)	(C)
70.	(A)	(B)	(C)		110.	(A)	(B)	(C)
71.	(A)	(B)	(C)		111.	(A)	(B)	(C)
72.	(A)	(B)	(C)		112.	(A)	(B)	(C)
73.	(A)	(B)	(C)		113.	(A)	(B)	(C)
74.	(A)	(B)	(C)		114.	(A)	(B)	(C)
75.	(A)	(B)	(C)		115.	(A)	(B)	(C)
76.	(A)	(B)	(C)		116.	(A)	(B)	(C)
77.	(A)	(B)	(C)		117.	(A)	(B)	(C)
78.	(A)	(B)	(C)		118.	(A)	(B)	(C)
79.	(A)	(B)	(C)		119.	(A)	(B)	(C)
80.	(A)	(B)	(C)		120.	(A)	(B)	(C)
81.	(A)	(B)	(C)					
82.	(A)	(B)	(C)					
83.	(A)	(B)	(C)					
84.	(A)	(B)	(C)					
85.	(A)	(B)	(C)					
86.	(A)	(B)	(C)					
87.	(A)	(B)	(C)					
88.	(A)	(B)	(C)					
89.	(A)	(B)	(C)					
90.	(A)	(B)	(C)					
91.	(A)	(B)	(C)					
92.	(A)	(B)	(C)					
93.	(A)	(B)	(C)					
94.	(A)	(B)	(C)					
95.	(A)	(B)	(C)					
96.	(A)	(B)	(C)					
97.	(A)	(B)	(C)					
98.	(A)	(B)	(C)					
99.	(A)	(B)	(C)					
100.	(A)	(B)	(C)					

EXAM 3
AFTERNOON SESSION

Questions 61–66 relate to Joan Fisher and Kim Weatherford.

Joan Fisher and Kim Weatherford are economists responsible for modeling security returns for Quincy Portfolio Managers, which is located in the southwestern United States. Fisher is the firm's chief economist and Weatherford is her assistant.

Fisher has been busy over the past week modeling the macroeconomic data of an emerging market. The data for the past 24 months is shown in Exhibit 1.

Exhibit 1: Time Series of Emerging Markets Data

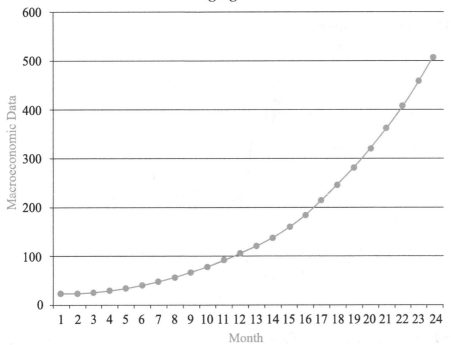

Fisher ponders how she can run a regression that will model the data for this country in the most appropriate way. She decides to regress the macroeconomic values against a time variable. The resulting plot of the residuals is shown in Exhibit 2.

Exhibit 2: Residual Plot from Emerging Markets Data

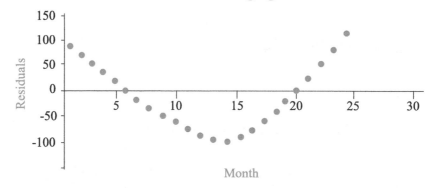

In addition to financial assets, Quincy Portfolio Managers also recommends the use of commodities as a portfolio diversifier. Weatherford has been examining price indices for silver in an attempt to determine whether silver returns are predictable. As an initial step, she uses an autoregressive first-order regression model on daily price data for silver over the past two years. The plot of the raw data and the results of the regression are shown in Exhibits 3 and 4.

Exhibit 3: Time Series of Silver Prices

Exhibit 4: Silver Price Regression Results

Regression Statistics	
Multiple R	0.99
R-Square	0.98
Adjusted R-Square	0.98
Standard Error	123.81
Observations	522.00
Durbin-Watson	2.39

Exhibit 4: Silver Price Regression Results (cont.)

ANOVA

	df	*SS*	*MS*	*F*	*Significance F*
Regression	1.00	365,730,065	365,730,065	23,859.63	0.00
Residual	520.00	7,970,771	15,328		
Total	521.00	373,700,837			

	Coefficients	*Standard Error*	*t-Stat*	*P-value*
Intercept	21.00	11.56	1.82	0.07
Slope	0.99	0.01	154.47	0.00

Fisher and Weatherford later discuss fluctuations in gold prices. Although the arithmetic and geometric mean returns for gold were negative for much of the 1980s and 1990s, Fisher and Weatherford believe that gold should perform better in the future due to higher expected inflation. After appropriate transformation of the data, they use an autoregressive first-order regression model to examine the characteristics of gold returns, the results of which are shown in Exhibit 5.

Exhibit 5: Gold Price Regression Results

Regression Statistics	
Multiple R	0.09
R-Square	0.01
Adjusted R-Square	0.01
Standard Error	123.95
Observations	520.00

ANOVA

	df	*SS*	*MS*	*F*	*Significance F*
Regression	1.00	66,742	66,742	4.34	0.04
Residual	518.00	7,958,144	15,363		
Total	519.00	8,024,887			

	Coefficients	*Standard Error*	*t-Stat*	*P-value*
Intercept	2.00	5.44	0.37	0.71
Slope	−0.09	0.04	−2.08	0.04

61. In order to *best* model the emerging markets data using linear regression, Fisher should use:
    A. an adjustment for multicollinearity.
    B. the natural log of the dependent variable.
    C. White's correction for the standard errors.

62. The *most likely* problem in Fisher's regression of the emerging market data and the *most appropriate* test for it in the regression are:

Problem	Test
A. Serial correlation	Durbin Watson
B. Serial correlation	Dickey Fuller
C. Cointegrated variables	Engle Granger

63. Is the use of the Durbin Watson statistic in Weatherford's silver regression appropriate and, if so, how should it be interpreted?
    A. No.
    B. Yes, and it appears that the error terms are positively correlated.
    C. Yes, and it appears that the error terms are negatively correlated.

64. Which of the following are the *most likely* problem in Weatherford's silver regression and the *most appropriate* test for it?

Problem	Test
A. Multicollinearity	Breusch Pagan
B. Multicollinearity	Dickey Fuller
C. Nonstationary data	Dickey Fuller

65. In order to *best* model the silver price data using an autoregressive first-order regression model, Weatherford should use:
    A. first differences of the data.
    B. the actual silver price levels.
    C. the predicted silver price levels.

66. Using the data for the gold regression, what is the mean reverting level and what is the two-step-ahead forecast if the current value of the independent variable is –0.80?

Mean reverting level	Two-step-ahead forecast
A. 1.830	1.75
B. 1.830	1.81
C. 2.072	1.81

Questions 67–72 relate to Iberia Corporation.

Bryan Stephenson is an equity analyst and is developing a research report on Iberia Corporation at the request of his supervisor. Iberia is a conglomerate entity with significant corporate holdings in various industries. Specifically, Stephenson is interested in the effects of Iberia's investments on its financial performance and has decided to focus on two investments: Midland Incorporated and Odessa Company.

Midland Incorporated
On December 31, 2007, Iberia purchased 5 million common shares of Midland Incorporated for €80 million. Midland has a total of 12.5 million common shares outstanding. The market value of Iberia's investment in Midland was €89 million at the end of 2008, and €85 million at the end of 2009. For the year ended 2008, Midland reported net income of €30 million and paid dividends of €10 million. For the year ended 2009, Midland reported a loss of €5 million and paid dividends of €4 million.

During 2010, Midland sold goods to Iberia and reported 20% gross profit from the sale. Iberia sold all of the goods to a third party in 2010.

Odessa Company
On January 2, 2009, Iberia purchased 1 million common shares of Odessa Company as a long-term investment. The purchase price was €20 per share, and on December 31, 2009, the market price of Odessa was €17 per share. The decline in value was considered temporary. For the year ended 2009, Odessa reported net income of €750 million and paid a dividend of €3 per share. Iberia considers its investment in Odessa as an investment in financial assets.

In addition, Iberia has a number of foreign investments, so Stephenson's supervisor has asked him to draft a report on accounting methods and ratio analysis. The following are statements from Stephenson's research report.

Statement 1: Under U.S. GAAP, Iberia cannot account for its investment in associates at fair value as that option is only available to venture capital firms, mutual funds, or similar entities.

Statement 2: In general, if the parent's consolidated net income is positive, the equity method reports a higher net profit margin than the acquisition method.

67.   Which of the following is the *most* appropriate classification of Iberia's investment in Odessa Corporation?
A. Held-to-maturity.
B. Held-for-trading.
C. Available-for-sale.

68. What amount should Iberia recognize in its 2009 income statement as a result of its investments in Midland and Odessa?
A. €1 million profit.
B. €2 million profit.
C. €3 million loss.

69. What amount should Iberia report on its balance sheet at the end of 2009 as a result of its investments in Midland and Odessa?
A. €84.4 million.
B. €101.4 million.
C. €102.0 million.

70. What adjustment, if any, must Iberia make to its 2010 income statement as a result of the intercompany transaction with Midland?
A. Sales and cost of goods sold should be reduced by Iberia's pro-rata ownership interest in the intercompany sale.
B. Midland's net income should be reduced by 20% of the gross profit from the intercompany sale.
C. No adjustment is necessary.

71. Is Stephenson's statement 1 correct?
A. Yes.
B. No, because under U.S. GAAP, all entities can account for their investment in associates at fair value.
C. No, because under U.S. GAAP, accounting of investment in associates at fair value is not allowed for any entity.

72. Is Stephenson's statement 2 correct?
A. Yes.
B. No. Net profit margin will be lower using the equity method.
C. No. Net profit margin will be the same using either the equity method or the acquisition method.

Questions 73–78 relate to Andrew Carson and Samilski Enterprises.

Andrew Carson is an equity analyst employed at Lee Vincent and Associates, an investment research firm. Carson is responsible for following Samilski Enterprises (Samilski), a publicly traded firm that produces motorcycles and associated mechanical parts. Samilski reports under U.S. GAAP.

Exhibit 1 shows selected financial data pertaining to Samilski's employee pension plan.

Exhibit 1: Selected Pension Plan Information for FY 20X9

	$ millions
Current service cost	118
Past service cost	36
Beginning PBO	1,022
Ending PBO	1,198
Interest cost	82
Actual return on plan assets	214
Employer contribution	102
Beginning plan assets	896

During fiscal year 20X9, a change in actuarial assumptions regarding employee life expectancy resulted in an actuarial loss of $128 million. Average employee service life is estimated to be 20 years. The discount rate and expected return on plan assets are 8% and 10% respectively. Carson believes that rate of compensation increase will be 5% as opposed to the 4% assumed by the plan.

73. If Samilski's expected rate of return on plan assets was the same as the discount rate used to compute the plan's benefit obligation, the resulting total periodic pension cost and PBO would *most likely* be:

Total periodic pension cost	PBO
A. Higher	Higher
B. Unchanged	Unchanged
C. Higher	Unchanged

74. The amount of benefits paid during the year is *closest* to:
    A. $76 million.
    B. $132 million.
    C. $188 million.

75. The ending fair value of plan assets is *closest* to:
    A. $1,024 million.
    B. $1,128 million.
    C. $1,412 million.

76. The total periodic pension cost is *closest* to:
    A. $62 million.
    B. $76 million.
    C. $150 million.

77. The amount of periodic pension cost reported in P&L if Samilski reported under IFRS would be *closest* to:
    A. $144 million.
    B. $152 million.
    C. $164 million.

78. For this question, assume that Samilski had changed their assumed level of compensation growth rate to the one estimated by Carson. Based on this change only, what will be the *most likely* effects on the next period's current service cost and net interest cost if Samilski reported under IFRS?
    A. Both will increase.
    B. Current service cost will increase while net interest cost will be unaffected.
    C. One will increase and the other will decrease.

Questions 79–84 relate to Kazmaier Foods.

The board members for Kazmaier Foods have gathered for their quarterly board of directors meeting. Presiding at the meeting is the Chairman and CEO for Kazmaier, Phil Hinesman. The other eight members of the board are also present, including Allen Kazmaier, the brother of Kazmaier's founder; Elaine Randall, Executive Vice President for Emerald Bank, which Kazmaier uses to obtain short-term financing; and Bill Schram, Kazmaier's President and Chief Operating Officer. Each of the directors was elected to serve on the board for a 4-year term. They were elected two at a time over the past three years. With the exception of Hinesman, Allen Kazmaier, Randall, and Schram, board members had no ties to Kazmaier prior to joining the board and had no personal relationships with management. In addition to the regular board meetings, the five independent board members get together annually, in a meeting separate from the regular board meetings, to discuss the company's operations.

Item 1 on the board meeting agenda is a discussion about the importance of corporate governance and how Kazmaier can improve its corporate governance system. Hinesman begins the discussion by saying, "A strong system of corporate governance is important to our shareholders. Studies have shown that, on average, companies with strong corporate governance systems have higher measures of profitability than companies with weak corporate governance systems." Randall adds her comment to the discussion: "The lack of an effective corporate governance system increases risk for our investors. If we do not have the appropriate checks and balances in place, our investors may be exposed to the risk that information used to make decisions about our firm is misleading or incomplete, as well as the risk that mergers or acquisitions the firm enters into will benefit management at the expense of shareholders."

After a lengthy discussion, the board agrees on five separate recommendations that will enhance its current system of corporate governance. One of these recommendations is to change the function and structure of the board's audit committee. Currently, the audit committee consists of Matthew Bortz, David Smith, and Ann Williams—three independent directors who each have backgrounds in finance and accounting. The board agrees that one more member should be added to the committee and that the committee should expand its list of responsibilities.

Item 2 on the agenda for the board of directors' meeting is a report from Kazmaier's Chief Financial Officer, Doug Layman. The following information was included in the material that was distributed to each board member before the meeting:

($ Millions)	20X0	20X1*
Net income	$98.50	$112.50
Cash flow from operations	$115.00	$132.00
Capital expenditures (FCInv)	$43.00	$150.00
Net borrowing	$22.00	$75.00
Dividends paid	$42.88	$45.00
Stock repurchases	$42.00	$3.00

*Estimated

Additional information:

Current share price:	$40.00
Shares outstanding:	56,250,000
Target debt-to-equity ratio:	1 to 1
Cost of equity:	8.0%
Constant growth rate:	5.2%

Layman tells the board that his analysis indicates that, based on a constant-growth dividend discount model, the current stable dividend policy would reduce the cost of equity by 1.2% and increase the value of the firm's stock, assuming that earnings, the cost of debt, and the constant growth rate don't change.

Item 3 on the agenda is the sale of Kazmaier's condiment packaging division to Sautter Packaging and Supply Company. Layman believes the sale will net the company $50 million, payable in cash. After discussing the pros and cons of selling the division, the directors agree that the sale is in the best interests of the company and its shareholders. The directors then move to a vote, and the sale of the condiment packaging division is approved unanimously. The committee then moves on to discuss what to do with the proceeds from the sale. Williams suggests that paying out the $50 million to shareholders as a special dividend would continue to give the firm flexibility in how it uses its excess cash. Smith tells the board that a share repurchase can be thought of as an alternative to a cash dividend, and that if the tax treatment between the two alternatives is the same, investors should be indifferent between the two. After debating the merits of special dividends and stock repurchases, Kazmaier's board authorizes the proceeds from the sale of the condiment packaging division to be used for the purchase of $50 million worth of outstanding shares.

An external agency recently included Kazmaier in a review of corporate governance systems to determine whether the structure of the board of directors was consistent with corporate governance best practices. The agency scored companies based on the following criteria:

Criterion 1: Composition of the board of directors.
Criterion 2: Chairman of the board of directors.
Criterion 3: Method of electing the board.
Criterion 4: Frequency of separate sessions for independent directors.

Each of the four criteria was weighted equally, with the firm receiving a positive mark for being in compliance with corporate governance best practice.

A month after the board meeting, the price of Kazmaier stock is still at $40 per share, and the sale of Kazmaier's condiment packaging division does not go through. In order to finance the approved share repurchase, Kazmaier is forced to borrow funds. Schram states, "I am concerned that the cost of the debt used to repurchase shares may cause a reduction in earnings per share."

Jennifer Nagy, a vice president in Kazmaier's finance division, tells Schram not to be concerned about using debt to finance the share repurchase because the rationale behind the repurchase is sound. Nagy then writes down some of the common rationales for share repurchases and hands them to Schram.

Rationale 1: Repurchasing shares can prevent the EPS dilution that comes from the exercise of employee stock options.

Rationale 2: Management can use a share repurchase to alter the company's capital structure by decreasing the percentage of equity.

Rationale 3: Like a dividend increase, a share repurchase is a way to send a signal to investors that Kazmaier's management believes the outlook for the company's future is strong.

79. Are the comments made by Hinesman and Randall about corporate governance systems correct?
     A. Both comments are correct.
     B. Only Hinesman is correct.
     C. Only Randall is correct.

80. Which of the following pairs of recommendations would be *best* in helping Kazmaier's audit committee comply with corporate governance best practices?
    A. The internal audit staff of the firm should report directly to the audit committee, all of the audit committee members should be independent, and the committee should meet with auditors at least annually without management present.
    B. At least 75% of the audit committee members should be independent, and all of the committee members should have a background in finance and accounting.
    C. All of the audit committee members should be independent and should meet with management at least annually to discuss findings in internal audits.

81. Based on the financial information distributed to the board members, the dividend per share for 20X1 based on a residual dividend approach should be *closest* to:
    A. $0.00.
    B. $0.22.
    C. $0.67.

82. Based on the financial information distributed to the board members, the FCFE coverage ratios for 20X0 and 20X1 are *closest* to:

	20X0	20X1
A.	2.19	1.27
B.	1.11	1.19
C.	1.35	2.75

83. Kazmaier's total score on the corporate governance report is *closest* to:
    A. 25%.
    B. 50%.
    C. 75%.

84. How many of Nagy's rationales for a share repurchase are valid?
    A. One.
    B. Two.
    C. Three.

Questions 85–90 relate to Henke Malfoy.

Henke Malfoy, CFA, is an analyst with a major manufacturing firm. Currently, he is evaluating the replacement of some production equipment. The old machine is still functional and could continue to serve in its current capacity for three more years. If the new equipment is purchased, the old equipment (which is fully depreciated) can be sold for $50,000 now but will be worthless in three years. The new equipment will cost $400,000, including shipping and installation. If the new equipment is purchased, the company's revenues will increase by $175,000 and costs by $25,000 for each year of the equipment's 3-year life. There is no expected change in net working capital.

The new machine will be depreciated using a 3-year MACRS schedule (note: the 3-year MACRS schedule is 33.0% in the first year, 45% in the second year, 15% in the third year, and 7% in the fourth year). At the end of the life of the new equipment (i.e., in three years), Malfoy expects that it can be sold for $10,000. The firm has a marginal tax rate of 40%, and the cost of capital on this project is 20%. In calculation of tax liabilities, Malfoy assumes that the firm is profitable, so any losses on this project can be offset against profits elsewhere in the firm. Malfoy calculates a project NPV of –$62,574.

85. The initial outlay for the project is *closest* to:
   A. $350,000.
   B. $370,000.
   C. $400,000.

86. The after-tax operating cash flow for the first year of operations with the new equipment (excluding the initial outlay) is *closest* to:
   A. $10,800.
   B. $132,000.
   C. $142,800.

87. What is the effect of taxes on the operating cash flow in year 2?
   A. Decrease by $7,200.
   B. Increase by $7,200.
   C. Increase by $12,000.

88. The combined after-tax operating cash flow and terminal year after-tax nonoperating cash flow in year 3 is *closest* to:
   A. $131,200.
   B. $151,200.
   C. $152,200.

89. Suppose for this question only that Malfoy has forgotten to reflect a decrease in inventory that will result at the beginning of the project. The *most likely* effect on estimated project NPV of this error:
    A. is to overestimate NPV.
    B. is to underestimate NPV.
    C. depends on whether the inventory is assumed to build back up to its previous level at the end of the project or the decrease in inventory is permanent.

90. What is the IRR based on Malfoy's NPV estimate, and should the project be accepted or rejected in order to maximize shareholder value?

IRR	Project
A. 8.8%	Accept
B. 8.8%	Reject
C. 21.5%	Accept

Questions 91–96 relate to Yi Tang.

Yi Tang updates several economic parameters monthly for use by the analysts and the portfolio managers at her firm. If economic conditions warrant, she will update the parameters even more frequently. As a result of an economic slowdown, she is going through this process now.

The firm has been using an equity risk premium of 5.2%, derived using historical estimates. By comparing the yields on nominal bonds and real bonds, Tang estimates the expected inflation rate to be 2.6%. She expects real domestic growth to be 3.0%. Tang believes that the markets are currently overvalued by 3%. The yield on the market index is 1.7%, and the expected risk-free rate of return is 2.7%.

Elizabeth Trotter, one of the firm's portfolio Managers, asks Tang about the effects of survivorship bias on estimates of the equity risk premium. Trotter asks, "Which method is most susceptible to this bias: historical estimates, Gordon growth model estimates, or survey estimates?"

Tang wishes to estimate the required rate of return for Northeast Electric (NE) using the Capital Asset Pricing Model (CAPM) and the Fama-French model. She uses the following information to accomplish this:

Factor	Risk Premium	Factor Sensitivity
Market	5.2%	0.83 (historical)
Size	3.2%	–0.76
Value	5.4%	–0.04
Liquidity	1.1%	0.20

Trotter has one final question for Tang. Trotter says, "We need to estimate the equity beta for VixPRO, which is a private company that is not publicly traded. We have identified a publicly traded company that has similar operating characteristics to VixPRO, and we have estimated the beta for that company using regression analysis. We used the return on the public company as the dependent variable and the return on the market index as the independent variable. What steps do I need to take to find the beta for VixPRO equity? The companies have different debt/equity ratios. The debt of both companies is very low risk, and I believe I can ignore taxes."

91.   The estimate of the equity risk premium using the Ibbotson-Chen model given the estimates determined by Tang is *closest* to:
A. 1.5%.
B. 4.2%.
C. 4.7%.

92. The *best* response to Trotter's question about survivorship bias is:
    A. survey estimates.
    B. Gordon model estimates.
    C. historical estimates.

93. The required rate of return for NE estimated with the CAPM is *closest* to:
    A. 5.7%.
    B. 6.0%.
    C. 7.0%.

94. The required rate of return for NE estimated with the Fama-French model is *closest* to:
    A. 4.4%.
    B. 4.7%.
    C. 9.0%.

95. Using the Blume method, the adjusted beta computed by Tang would be *closest* to:
    A. 0.90.
    B. 0.96.
    C. 1.03.

96. What response should Tang give Trotter about estimating the equity beta for VixPRO?
    A. Estimate the beta for VixPRO by regressing the returns for VixPRO against an index of non-traded equity market securities.
    B. Estimate the VixPRO beta by multiplying the public company beta times the ratio of the equity risk premium of the market to the risk-free rate of return.
    C. Estimate the unlevered beta for the public company based on its debt/equity ratio. Then, use that unlevered beta to estimate the equity beta for VixPRO based on the VixPRO debt/equity ratio.

Questions 97–102 relate to Shirley Nolte.

Shirley Nolte, CFA, is a portfolio manager for McHugh Investments. Her portfolio includes 5,000 shares of Pioneer common stock (ticker symbol PNER), which is currently trading at $40 per share and does not pay any dividends. Pioneer is an energy and petrochemical business that operates or markets its products in the United States, Canada, Mexico, and over 100 other countries around the world. Pioneer's core business is the exploration, production, and transportation of crude oil and natural gas. Pioneer also manufactures and markets petroleum products, basic petrochemicals, and a variety of specialty products.

Nolte would like to fully hedge her exposure to price fluctuations in Pioneer common stock over the next 90 days. She determines that the continuously compounded risk-free rate is 5%. She also gathers some information on exchange-traded options available on Pioneer stock. This data is shown in Exhibit 1.

Exhibit 1: Exchange-Traded Options on Pioneer Stock

Maturity	Exercise Price	Call Option Price	Call Option Delta	Put Option Price
1-month	$40	$2.84	0.54	$2.67
3-month	$40	$5.00	0.58	$4.50
6-month	$40	$7.14	0.61	$6.15
9-month	$40	$8.81	0.63	$7.34

She also concludes that the 9-month put option is mispriced relative to the 9-month call option, and an arbitrage opportunity is possible, but that the 3-month put option is correctly priced relative to its comparable call option. She also estimates the gamma of the 3-month call option to be 0.023. Nolte is concerned about gamma risk of any hedging strategy she uses.

One year at-the-money calls on the stock of Delpha (current price $60) are trading at $6.90. Nolte believes that over the next year, the stock could either appreciate or depreciate by 15%.

97. Which of the following positions will *best* delta hedge Nolte's long position in Pioneer?
     A. Short 9,259 1-month call options.
     B. Short 8,197 3-month call options.
     C. Short 7,937 6-month call options.

98. If Nolte hedges the position with the 3-month call options, she:
     A. will have to continuously rebalance the position in order to maintain the delta hedge.
     B. can offset the cost of the hedge and maintain the hedged position by buying an equivalent amount of 3-month put options.
     C. will perfectly hedge the position over the 90-day investment horizon and won't need to rebalance the position only if the stock price of Pioneer remains at $40 for 90 days.

99. Violation of which BSM assumption is *most likely* to lead to gamma risk?
     A. The volatility of the returns on the underlying asset is constant and known.
     B. Markets are frictionless; there are no transaction costs.
     C. The price of the underlying changes smoothly.

100. Assuming that Nolte establishes a delta hedge on Pioneer stock using 3-month call options, the gamma of this delta hedged portfolio would *most likely* be:
     A. positive.
     B. negative and would increase with the stock's price.
     C. negative and would decrease as the stock's price increases.

101. Is Nolte correct in her analysis of the relative pricing of the 3-month put option and the 9-month put option?
     A. Nolte is correct on both options.
     B. Nolte is only correct on the 3-month option.
     C. Nolte is only correct on the 9-month option.

102. For this question only, assume that the periodically compounded risk-free rate is 5%. An arbitrage profit can *most likely* be earned by:
     A. buying Delpha calls and shorting Delpha stock.
     B. buying Delpha stock and Delpha calls.
     C. buying Delpha stock and writing Delpha calls.

Questions 103–108 relate to Trent Black.

Trent Black is a government fixed-income portfolio manager, and on January 1, he holds $30 million of fixed-rate, semi-annual pay notes. Black is considering entering into a 2-year, $30 million semi-annual pay interest rate swap as the fixed-rate payer. He must first determine the swap rate. Black notes the term structure shown in Figure 1:

Figure 1: Term Structure of LIBOR (USD and CHF) on January 1

Term (days)	CHF		USD	
	LIBOR	Discount Factor	LIBOR	Discount Factor
180	−0.65%	1.0033	3.25%	0.9840
360	−0.55%	1.0055	3.35%	0.9676
540	−0.20%	1.0030	3.60%	0.9488
720	0.10%	0.9980	3.85%	0.9285
900	0.30%	0.9926	4.00%	0.9091
1,080	0.55%	0.9838	4.10%	0.8905
1,260	0.88%	0.9701	4.25%	0.8705

Black is also evaluating a USD fixed for CHF fixed, 3-year, semiannual currency swap on a notional of USD 10 million. The current exchange rate is CHF/USD 0.97.

Black is additionally evaluating receiver and payer swaptions on the previously mentioned $30 million interest rate swap. The swaptions are European-style swaptions that mature in 240 days. Black anticipates a decline in interest rates and would like to use the swaptions to profit from his interest rate forecast.

Black is concerned about the value of a two-year semiannual pay fixed, receive equity swap the firm entered into six months ago (first settlement just occurred). The fixed rate was set at 3% and the equity index was at 1500 at inception. The index is currently at 1700 and the notional principal is $5 million.

On July 1, immediately after the first settlement, Black observes that the 18-month semiannual swap fixed rate is 4.62%. The term structure of LIBOR is given in Figure 2.

Figure 2: USD LIBOR Term Structure on July 1

Days	Annual Rate (%)	Discount Factor
60	3.31	0.9945
180	3.66	0.9820
360	4.21	0.9596
480	4.69	0.9411
540	4.74	0.9336
720	5.00	0.9091

103. The annualized fixed rate for the $30 million swap on January 1 is *closest* to:
  A. 3.73%.
  B. 3.80%.
  C. 3.91%.

104. For this question only, assume the annualized fixed rate on the $30 million swap is 3.80%. The amount of the first net payment due on this swap is *closest* to:
  A. $82,500.
  B. $165,000.
  C. $285,000.

105. For this question only, assume that the original 2-year $30 million notional swap was entered into at a fixed rate of 4.0%. Based on the information in the case and Figure 2, the value of the swap on July 1 to Black is *closest* to:
  A. $267,390.
  B. $270,000.
  C. $346,572.

106. The CHF fixed payment to be made periodically by the USD receiver is *closest* to:
  A. CHF 26,200.
  B. CHF 52,381.
  C. CHF 54,000.

107. Which position (long or short) should Black take in the payer and receiver swaptions based on his interest rate forecast?

	Payer swaption	Receiver swaption
A.	Short	Short
B.	Long	Short
C.	Short	Long

108. Using the information in Figure 1, the value of the equity swap to the firm is *closest* to:
  A. $19,230
  B. $38,500
  C. $705,167

Questions 109–114 relate to IGS.

The New York-based Irwin Goldreich Schmidt (IGS) is a mid-sized private equity firm with $300 million capital raised from its investors. Amid a turbulent year, the firm has recently dropped its unsuccessful $100 million bid for a Norwegian media company and is now aggressively searching for new venture or buyout investments in the Eurozone. After several months of intense search, IGS believes it identified two potential investments:

1. Sverig, a rapidly expanding Swedish start-up construction company.

2. L'Offre, a struggling French department store in existence since the late 19th Century.

Following several rounds of successful negotiations, IGS makes a $20 million investment in Sverig and a $100 million leveraged buyout investment in L'Offre, committing to an additional $100 million for possible future capital drawdowns. It retains all of Sverig's managers but replaces L'Offre's management team with experienced IGS managers, many of whom are former company senior executives.

IGS also sets up Sverig-L'Offre Private Equity Fund (SLPEF), a fund to manage both firms. The fund manager's compensation is set at 20% of profits net of fees. IGS also specifies that the manager's profits are calculated on the entire portfolio when portfolio value exceeds invested capital by 30%.

Despite the market's recent turbulence, Sverig's original founders are extremely optimistic and believe the firm could be sold for $400 million in six years. To achieve this, they speculate the firm needs another capital infusion of $40 million in four years in addition to the $20 million capital investment today. Given the high risk of the firm, SLPEF's private equity investors decide that a discount rate of 40% for the first four years and 30% for the last two years is appropriate. The founders of Sverig want to hold 5 million shares.

109. If total proceeds net of fees to SLPEF are worth $180 million upon exit in a year, the fund's general partner (GP) under the total return using invested capital method would receive a compensation of:
   A. $0.
   B. $12 million.
   C. $36 million.

110. An appropriate equity valuation technique for Sverig and L'Offre, respectively, would be the:

Sverig	L'Offre
A. Relative value approach	Venture capital method
B. Venture capital method	DCF method
C. DCF method	Relative value approach

111. Common risk factor(s) faced by both IGS investors and the managers of the private equity firm is(are):
    A. market risk but not agency risk.
    B. agency risk but not market risk.
    C. both market and agency risk.

112. SLPEF's general partner's (GP's) share of fund profits, and management's right to sell their equity interest in the event of an acquisition, respectively, are called:

Profits to the GP	Management's right to sell
A. Carried interest	Ratchet
B. Ratchet	Distribution waterfall
C. Carried interest	Tag-along, drag-along clause

113. Sverig's post-money valuation at the first round of financing, using the NPV venture capital method, is *closest* to:
    A. $61.61 million.
    B. $50.08 million.
    C. $51.20 million.

114. The appropriate stock price after the first-round of financing for Sverig's first-round investors is *closest* to:
    A. $6.24.
    B. $8.32.
    C. $6.02.

Questions 115–120 relate to Millennium Investments and Richie Shepard.

Millennium Investments (MI), an investment advisory firm, provides asset allocation recommendations for its clients. Richie Shepard, senior analyst at MI, is using a two-factor macroeconomic model to evaluate a portfolio of two stocks: WMB and REL. The two factors in the model are surprises in inflation and in real GDP growth rate (both given in percentages). The portfolio is invested 60% in WMB. Factor sensitivity and other information for the two stocks are shown in Exhibit 1.

Exhibit 1: WMB and REL

Stock	E(R)	Inflation	GDP Growth Rate
WMB	9%	–2.2	+3.0
REL	10.8%	–1.0	+3.3

Another stock (not in the portfolio), PSL, has a factor sensitivity of –0.9 to inflation and +1.2 to GDP growth rate.

Shepard is also looking at evaluating three portfolios using a single-factor model. Information about the three portfolios is shown in Exhibit 2.

Exhibit 2: Portfolio Factor Sensitivity and Expected Return

Portfolio	Expected Return	Factor Sensitivity
X	0.10	1.00
Y	0.12	1.25
Z	0.15	1.50

Shepard is meeting with a client to discuss inclusion of actively managed funds in that client's portfolio. To prepare for the meeting, Shepard prepares a presentation to illustrate the merits and risks of this change. Shepard cannot recall the term that is used to capture the sum of active factor risk and active specific risk.

Shepard feels that the economy is finally out of recession and poised for robust growth over the next three to five years.

115. Using the information in Exhibit 1, the expected return on the portfolio is *closest* to:
   A. 8.4%.
   B. 9.2%.
   C. 9.7%.

116. Using information in Exhibit 1, the portfolio's sensitivity to inflation is *closest* to:
   A. −1.1.
   B. −1.7.
   C. −2.2.

117. Last year, PSL's actual return was 8% (0.5% unexplained by the model). Inflation surprise, as well as GDP growth rate surprise, was +0.5%. PSL's expected return was *closest* to:
   A. 7.35%.
   B. 7.50%.
   C. 8.50%.

118. Using information in Exhibit 2, taking advantage of an arbitrage opportunity would *most likely* require shorting:
   A. portfolio X.
   B. portfolio Y.
   C. portfolio Z.

119. The term that Shepard cannot recall is *most likely*:
   A. active total risk.
   B. active risk squared.
   C. alpha risk.

120. Based on Shepard's economic outlook, it can be *most appropriately* concluded that:
   A. government bonds will outperform corporate bonds.
   B. higher-rated corporate bonds will outperform lower-rated corporate bonds.
   C. lower-rated corporate bonds will outperform higher-rated corporate bonds.

End of Afternoon Session

Exam 1
Morning Session Answers

To get valuable feedback on how your score compares to those of other Level II candidates, use your Username and Password to gain Online Access at schweser.com and choose the menu item *"Practice Exams Volume 2 (Enter answers from book)."*

1. C	21. B	41. A
2. B	22. A	42. C
3. B	23. A	43. A
4. C	24. C	44. C
5. B	25. B	45. C
6. B	26. A	46. A
7. B	27. B	47. B
8. A	28. B	48. C
9. B	29. A	49. B
10. B	30. B	50. C
11. B	31. B	51. B
12. C	32. A	52. B
13. A	33. B	53. C
14. C	34. A	54. B
15. A	35. A	55. C
16. C	36. C	56. C
17. B	37. A	57. C
18. C	38. C	58. C
19. A	39. B	59. A
20. B	40. C	60. B

Exam 1
Morning Session Answers

1. **C** The ROS principle of Reasonable and Adequate Basis requires that appropriate due diligence be performed and that recommendations be substantiated. Moreover, the ROS states that supervisory procedures must be in place to ensure compliance with the policy. If the report is released with the supervisor's revision, Blackwell should insist that her name be removed. (Study Session 1, LOS 3.b)

2. **B** Standard III(A) Loyalty, Prudence, and Care. Unusual proposals, such as hostile takeovers and executive changes, may require more review than routine matters such as renewing stock-repurchase agreements. Money managers should provide a means to review complex proxies. Establishing evaluation criteria and disclosing the firm's proxy voting policies and procedures to clients are basic elements of a proxy-voting policy. Client wishes regarding proxy voting should always be followed. (Study Session 1, LOS 2.a)

3. **B** Analysts may undertake research related to firms with which they also have an investment banking relationship. The research must remain objective and unbiased to avoid violating the Research Objectivity Standards. Furthermore, the research report must fully disclose the nature of the investment banking relationship and any potential conflict of interest. (Study Session 1, LOS 3.b)

4. **C** Firms have a fiduciary obligation to their clients to publish adequate and timely information on the companies under coverage. The ROS recommends that firms should publish research reports on covered stocks on a regular basis. At least five months had passed without a published research report from Blanchard regarding a major news story affecting Patel shares. While Baldwin was correct to discuss the reason for dropping coverage, he did not comply with ROS recommendations because he did not publish a timely and/or final report on Patel. It is recommended that firms publish a final research report when dropping coverage discussing the reason and disclosing the analyst's final rating. (Study Session 1, LOS 3.b)

5. **B** Standard III(B) Fair Dealing requires firms to notify clients of changes in investment advice before executing trades that go counter to that advice. While equal dissemination is usually impossible, it is an admirable goal. Firms should establish dissemination guidelines that are fair to all clients. Trading disclosures and confidentiality regarding investment rating changes are sensible precautions that meet the spirit of the fair dealing Standard. Maintaining client lists that detail client holdings will simplify the process of deciding how to best disseminate a change in investment recommendation. (Study Session 1, LOS 2.a)

6. **B** Method 2 is the best answer. Quintux should cover the cost of the trading error, and if Borchard is willing to accept investment research in lieu of cash, that's all the better for Quintux. If Quintux compensates Borchard with extra trades, its clients are covering the costs of the error, which may violate Standard III(A) Loyalty, Prudence, and Care if directing future trades to Borchard is not in the clients' best interest. By accepting the CBX shares it did not request and allocating the shares to all client accounts rather than paying for the error, Quintux is violating Standard III(C) Suitability, since the shares are not likely to be appropriate for all of its client accounts and may not be suitable for any

©2017 Kaplan, Inc.

accounts since the shares were obtained as a result of a trading error, not an intentional investment action. Passing on client names is a violation of Standard III(E) Preservation of Confidentiality. (Study Session 1, LOS 2.a)

7. **B** Statement 1: Correct, although not all the shares will be offered.

Statement 2: Incorrect because shares are not automatically issued to existing shareholders under a carve-out.

Statement 3: Correct since the results of the business sector will be more easily identifiable once the sector represents a separate company.

Statement 4: Correct for all strategies under consideration.

Statement 5: Incorrect—with a carve-out the "selling" corporation may (usually does) maintain some control of the business that has been split out into a separate company.

(Study Session 8, LOS 26.n)

8. **A** Debian s/h gain = gain_T = TP = $P_T - V_T$ = \$90m – \$85m = \$5m

Fedora s/h gain = gain_A = S – TP = 8 – 5 = \$3m.

Synergies are not directly given, but you are given that Fedora's value post merger (after paying the \$5m takeover premium) increases by \$3 million. Synergies must then be \$5m + \$3m = \$8m.

Alternatively, the change in Fedora's value post merger, (\$135m – \$132m) = \$3m, would give the gains to the acquirer in the case of a cash merger.

Note: The total gains = value of combined entity – value of both companies prior to merger

(\$135m + \$90m) – (\$85m + \$132m) = \$8m

Note: The value of the combined entity in a stock merger must include the \$90 million in cash that was paid by Fedora to Debian. For computing the total gains to merger in a cash transaction, we need to add the \$90 million that would be paid out to the seller. (Study Session 8, LOS 26.k)

9. **B** Value of Fedora and Ubunta post cash acquisition (given) = \$135 million.

Value of Fedora and Ubunta post stock acquisition = \$135 million + \$90 million cash = \$225 million.

Number of shares outstanding post stock acquisition = 5 + 3 = 8 million.

Value of shares received based on their likely post-acquisition price = [(225m) / 8m] × 3m = \$84,375,000.

Gain to Debian's shareholders is therefore \$84,375,000 – \$85,000,000 = –\$625,000.

(Study Session 8, LOS 26.k)

10. **B**

New value of their 5m shares = (\$225m / 8m) × 5m	= \$140,625,000
Old value of their 5m shares	= \$132,000,000
Gain	= \$8,625,000

(Study Session 8, LOS 26.k)

11. **B** Attribute 1: This attribute is incorrect. An effective corporate governance system defines the rights (not the responsibilities) of shareholders and other stakeholders.

    Attribute 2: This attribute is correct. An effective corporate governance system provides for fairness and equitable treatment in all dealings between managers, directors, and shareholders.

    (Study Session 8, LOS 25.a)

12. **C** Using comparable company analysis:

Using P/E ratio: 25 × 1.50 =	37.50
Using P/B ratio: 2 ×18 =	36.00
Average	36.75
Add: 30% premium	11.03
Estimated takeover price	$47.78

    Using comparable transaction analysis:

Using P/E ratio: 30 × 1.50 =	$45.00
Using P/B ratio: 2.80 × 18 =	50.40
Average	$47.70

    Note: No additional premium is applied for comparable transactions.

    (Study Session 8, LOS 26.j)

13. **A** FCFE = NI + depreciation – FCInv – WCInv + net borrowing
    = 7.0 + 3.5 – 3.2 – 0.4 + (2.4 – 2.0)
    = LC7.3 million, or LC7,300,000
    (Study Session 11, LOS 31.d)

14. **C** FCFF = FCFE + Int(1 – tax rate) – net borrowing = 7.3 + 5.0(1 – 0.34) – (2.4 – 2.0) = LC10.2 million, or LC10,200,000. (Study Session 11, LOS 31.d)

15. **A** Given the assumptions stated in the problem, this is a simple single stage valuation. Using the firm's modified build-up methodology, the real required rate of return is 8% (= country real rate + industry adjustment + firm adjustment = 3% + 3% + 2%). The real growth rate is $\left[\left(\dfrac{1.12}{1.08738}\right)-1\right]=3\%$. FCFE is LC7,3000,000 from an earlier question.

    Hence, the value of PCC equity is:

    $$V_0 = \frac{\text{FCFE}\times(1+g)}{r-g} = \frac{7,300,000\times 1.03}{0.08-0.03} = \text{LC}150,380,000$$

    (Study Session 11, LOS 31.j)

16. **C** *Dividend policy change*: A change in dividend policy will have no direct impact on future FCFE. Note that dividend payments are a use of equity cash flows, not a reduction in FCFE. It is possible that an increase in dividends could reduce the long-term growth rate of the firm, thus reducing firm value. However, holding all other factors constant, an increase in dividends will not affect FCFE forecasts.

    Net change in debt: The increase in debt, LC400,000, will increase future interest expense and decrease future FCFE, but the amount is small, relative to net income of LC7,000,000. (Study Session 11, LOS 31.g)

17. **B** Since the company's capital structure is reasonably stable and FCFE is positive, FCFE is a simpler approach to valuation than FCFF, EVA, or residual income, and is preferred in this case. (Study Session 11, LOS 31.a)

18. **C** Both statements are correct. EBITDA is in fact a poor proxy for FCFF because it does not incorporate the cash taxes paid by the firm. EBITDA also fails to reflect the investment in working capital and the investment in fixed capital. EBITDA is an even worse proxy for FCFE than as a proxy for FCFF. EBITDA does not reflect after-tax interest costs or other cash flows that shareholders care about, such as new borrowing or the repayment of debt. (Study Session 11, LOS 31.h)

19. **A** Free cash flow to the firm can be calculated in various ways. One approach to calculate FCFF is to start with net income:

    FCFF = NI + NCC + Int(1 – tax rate) – FCInv – WCInv
    NI = $164,497   (income statement)
    NCC = Noncash charges = $56,293   (income statement)
    Int = Interest = $20,265 + $5,223 = $25,488   (income statement)
    FCInv = Fixed capital investment = $143,579   (additional information)
    WCInv = Working capital investment = $7,325   (additional information)

    Putting it all together:

    FCFF = $164,497 + $56,293 + $25,488(1 – 0.3) – $143,579 – $7,325 = $87,728
    (Study Session 11, LOS 31.d)

20. **B** FCFE can be expressed in terms of FCFF as follows:

    FCFE = FCFF – Int(1 – tax rate) + net borrowing

    Therefore, the amount by which FCFF exceeds FCFE can be written as:

    FCFF – FCFE = Int(1 – tax rate) – net borrowing

    Int = $25,488

    Net borrowing = $5,866 – $33,275 = –$27,409 (additional information)

    Therefore: FCFF – FCFE = $25,488(1 – 0.3) – (–$27,409) = $45,251
    (Study Session 11, LOS 31.d)

21. **B** The cost of equity can be determined from the capital asset pricing model. We get:

    $r = R_f$ + beta[market risk premium] = 4.5% + 1.10[5%] = 10%.

    The sustainable growth rate can be found from: g = ROE × b

    $$\text{ROE} = \frac{\text{net income}}{\text{beginning total equity}} = \frac{\$164,497}{\$1,019,869} = 0.16129$$

    b = retention rate = 1 – ($82,248.50 / $164,497) = 0.5

    g = 0.16129 × 0.5 = 0.0806 = 8.06%

    (Study Session 10, LOS 30.o)

22. **A** When depreciation is the only noncash charge, FCFF can be estimated from:

$$FCFF = EBIT(1 - \text{tax rate}) + Dep - FCInv - WCInv$$

$$EBIT_{2019} = \$4,052,173 \times 1.06 \times 0.064 = \$274,899$$

Therefore: $FCFF_{2019} = \$274,899 (1 - 0.3) + \$60,000 - \$36,470 - \$24,313 = \$191,646$

(Study Session 11, LOS 31.d)

23. **A** This is a two-stage FCFE model. The required return on equity is 10% (from previous problem), and the long-term growth rate after 2 years is 5%.

$$\text{value of equity} = \frac{\$0.21}{1.1} + \frac{\$0.23}{1.1^2} + \left(\frac{\$0.23 \times 1.05}{0.1 - 0.05} \times \frac{1}{1.1^2} \right)$$

$$= \frac{\$0.21}{1.1} + \frac{\$0.23}{1.1^2} + \left(\$4.83 \times \frac{1}{1.1^2} \right) = \$4.37$$

Financial calculators can perform this calculation more quickly and accurately. The appropriate keystrokes are:

$CFO = 0$; $C01 = \$0.21$; $C02 = \$0.23 + \$4.83 = \$5.06$; $I = 10.0$; $CPT \rightarrow NPV = \$4.37$

Notice that the second cash flow combines the FCFE for the second year with the present value of the series of constantly growing FCFE terms that begin at the end of the third year. This approach is valid since the timing of these two cash flows is the same (i.e., the end of the second year). (Study Session 11, LOS 31.j)

24. **C** Dividends, share repurchases, and changes in the number of shares outstanding do not have an effect on either FCFE or FCFF. Therefore, only the new convertible debt offering will have a significant influence on the current level of FCFE because net borrowing changes FCFE. (Study Session 11, LOS 31.i)

25. **B** FCFE = CFO − FCInv + Net borrowings
CFO = 1042 (given), Net borrowings is change in long-term debt and notes payable.
FCInv = CF from investing = 648
FCFE = 1042 − 648 + [(2,070 + 644) − (2,020 + 600)] = €488 million.

Please note that CF from investing activities and FCInv may not be always the same, but in the curriculum (and for this question), they are treated as same. (Study Session 11, LOS 31.d)

26. **A**   FCFF = CFO + Int(1 − Tax rate) − FCInv = 1042 + 150(0.7) − 648 = €499

Overall growth rate for cosmetics industry = 3.5%

	Percentage	Cost
Debt	50%	4.50%
Equity	50%	8.50%
WACC		6.50%
Cosmetics industry growth rate		3.50%

$$\frac{499 \times (1 + 0.035)}{0.065 - 0.035} = 17{,}216 \text{ million}$$

(Study Session 11, LOS 31.i,j)

27. **B**   To value Hermosa stock, use the following information and apply the two-stage growth model. FCFE for the fiscal year is €136 million. Growth rate for the first 3 years is 14.0%; growth rate after 3 years is 5.5%. For CAPM, expected return on market = 8.5% (since Schön with a beta of 1 should have the same expected rate of return as the market).

Cost of equity (Hermosa) = 0.025 + 1.2 × (0.085 − 0.025) = 9.70%.

	Yr 1	Yr 2	Yr 3
FCFE (in € millions)[1]	155.3	177.0	201.8
Terminal Value			5,069[2]
Total cash flow (in € millions)	155.3	177.0	5,270.8
Cost of Equity		9.70%	

[1]$FCFE_1 = FCFE_0(1 + g) = 136.23(1 + 0.14) = 155.3$

[2]Terminal value = $\dfrac{201.8(1.055)}{(0.097 - 0.055)} = 5069$

For the calculator inputs for NPV function, CF0 = 0, CF1 = 155.3, CF2 = 177.0, CF3 = 5,270.5
I/Y = 9.7

Estimated value is €4,281.26 million. Divide this value by 200 million shares for €21.40 per share. (Study Session 11, LOS 31.j)

28. **B**   Free cash flow to equity values Schön's stock at €17,100,000,000 / 1,000,000,000 or €17.10 per share. This is greater than the market price per share of €15.42; the stock is selling at a price below the implied value which means the stock is undervalued. (Study Session 11, LOS 31.m)

29. **A**   The luxury skin care segment's price-to-earnings ratio is 22.9X. The trailing P/E ratio for Hermosa is €22.78 divided by the earnings per share of €193 / 200 or €0.97. Trailing P/E = €22.78 / €0.97 = 23.6X. Hermosa seems to be slightly overvalued relative to the segment. (Study Session 11, LOS 32.a)

30. **B**   Approach #2 is the best. The free cash flow to firm approach takes a control perspective in valuation as is appropriate in a buyout. Dividend discount models take a minority perspective, and Hermosa does not pay dividends so Approach #1 is unsuitable. Relative valuation approaches, such as trailing P/E, also focus on market price and hence are based on minority investor perspective. (Study Session 11, LOS 32.d,f)

31. **B**   Since the required return (12%) as determined by CAPM is greater than Lear's expected return (10%), then Taylor's stock is overvalued. (Study Session 9, LOS 28.a)

32. **A**   Required return under FFM = risk-free rate + market beta (equity risk premium) + size beta (small-cap return premium) + value beta (value-return premium)

    = 3.4% + 0.7(5.5%) + −0.3(3.1%) + 1.4(2.2%) = 9.4%

    Note: The liquidity factor is only applicable to the Pastor-Stambaugh (PS) model. The PS model is otherwise the same as the FFM, save for the addition of the liquidity factor. (Study Session 9, LOS 28.d)

33. **B**   The Gordon growth model is a popular method to generate forward-looking estimates using current information and expectations concerning economic and financial variables.

    A historical estimate of the equity risk premium consists of the difference between the historical mean return for a broad-based equity market index and a risk-free rate over a given time period.

    A macroeconomic model estimate of the equity risk premium is based on the relationships between macroeconomic variables and financial variables.
    (Study Session 9, LOS 28.b,c,d)

34. **A**   The build-up method is usually applied to closely held companies (such as Densmore) where betas are not readily obtainable.

    The risk premium approach requires betas for its calculations; betas are generally not readily available for closely held companies.

    The bond-yield plus risk premium method is appropriate only if the company has publicly traded debt. The method simply adds a risk premium to the yield to maturity of the company's long-term debt. (Study Session 9, LOS 28.d)

35. **A**   Neither of Saunder's statements is correct. *Confidence risk* represents the unexpected change in the difference between the return of risky corporate bonds and government bonds. *Business cycle risk* represents the unexpected change in the level of real business activity. (Study Session 9, LOS 28.d)

36. **C**   A weakness (not strength) of the CAPM is its low explanatory power in some cases. Multifactor models usually have higher explanatory power than the CAPM since they use more than one factor, whereas CAPM uses only one factor.

    A weakness (not strength) of multifactor models is that they are typically more complex to use. (Study Session 9, LOS 28.f)

37. **A**   We have to bootstrap the three-year spot rate (S_3) given the par curve.

S_1 = par rate for a one-year bond = 1.50%.

Value of two-year (par) bond = $100 = \dfrac{2}{(1+S_1)} + \dfrac{102}{(1+S_2)^2} = \dfrac{2}{(1.015)} + \dfrac{102}{(1+S_2)^2}$

Hence, $(1 + S_2)^2 = 102 / 98.03 = 1.04$ and $S_2 = 2.005\%$

Value of a three-year (par) bond = 100

$$= \dfrac{2.25}{(1+S_1)} + \dfrac{2.25}{(1+S_2)^2} + \dfrac{102.25}{(1+S_3)^3} = \dfrac{2.25}{(1.015)} + \dfrac{2.25}{(1.02005)^2} + \dfrac{102.25}{(1+S_3)^3}$$

Hence, $(1+S_3)^3 = 102.25 / 95.62 = 1.0693$ and $S_3 = 2.259\%$

(Study Session 12, LOS 35.c)

38. **C** $[1+f(2,1)]^1 = (1 + S_3)^3 / (1 + S_2)^2$

From the earlier computations, we know that $S_2 = 2.005\%$ and $S_3 = 2.259\%$.

$[1+f(2,1)]^1 = (1.02259)^3 / (1.02005)^2 = 1.0277 \rightarrow f(2,1) = 2.77\%$

(Study Session 12, LOS 35.c)

39. **B** $F_{(3,3)} = \$0.9151$ (given)

$P_3 = 1 / (1 + S_3)^3 = 1 / (1.02259)^3 = \$0.9352$

$P_6 = F_{(3,3)} \times P_3 = 0.9151 \times 0.9352 = \$0.8558$

(Study Session 12, LOS 35.b)

40. **C**   Bond A is a three-year bond, callable in one year. Callable bonds are sensitive to par rates corresponding to their call date (particularly if their coupon rate is relatively high) and to the par rates corresponding to their maturity date (especially if the coupon rate is relatively low). (Study Session 12, LOS 35.k)

41. **A**   Callable bonds exhibit negative convexity due to price compression that occurs when the call option is in the money. Hence, bond A would exhibit negative convexity. Also, the upside potential for a callable bond (that is realized when interest rates fall) is limited due to the embedded short call. (Study Session 12, LOS 35.k,l)

42. **C**

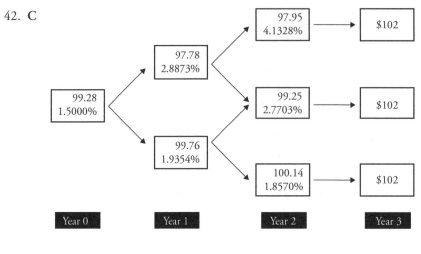

$$V_{2,UU} = \frac{102}{(1.041328)} = \$97.95$$

$$V_{2,UL} = \frac{102}{(1.027703)} = \$99.25$$

$$V_{2,LL} = \frac{102}{(1.01857)} = \$100.14$$

$$V_{1,L} = 0.5\left(\frac{99.25+2+100.14+2}{(1.019354)}\right) = \$99.76$$

$$V_{1,U} = 0.5\left(\frac{99.25+2+97.95+2}{(1.028873)}\right) = \$97.78$$

$$V_0 = 0.5\left(\frac{99.78+2+99.76+2}{(1.015)}\right) = \$99.28$$

Note that the option was never exercised. (Study Session 13, LOS 37.c)

43. **A**
Expected stock price:	= \$38.80
Expected loss using Dec 39: [(41.28 − 39) + 4.20] × 140,000	= \$907,200
Expected loss using Dec 38: [(41.28 − 38.80) + 3.62] × 140,000	= \$854,000
Dec 38 loss smaller by: 907,200 − 854,000	= \$53,200

    (Study Session 14, LOS 42.e)

44. **C** To hedge the return on an equity portfolio, AHI would pay equity and receive the floating rate (LIBOR). However, if the return on the equity portfolio was negative, it would receive this return (i.e., "pay" a negative return) and also receive 90-day LIBOR. (Study Session 14, LOS 42.a)

45. **C** The number of contracts required is based on the multiplier and the current price of the index. Given the index level is 2,250, the number of contracts required is:

    $10,000,000/ ($250 × 2,250) = 17.77. (Study Session 14, LOS 42.a)

46. **A**   Current stock price = $79
Price after a 10% decrease = 79 × 0.9   = $71.10
Price after a 10% increase = 79 × 1.10   = $86.90

Call option with intrinsic value of $1:
Intrinsic value = stock price − exercise price
or $1.00 = 79 − exercise price
Exercise price = $78.00

A long straddle involves buying a put and call at the same strike with the same expiry; hence, Ramiro will use Dec 78 calls and Dec 78 puts.
Total premium paid = 4.60 + 3.22 = 7.82
Breakeven prices: = 78 + 7.82   = 85.82
                      = 78 − 7.82   = 70.18

For a 10% decrease in price to $71.10, the straddle would not breakeven (loss of $0.92).

For a 10% increase in price to $86.90, the straddle would show a profit (profit of $1.08).

(Study Session 14, LOS 42.g)

47. **B**   A short calendar spread using calls involves buying (long) the short dated call option and selling (short) the longer dated call option. This would result in an inflow of 3.62 − 2.85 = $0.77. (Study Session 14, LOS 42.i)

48. **C**   The payoff on a synthetic call is replicated using a long position in the underlying stock plus a long position in corresponding put option.

Alternatively, if Ramiro's position moved by $4.20 as a result of a $10.00 movement in the underlying stock, his position must have a delta of $4.20 / $10.00 = 0.42.

This corresponds to a Dec 82 call option delta. The synthetic call is made up of the long underlying and long Dec 82 put. Note that the delta of this position is also 0.42 (the underlying has a delta of 1, the put delta is −0.58). (Study Session 14, LOS 42.b)

49. **B**   For two up-moves, $45(1.15)^2 = \$59.51$. For two down-moves,

$45(0.87)^2 = 34.06$.

For two up-moves, the intrinsic call value is $59.51 − $40 = $19.51.

For two down-moves, the call is out-of-the-money, intrinsic value = $0. For an up and a down-move the stock price is unchanged at 45, so the intrinsic value of the calls is $45.00 − $40.00 = $5.

The risk neutral probabilities for the decision tree: $\pi_U = \dfrac{1.04 - 0.87}{1.15 - 0.87} = 0.607$ and $\pi_D = 1 - \pi_U = 0.393$.

The probability weighted present value of the option payoff if there are two up-moves is $\dfrac{0.607^2 (19.51)}{1.04^2} = \$6.65$.

For up-down and down-up (which are equal probabilities), the probability weighted present value of the payoff is $\dfrac{(2)(0.607)(0.393)(\$5.00)}{1.04^2} = \$2.21$.

Sum these to get the option value, $8.86. (Study Session 14, LOS 41.b)

50. **C**   To form a delta neutral portfolio Loper needs to write $\dfrac{1,000}{0.83}$ = 1,204.82, or 1,205 calls. (Study Session 14, LOS 41.l)

51. **B**   The payoff is zero for a down-move and 11.75 for an up-move. Since the probability of an up-move is 0.607, the present value is $\dfrac{(0.607)11.75}{1.04} = \$6.86$. (Study Session 14, LOS 41.b)

52. **B**   The possibility of early exercise is not valuable for call options on non-dividend paying stocks, so the value of the American call is the same as the value of the European call, and the difference in value is zero. (Study Session 14, LOS 41.b)

53. **C**   The first assumption listed in the vignette should read, "The volatility of the return on the underlying stock is known and constant." The other listed assumptions are correct. (Study Session 14, LOS 41.f)

54. **B**   Dividends on the underlying stock decrease the value of call options and increase the value of put options, all else equal. By ignoring them in his valuation, Loper will likely overvalue a long call option and undervalue a long put. (Study Session 14, LOS 41.b)

55. **C**   The investment process requires consideration of risk and return concurrently. While maximization of returns is always preferable, an investor's risk tolerance must also be determined and included in the investment decision. Recall that risk and return objectives are closely related to one another because of the trade-off between risk and return. Therefore, Statement 1 is incorrect, and Statement 4 is correct. (Study Session 16, LOS 47.e)

56. **C**   Specific factors that determine an investor's ability to accept risk include required spending needs, financial strength, and long-term wealth targets. Behavioral factors affect an individual investor's willingness to accept risk. (Study Session 16, LOS 47.e)

57. **C**   Strategic asset allocation requires investment managers to consider all sources of income and risk. It also requires an analysis of capital market conditions and specific risk and return characteristics of individual assets. Therefore, Statement 2 is incorrect, and Statement 3 is correct. (Study Session 16, LOS 47.d)

58. **C**   Responses A and B are appropriate considerations related to tax considerations. Although investors should rely on accountants and other advisors for tax advice, portfolio managers also need to pay attention to the tax consequences of their investment recommendations and relay those consequences to the investor so proper tax planning can occur. (Study Session 16, LOS 47.e)

59. **A**   The most important portfolio constraints faced by individual investors include liquidity, investment horizon, and unique needs. Legal and regulatory factors are less important for individual investors than they are for institutional investors. (Study Session 16, LOS 47.e)

60. **B**   Investment policy statements should be transportable, foster discipline, and discourage short-term strategy shifts. (Study Session 16, LOS 47.c)

Exam 1
Afternoon Session Answers

To get valuable feedback on how your score compares to those of other Level II candidates, use your Username and Password to gain Online Access at schweser.com and choose the menu item *"Practice Exams Volume 2 (Enter answers from book)."*

61. A	81. C	101. C
62. C	82. B	102. C
63. C	83. A	103. C
64. C	84. A	104. C
65. B	85. B	105. B
66. A	86. C	106. B
67. C	87. C	107. B
68. C	88. C	108. C
69. B	89. C	109. A
70. A	90. C	110. C
71. C	91. A	111. B
72. C	92. B	112. C
73. A	93. B	113. B
74. C	94. B	114. B
75. B	95. C	115. C
76. C	96. A	116. B
77. B	97. C	117. A
78. B	98. B	118. B
79. C	99. B	119. A
80. B	100. B	120. C

EXAM 1
AFTERNOON SESSION ANSWERS

61. **A** By implying that the composite's past performance is representative of future performance, Burton is in violation of Standard III(D) Performance Presentation. A member or candidate should give a fair and complete presentation of performance and not state or imply that clients will obtain a rate of return that was generated in the past.

    Burton's references to the CFA program in his marketing materials were acceptable according Standard VII(B) Reference to CFA Institute, the CFA Designation, and the CFA Program. The Standard states that members and candidates may make references to the rigor of the program and the commitment of members and candidates to ethical and professional standards. However, statements must not exaggerate the meaning or implications of the designation, membership in CFA Institute, or candidacy. (Study Session 1, LOS 2.a)

62. **C** According to CFA Institute Standards of Professional Conduct, client brokerage is the property of the client; client-directed brokerage does not violate the duty of loyalty to clients. Members should disclose to the clients if such arrangements does not result in best execution for the clients (but this stipulation is not applicable in this case). (Study Session 1, LOS 2.a)

63. **C** Standard VI(C) Referral Fees states that members and candidates must disclose to their clients and prospective clients any compensation or benefit received for the recommendation of services. In this case, Burton may accept a referral fee if he discloses it to the client so that the client may evaluate any partiality shown in the recommendation. (Study Session 1, LOS 2.a)

64. **C** According to Requirement 4.0 Investment Banking of the CFA Institute Research Objectivity Standards, firms must prohibit communication between members of the research and investment banking divisions. Recommended compliance procedures for Requirement 4.0 include prohibiting analysts from participating in marketing road shows. Therefore, while Security Bank complies with all of the requirements of the Standards, it does not comply with all of the recommendations.

    Under Requirement 10.0 Disclosure, firms are required to disclose all conflicts of interest to which the firm or its covered employees are subject, including whether the firm engages in any investment banking or other corporate finance activities. Therefore, "publicly revealing" the relationship is not a violation of the client's confidentiality. (Study Session 1, LOS 3.b)

65. **B** Standard V(A) Diligence and Reasonable Basis states that the member or candidate must exercise diligence, independence, and thoroughness before making an investment recommendation. The Standard also requires that members and candidates have a reasonable and adequate basis supported by research and investigation for any investment recommendations or actions. Burton made his purchase recommendation to Crossley purely on the basis of the Security Bank road show and did not perform his own evaluation to determine whether or not the SolutionWare IPO was a good investment opportunity. Burton has therefore violated Standard V(A).

©2017 Kaplan, Inc.

Standard III(C) Suitability was also violated because there is no indication that Burton made any effort to determine if the investment was appropriate for Crossley's portfolio. Burton should have determined that the investment was consistent with Crossley's written objectives and constraints before he recommended the investment. Even though he later determined that the investment was suitable, he did not know this was the case before he told Crossley that he should purchase shares in the IPO. Standard III(B) Fair Dealing (and not I(B) Independence and Objectivity) would also be violated if Burton did not afford all the clients for whom the IPO was suitable to participate in the offering. Standard III(B) Fair Dealing (and not standard I(B)) would also be violated if Burton did not extend IPO participation to all portfolios meeting suitability criteria. (Study Session 1, LOS 2.a)

66. **A**   Standard VI(B) Priority of Transactions clearly states that investment transactions for clients must have priority over members' and candidates' transactions. Members and candidates can profit from personal investments as long as the client is not disadvantaged by the trade. By taking a portion of the IPO shares for his own account, Burton has ensured that Crossley's order will not be completely filled. It does not matter that the trade allocation was done on a pro-rata basis; Burton should have placed his client's transaction ahead of his own. (Study Session 1, LOS 2.a)

67. **C**   The best formulation for Smith's retail sales data would include the intercept, the lag one coefficient, and the lag twelve coefficient. First, note that in the second regression, all of these are statistically significant, with a p-value of less than 1%. Also, the second regression that included the lag twelve term has a higher adjusted R-square at 0.92 compared to 0.83 in the first regression that omits the lag twelve term. Lastly, we should suspect that the lag twelve term is appropriate because this is seasonal, monthly data.

We could have also looked at the significance of the autocorrelations if they had been provided. If any are significant in either regression, another lag term would be added to the autoregressive model. (Study Session 3, LOS 11.d, l)

68. **C**   To forecast the sales this month, we first calculate the change in the log of sales last month:

$\Delta \ln \text{sales}_{t-1} = \ln(6{,}270) - \ln(6{,}184) = 8.7435 - 8.7297 = 0.0138$

Next, use this change in the regression model to obtain the forecasted change for this month:

$\Delta \ln \text{sales}_t = 0.052 + 0.684(0.0138) = 0.0614$

Add the forecasted change to last month's log sales to obtain this month's forecasted log sales:

$\ln \text{sales}_t = 0.0614 + 8.7435 = 8.8049$

Lastly, convert the forecasted log value to a dollar value by taking its antilog:

$\text{sales}_t = e^{8.8049} = \$6{,}667$

(Study Session 3, LOS 11.d)

69. **B** Smith is correct. The first step in testing for an ARCH process is to take the residuals from the original autoregressive model and then square them.

    Sims is incorrect. The next step in determining whether an ARCH process exists is to regress the squared residuals from this period against the squared residuals from the previous period as follows:

    $$\varepsilon_t^2 = b_0 + b_1\varepsilon_{t-1}^2$$

    If b_1 is statistically different from zero, then we conclude that the regression model contains an ARCH process. (Study Session 3, LOS 11.m)

70. **A** Neither the lag two term nor the lag four term should be included. To determine the significance of the autocorrelation of the residuals, we need the standard error, which is calculated as one over the square root of the number of observations. There are 36 quarters of inflation data. One quarter is lost because we have a lag one term, so there are 35 observations in the regression. Therefore, the standard error is $\dfrac{1}{\sqrt{35}} = 0.1690$.

    The t-statistics are the autocorrelations divided by the standard error which results in:

Lag	Autocorrelation	Standard Error	t-Statistic
1	0.0829	0.1690	0.49
2	0.1293	0.1690	0.76
3	0.0227	0.1690	0.13
4	0.1882	0.1690	1.11

    The critical t-value is 2.03 for a two-tail test, so none of the t-statistics indicate that the autocorrelations are significantly different from zero. Therefore, we do not need to include additional lag terms. (Study Session 3, LOS 11.d)

71. **C** In the first regression, the Federal Funds rate in the United States has a unit root, but the bond yield in the European Union does not. So the former data series is not covariance stationary, but the latter is. In this case, the regression results will not be valid.

    In the second regression, both the Federal Funds rate in the United States and the bond yield in Great Britain have a unit root. So both data series are not covariance stationary. However, because they are cointegrated, the regression results will be valid.

    To sum up the possibilities you may face on exam day:
    - If neither data series has a unit root, the regression results are valid.
    - If only one data series has a unit root, the regression results are invalid.
    - If both data series have a unit root and they are cointegrated, the regression results are valid.
    - If both data series have a unit root and they are not cointegrated, the regression results are not valid.

    (Study Session 3, LOS 11.k, n)

72. **C** To test whether two variables are cointegrated, we regress one data series on the other and examine the residuals for a unit root using the Dickey-Fuller/Engle-Granger test. If we reject the null hypothesis, the error terms of the two data series are covariance stationary and cointegrated. The regression results will be valid. (Study Session 3, LOS 11.n)

73. **A** Hoskins's statement is likely to be correct. If the Maldavian government is considering taxing stock market transactions, then this will limit future economic growth. Economic growth is dependent in part on markets, because markets facilitate business transactions between buyers and sellers.

    Lanning's statement is also likely to be correct. If the president of Petria nationalizes the oil industry, then private property will be seized and property rights will not have been respected. Without property rights, firms and individuals have little incentive to make investments that could lead to future economic growth. (Study Session 4, LOS 14.a)

74. **C** Hoskins's reasoning is incorrect because although labor productivity will increase, the increase will result from a movement *along* the productivity curve. An upward shift in the productivity curve requires an advancement in technology. (Study Session 4, LOS 15.d)

75. **B** Felicia has lower capital to labor ratio and would benefit more from capital deepening. Removal of restrictions on the inflow of capital would lead to more investment and hence capital deepening—again benefiting Felicia more. (Study Session 4, LOS 14.d)

76. **C** GDP growth rate = growth rate in TFP + α (long-term growth rate of capital) + $(1 - \alpha)$ (long-term growth rate of labor).
    $(1 - \alpha) = 0.52$ and thus $\alpha = 0.48$
    $3.9\% = \Delta TFP + (0.48)(1.4) + (0.52)(1.9) \rightarrow \Delta TFP = 2.24\%$
    (Study Session 4, LOS 14.e)

77. **B** Under the classical growth theory, the Tiberian economy will settle at a subsistence level. The high growth in the economy will result in a higher population. The higher population will eventually result in decreased returns to labor and decreased labor productivity. No permanent increase in labor productivity will result and per capita GDP will settle at a subsistence level. (Study Session 4, LOS 14.i)

78. **B** Under the endogenous growth theory, the Tiberian GDP growth rate can continue to increase because technological advances will be shared by many sectors of the economy. Increasing R&D investment, for example, results in benefits not just to the firm making the investment but also to other firms. As these benefits flow to other firms, the economy becomes more productive and the long-term economic growth rate can continue to increase. (Study Session 4, LOS 14.i)

79. **C** The balance sheet accrual ratio is the year-over-year increase in net operating assets divided by average net operating assets. An increase in payables (a liability) will tend to decrease (reduce the change in) net operating assets, while an increase in inventory will tend to increase (increase the change in) net operating assets. Cash is not an operating asset and does not affect the ratio. (Study Session 6, LOS 20.e)

80. **B**   The unadjusted interest coverage ratio is calculated as follows:

$$\text{interest coverage} = \frac{\text{EBIT}}{\text{interest expense}} = \frac{10,876.00}{693.00} = 15.69$$

To adjust the interest coverage ratio for the operating lease, we need to take EBIT and add back the lease/rental expense (the lease payment amount) and subtract an estimate of depreciation for the machinery. Then, we need to add the appropriate interest expense for the operating lease to the overall interest expense.

To compute the interest expense and depreciation for the operating lease, we must first calculate the present value of the operating lease as follows:

PMT   = 2,000
I/Y   = 9
N   = 5
FV   = 0
CPT→PV = 7,779.30

Depreciation and interest expense are then calculated as:

$$\text{depreciation} = \frac{7,779.30}{5} = 1,555.86$$

$$\text{interest expense} = 7,779.30 \times 0.09 = 700.14$$

The adjusted interest coverage ratio is:

$$\text{interest coverage}_{(\text{adjusted})} = \frac{\text{EBIT} + \text{operating lease rent expense} - \text{depreciation}}{\text{interest expense} + \text{interest expense}}$$

$$\text{interest coverage}_{(\text{adjusted})} = \frac{10,876.00 + 2,000.00 - 1,555.86}{693.00 + 700.14} = 8.13$$

(Study Session 6, LOS 20.c)

81. **C**   The elimination of the securitization of receivables as an off-balance-sheet item would result in Konker having to report the transaction as securitized borrowing, replacing the receivables on the balance sheet, and reporting a liability equal to the proceeds of the securitization transaction. The impact on Konker's balance sheet would be an increase in assets, and an increase in liabilities. The change in equity from reporting the transaction in this way is likely to be small. Financial leverage would increase, and the consequent increase in interest expense from the liability would decrease the interest coverage ratio. (Study Session 5, LOS 16.c, Study Session 6, LOS 20.d)

82. **B**   Removing the effects of the income reported under the equity method involves removing the income and the equity asset reported on the balance sheet. The decrease in total assets will increase the asset turnover ratio. The tax burden term is net income divided by earnings before tax so that the decrease in net income from removing the equity income will decrease the term (an apparently greater reduction in ROE due to taxes). Neither interest expense nor operating earnings (EBIT) are affected by the appropriate adjustments, so the interest coverage ratio is unaffected. (Study Session 6, LOS 20.b)

©2017 Kaplan, Inc.

83. **A** The fact that Konker is growing the Industrial division most rapidly (highest capex percent to asset percent ratio) is a likely cause for concern and further investigation, since this division has the lowest operating return on assets. The decrease in the operating ROA for the Capital division is not particularly troublesome as it mirrors the pattern for the other divisions and likely just reflects year-to-year variation in profitability. The fact that the percent of capex for the Defense division is less than its percent of total assets is not a primary cause for concern since that division has a lower operating ROA, and growth in capital assets likely follows contract awards in the defense industry, rather than drives business. Also, the apparent overinvestment in the Industrial division will decrease the capex percent for other divisions, other things equal. (Study Session 6, LOS 20.b)

84. **A** Volatile accruals ratios are an indicator that a firm may be manipulating earnings. Additionally, increasing accruals ratios may be a sign that a firm may be manipulating earnings. Lower accrual ratios represent higher earnings quality. (Study Session 6, LOS 20.b)

85. **B** The assets and liabilities of the purchased firm are included on the balance sheet of the acquiring firm under either method. Under the pooling method, there is no adjustment of balance sheet asset and liability values to their fair values. Under the acquisition method, assets and liabilities acquired are reported at fair value at the time of the purchase. There is no goodwill reported under the pooling method; the purchase price is not reflected on the balance sheet of the acquiring firm. (Study Session 5, LOS 16.a)

86. **C** Under the acquisition method, the investee firm's revenue and expenses would be reported on Fisher's income statement, increasing both expenses and revenues. Under the equity method, Fisher's revenue and expenses are reported without adjustment, and the proportion of income from the purchased firm is reported separately, so that net income is the same under either method. (Study Session 5, LOS 16.a)

87. **C** Goodwill is not amortized under IFRS or U.S. GAAP. The test for impairment is different under IFRS than under U.S. GAAP. Impairment losses cannot be reversed under U.S. GAAP nor under IFRS. (Study Session 5, LOS 16.b)

88. **C** All business combinations (e.g., merger, purchase, or consolidation) are reported under the acquisition method. Identifiable assets and liabilities must be reported at fair value at the time of the acquisition. Under IFRS, Fisher has the option of calculating the goodwill for the acquisition under either the full goodwill or partial goodwill methods. Goodwill is less under the partial goodwill method. (Study Session 5, LOS 16.b)

89. **C** U.S. GAAP requires that unrealized gains and losses on available-for-sale securities be reported in comprehensive income as part of shareholders' equity. The appropriate adjustment to Fisher's statements is to decrease net income by the amount of the gain. Lower net income will result in lower ROA and ROE (lower numerators). Lower net income results in lower retained earnings. However, the gain increases other comprehensive income; thus, total equity does not change. In summary, assets, liabilities and total equity are not affected by the adjustment; thus, asset turnover, debt-to-equity and debt-to-total capital are not impacted. (Study Session 5, LOS 16.a,b)

90. **C** The acquisition method results in higher assets and higher sales, but the same net income. Therefore, both ROA (net income divided by assets) and net profit margin (net income divided by sales) will decrease. (Study Session 5, LOS 16.c)

91. **A** Exposure under the current rate method is equity. Beginning equity is positive (R4,000) and the change in equity during the year is positive (R6,000 – R4,000 = R2,000). Because the Rho appreciated during the year, the current rate method will report a translation gain for 2018. Under the current rate method, gains and losses are reported as part of the cumulative translation adjustment in the equity section of the balance sheet. (Study Session 5, LOS 18.e,f)

92. **B** Exposure under the temporal method is cash and accounts receivable minus current liabilities and long-term debt. Beginning exposure is negative (R5,000 – R11,000 = –R6,000) and the change in exposure is also negative [–R6,300 – (–R6,000)] = –R300. Because the Rho appreciated during the year, the temporal method will report a translation loss for 2018. Gains and losses are reported on the income statement under the temporal method. (Study Session 5, LOS 18.e,f)

93. **B** If the Rho is appreciating, mixed ratios, like return on assets and total asset turnover (using end-of-period balance sheet figures), calculated from the local currency statements, will be larger than the same ratios calculated from the reporting currency statements that were translated using the current rate method. For example, under the current rate method, net income will be translated at the lower average rate ($0.42) and assets will be translated at the higher ending rate ($0.45). Therefore the original return on assets (net income divided by total assets) from the Rho statements will be higher than the ratio after it is translated into the reporting currency. (Study Session 5, LOS 18.e,f)

94. **B** With the Rho appreciating, fixed asset turnover will be lower under the current rate method. (Study Session 5, LOS 18.e,f)

95. **C** This is an example of transaction exposure for Wayward. The translation of Wayward's Del-denominated receivables to Rho would occur at the current exchange rate (i.e., the exchange rate at balance sheet date) and any gains or losses would be reflected in the income statement. (Study Session 5, LOS 18.b)

96. **A** The quick ratio (cash and receivables divided by current liabilities) is a pure balance sheet ratio, which means both numerator and denominator will be translated at the current exchange rate and the ratio will be the same before and after translation. The result is the same for the interest coverage ratio (EBIT divided by interest expense) because it is a pure income statement ratio; both the numerator and denominator will be translated at the average rate over the reporting period and the ratio will be the same before and after translation. (Study Session 5, LOS 18.e,f)

97. **C**

Employer contributions	306
Opening Funded Status	810
Closing Funded Status	493
Change in Funded Status	(317)
TPPC = contributions – Δ funded status	€623

(Study Session 5, LOS 17.c)

98. **B** Income statement (U.S. GAAP)

Service cost		170
(+) Interest cost	(4.5%)	365
(–) Expected return on assets	(3%)	(268)
(=) Periodic pension cost in P&L		267

Since beginning actuarial losses were less than 10% of the greater of beginning PBO or beginning plan assets, there would be no amortization. (Study Session 5, LOS 17.c).

©2017 Kaplan, Inc.

99. **B** Under IFRS interest income/expense is calculated by applying the discount rate to the opening funded status. Since the plan is overfunded, Clear is reporting net interest income.

Opening funded status:	$8920 - 8110 = 810$
Net interest income:	$810 \times 0.045 = 36.45$
Operating profit as reported:	234
Less net interest income:	(36.45)
Adjusted operating profit:	197.55
Adjusted margin:	$197.55/9777 = 2.02\%$

(Study Session 5, LOS 17.e)

100. **B** If the employer contributions are lower than the total periodic pension cost, the company is effectively borrowing from the pension plan. The after-tax difference should be deducted from CFO and added to CFF. (Study Session 5, LOS 17.f)

101. **C** Under IFRS, Remeasurement gains/losses are never amortized into the income statement, they remain in other comprehensive income.

Under U.S. GAAP actuarial gains and losses are amortized using the corridor approach. Amortization removes a gain or loss from OCI and shows it in the income statement. Therefore it has no overall impact on equity. (Study Session 5, LOS 17.c)

102. **C** The expense of the employee stock option scheme will be shown as employee compensation expense in the income statement and hence reduce retained earnings. However, there is an offsetting increase in paid-in capital and hence no overall impact on equity. (Study Session 5, LOS 17.h)

103. **C** initial investment outlay
$$= \text{purchase price} + \text{increase in net working capital}$$
$$+ \text{shipping and installation costs}$$
$$= \$700,000 + (\$50,000 - \$20,000) + \$100,000 = \$830,000$$

terminal year after-tax non-operating cash flow (TNOCF)
$$= \text{Sal}_T + \text{NWCInv} - T(\text{Sal}_T - B_T)$$
$$= 75,000 + 30,000 - 0.4(75,000 - 0)$$
$$= 75,000$$

after-tax operating cash flow (Year 4)
$$= (S - C)(1 - T) + DT$$
$$= (\$750,000 - \$225,000 - \$75,000)(1 - 0.4) + (0.4)(\$56,000) = \$292,400$$

The book value at the end of Year 4 is $0 because total depreciation over the four years was $800,000.

total CF (Year 4) = $292,400 + $75,000 = $367,400

(Study Session 7, LOS 21.a)

104. **C** Both recommendations are incorrect. The $100,000 is a sunk cost and is thus not a relevant cash flow. Using straight-line depreciation will reduce the present value of the depreciation tax shield and reduce the NPV. (Study Session 7, LOS 21.a)

105. **B** By ignoring the initial $30,000 cash inflow (recall that you are asked to assume it is an inflow), he has underestimated project NPV by $30,000. By ignoring the terminal cash outflow of $30,000, he has overestimated the project NPV by $\frac{\$30,000}{1.08^4} = \$22,050$

The net effect is to underestimate NPV by $30,000 − 22,050 = $7,950.

(Study Session 7, LOS 21.a)

106. **B** The overall NPV of Project 1 = project NPV − option cost + option value

overall NPV = −$7 million − $3 million + $9 million = −$1 million

Without the option, the NPV of the production facility is negative, and the real option does not add enough value to make the overall project profitable.

Holbrook is incorrect that he needs to wait for more information to make the decision on Project 2. If the NPV of the project without the option is positive, the analyst knows that the project with the option must be even more valuable, and determining a specific value for the option is unnecessary. A real option adds value to a project, even if it is difficult to determine the monetary amount of that value. (Study Session 7, LOS 21.f)

107. **B** economic income = cash flow − economic depreciation

economic depreciation = beginning market value − ending market value

market value at time t = present value of all remaining cash flows discounted at the WACC

$$\text{Year 3 beginning market value} = \frac{CF_3}{(1+\text{WACC})^1} + \frac{CF_4}{(1+\text{WACC})^2}$$

$$= \frac{\$318,000}{(1.08)^1} + \frac{\$367,400}{(1.08)^2} = \$294,444 + \$314,986 = \$609,430$$

$$\text{Year 3 ending market value} = \frac{CF_4}{(1+\text{WACC})^1} = \frac{\$367,400}{(1.08)^1} = \$340,185$$

Year 3 after-tax operating cash flow (given) = $318,000

Year 3 economic depreciation = $609,430 − $340,185 = $269,245

Year 3 economic income = $318,000 − $269,245 = $48,755

(Study Session 7, LOS 21.h)

108. **C** Comment 1 is incorrect. Interest should not be included in a project's cash flows when conducting NPV analysis because it is a financing cost that is reflected in the discount rate use to compute NPV.

Comment 2 is incorrect. In theory, when discounted at the WACC, the present value of the economic profits from a project equals the NPV of the project. For a given period, economic profit = NOPAT − $WACC, where NOPAT is net operating profit after taxes and $WACC is the dollar cost of the capital used during the period. Economic profit reflects the income earned by all capital providers. (Study Session 7, LOS 21.a,i)

109. **A** Structural models require that the company's assets trade in a frictionless arbitrage free market. (Study Session 13, LOS 38.f)

110. **C** Reduced form models assume that given the macroeconomic state variables, a company's default represents idiosyncratic risk. Structural models assume a constant (non-stochastic) risk-free rate and that the time T value of the assets is characterized by a lognormal distribution. (Study Session 13, LOS 38.f)

111. **B** Ratings tend to be stable over time, which reduces their correlation to default probabilities; hence, Point 1 is incorrect. (Study Session 13, LOS 38.c)

112. **C** The maximum amount an investor would to pay to remove the credit risk is the present value of the expected loss. (Study Session 13, LOS 38.d)

113. **B** The time value of money discount will always reduce the present value of expected loss. Because the present value of expected loss in this case is higher than the expected loss, the risk premium for risk of credit loss must be larger than the time value of money discount. (Study Session 13, LOS 38.d)

114. **B** Under the option analogy of the structural model, risky debt can be viewed as a portfolio comprising a long position in risk-free debt and a short put option on the company's asset with a strike price equal to the face value of the risky debt. When the asset volatility increases, the value of the put option increases and the value of the portfolio with short exposure to the put option will decrease. Hence the computed value of risky debt will be lower. (Study Session 13, LOS 38.d)

115. **C** Using direct capitalization:

Cap rate data:

Office Building	Craig Court	Kenton Place	Hester Oasis
Cap rate	$2.56 / $32.0 = 8.0%	$1.80 / $24.0 = 7.5%	$3.15 / $45.0 = 7.0%

The average cap rate for the three apartment buildings is 7.5%. The estimated value of Parkway Terrance is calculated as the NOI of $3,300,000 divided by the cap rate of 7.5%, or $44.0 million. (Study Session 15, LOS 43.g)

116. **B** Using the sales comparison approach:

Variable	Craig Court	Kenton Place	Hester Oasis
Sale price	$32,000,000	$24,000,000	$45,000,000
Size	200,000	150,000	300,000
Sale price per sq ft	$160.00	$160.00	$150.00
Age adjustment	-4.5%	0.0%	+4.5%
Condition adjustment	+7.5%	0.0%	0.0%
Location adjustment	0.0%	+7.5%	+7.5%
Date of sale adjustment	+4.5%	+2.5%	+8.0%
Total adjustments	+7.5%	+10.0%	+20.0%
Adjusted sales price psf	$160 × (1 + 0.075) = $172.00	$160 × (1 + 0.100) = $176.00	$150 × (1 + 0.200) = $180.00

Average sales price per square foot is $176.00. The sales comparison method estimates the value of the property at 240,000 square feet × $176.00 = $42.2 million.
(Study Session 15, LOS 43.i)

117. **A**

	Parkway Terrace	Standards
NOI	$3,300,000	
Equity[1]	$10,000,000	
Annual Debt Service	$166,750 × 12 = $2,001,000	
Equity Dividend Rate	= ($3,300,000 − $2,001,000) / $10,000,000 = 13.0%	13.0% is less than 25.0%
DSCR	$3,300,000/$2,001,000 = 1.65X	1.65X exceeds 1.50X
Cash flows (PMT)	$3,300,000 − $2,001,000 = $1,299,000	
Equity (PV)	$10,000,000	
Sales Price − Outstanding Loan in 10 Years (FV)	$60,000,000 − $21,797,543 = $38,202,457	
Sales Date (N)	10	
Levered IRR[2]	22.6%	22.6% exceeds 20.0%

1. LTV = 75% (given), Equity = 25% of 40 million.
2. Levered IRR calculation: N = 10; PV = −10,000,000; PMT = 1,299,000;
   FV = 38,202,457; CPT → I/Y = 22.56%

(Study Session 15, LOS 43.m)

118. **B**

Value of land (given)	$12,500,000	

Replacement cost, including constructor's profit

Building costs (psf)	$175	
Total area	240,000	$42,000,000
Developer's profit	$15	$3,600,000
		$45,600,000
Reduction for curable deterioration		−$5,000,000
		$40,600,000

Reduction for incurable deterioration

Total economic life	50	
Remaining economic life	40	
Effective age	10	
Ratio of effective to total	20.0%	
Reduction for incurable deterioration		−$8,120,000
		$32,480,000
Reduction for total obsolescence		−$4,000,000
Total building value		$28,480,000
Total Cost Estimate		$40,980,000

(Study Session 15, LOS 43.i)

119. **A** The economic outlook on home prices and population trends indicate favorable conditions going forward. Shorter leases would allow rents to be adjusted upwards as demand for rentals increase, so Lundy's comment is correct. For a buyer of real estate, low interest rates along with a high loan-to-value (LTV) will maximize the potential for high levered returns. Tenants will benefit from longer leases in a high demand environment; this would not benefit the investors so Park's comment is incorrect. (Study Session 15, LOS 43.c,d)

120. **C** Appraisal lag tends to smooth the reported returns of real estate indices, resulting in an artificially low correlation with other asset classes. Appraisal lag can be mitigated by unsmoothing the index or by using a transaction-based index. Using more-recent appraisals still relies on appraisal-based data. (Study Session 15, LOS 43.k)

Exam 2
Morning Session Answers

To get valuable feedback on how your score compares to those of other Level II candidates, use your Username and Password to gain Online Access at schweser.com and choose the menu item *"Practice Exams Volume 2 (Enter answers from book)."*

1. B	21. C	41. B
2. A	22. C	42. A
3. A	23. A	43. B
4. C	24. B	44. C
5. C	25. C	45. A
6. C	26. A	46. A
7. C	27. C	47. A
8. A	28. B	48. C
9. A	29. B	49. B
10. B	30. A	50. C
11. C	31. B	51. A
12. A	32. A	52. C
13. B	33. A	53. B
14. A	34. A	54. C
15. C	35. A	55. C
16. C	36. C	56. C
17. C	37. C	57. B
18. B	38. C	58. B
19. C	39. A	59. A
20. C	40. A	60. B

Exam 2
Morning Session Answers

1. **B** **Standard I(B).** Attending the conference would be appropriate, but Gillis must avoid any situation that would affect her independence in order to properly comply with Standard I(B) Professionalism – Independence and Objectivity. Since Gingeria is remotely located, it is reasonable for the government to pay her travel expenses. However, the gift of emeralds must be refused. The fact that the host is a sovereign government does not matter—the obvious objective is to give the analysts a favorable bias toward the currency and the proposed reforms. (Study Session 1, LOS 2.a)

2. **A** **Standard V(C).** Gillis's reports may not be specific investment recommendations, but because they are client communications, she should keep either electronic or hard copy records of her conversations with the government officials and copies of the research reports she used in developing her weekly summary reports, in order to comply with Standard V(C) Investment Analysis, Recommendations, and Actions – Record Retention. (Study Session 1, LOS 2.a)

3. **A** **Standard VI(B).** Gillis is attempting to trade ahead of her employer and her clients in violation of the Standards. She was wrong to take the long position in anticipation of a positive recommendation and wrong to sell the position before issuing her negative recommendation. These trades were wrong regardless of whether they were disclosed. In accordance with Standard VI(B) Conflicts of Interest – Priority of Transactions, client interests must take precedence over personal interests. (Study Session 1, LOS 2.a)

4. **C** **Standard I(A).** Warning Gillis and/or reporting the violation up Trout's management structure are inadequate solutions. Limiting the trading activity and increased monitoring to prevent future violations are more appropriate initial responses, in accordance with Standard I(A) Professionalism – Knowledge of the Law. (Study Session 1, LOS 2.a)

5. **C** **Standard VI(B).** The main problem in this case appears to be that there is no system to identify potential front-running violations before they occur. Standard VI(B) Conflicts of Interest – Priority of Transactions recommends both preclearance of trades and duplicate trade confirmations as procedures for compliance. (Study Session 1, LOS 2.a)

6. **C** **Standards II(B) and V(B).** The strategy based on interest rate parity would provide riskless profits until the prices moved into equilibrium and the forward rates accurately reflected the interest rate differentials. Trout's guarantee is therefore accurate. The low transaction costs available to Trout are a competitive advantage that can be exploited without violating Standard II(B). (Study Session 1, LOS 2.a)

7. **C** We want to convert ¥ to NT$ (via USD). Since we are not given the starting ¥ position, we start with a hypothetical ¥1,000 contract size. The quotes given are $/¥ and $/NT$. To convert ¥ to $ (i.e., going "up the quote") use the bid price (and multiply). To convert from $ to NT$ we use the offer price (and divide).

Step 1: Convert 1,000 yen to USD at $0.008852 to obtain $1,000 \times 0.008852 = \$8.852$.

Step 2: Convert $8.852 to NT$ at $0.02876 to get $8.852 / 0.02876 = $ NT$ 307.7886.

Now, we want NT$ 10 million or $10,000,000 / 307.7886 = 32,489.8323$ ¥ contracts or ¥32,489,832. (Study Session 4, LOS 13.b)

8. **A** Surratt is correct. Market conditions affect currency spreads such that the bid-ask spread on foreign currency quotations increases as exchange rate volatility (uncertainty) increases. In this example, an economic crisis in the Asian markets would create uncertainty, thereby impacting the $/¥ and $/NT$ exchange rates and increasing the bid-ask spread.

Castillo is incorrect. Bank and other currency dealer positions are not considered to directly impact the size of foreign currency spreads.

In this example, it is true that the dealer would likely reduce her yen ask (selling price) if she wanted to unload an excess inventory of yen. However, the dealer would also probably reduce her bid (buying price) so that she did not buy any additional yen. The result would be that the spread would remain relatively unchanged. (Study Session 4, LOS 13.a)

9. **A** Surratt is correct. Under the Mundell-Fleming model, restrictive monetary policy reduces the growth rate of the money supply and will lead to appreciation of a country's currency. Restrictive monetary policy will increase the interest rate and, consequently, the demand for domestic physical and financial assets. This increase in financial inflows (increase in the financial account) increases the demand for the domestic currency for investment purposes leading to its appreciation. Choice C is incorrect because we are given in the vignette that the foreign interest rates remain constant. (Study Session 4, LOS 13.k)

10. **B** Castillo is incorrect with respect to the impact of unanticipated restrictive fiscal policies on the value of the dollar.

A reduction in the budget deficit means that government borrowing will decline, which reduces interest rates and causes investment funds to flow out of the country. As a result, the value of the dollar tends to decline. (Study Session 4, LOS 13.k)

11. **C** The 90-day USD and SF interest rates are 18% / 4 = 4.5% and 12% / 4 = 3% respectively.

Using CIRP, $F = S (1+R_\$) / (1+R_{SF}) = 0.85 (1.045) / (1.03) = \$0.8624 / $ SF, which is greater than the market forward price of $0.80/SF. This implies that SF is trading at a bargain price in the forward market—buy it!

At t = 0	*Cash flow*
Buy (i.e., long position in) SF in forward market at $0.80/SF	$0
Sell 1,176,471 SF in the spot at $0.85/SF	$1,000,000
	(1,176,471 SF)
Borrow 1,176,471 SF for 90 days @ 12% annual rate	1,176,471 SF
Invest $1 million for 90 days @ 18% annual rate	($1,000,000)
Total cash flows at t = 0	0

t = 90	*Cash flow*
Receive USD with interest	$1,045,000
Convert USD 969,412* into SF at previously locked-in forward rate of $0.80/SF	($ 969,412) SF 1,211,765
Repay the SF loan taken at t = 0	(1,211,765)
Total cash flows at t = 90	$ 75,588

*This is the amount needed to repay the SF loan (with interest) after conversion.

(Study Session 4, LOS 13.e)

12. **A** Only factor 3 is correct. Factor 1 incorrectly specifies the size of expected future deficits rather than size of initial current account deficit. Factor 2 incorrectly specifies influence on domestic prices in general rather than domestic prices of traded goods (i.e., imports/exports). (Study Session 4, LOS 13.j)

13. **B** Funded status equals fair value of plan assets minus PBO (395 − 635 = −240). Because the funded status is negative, Iron Parts would report a liability of $240 million. (Study Session 5, LOS 17.b)

14. **A** The discount rate increased from 5.5% to 6.0%. An increase in the discount rate will result in lower service cost. Lower service cost will result in a *lower* PBO. A lower PBO will result in a higher funded status (more funded). Lower service cost will result in lower pension expense and *higher* retained earnings. The impact on interest cost cannot be determined without more information. (Study Session 5, LOS 17.d)

15. **C** $327 beginning balance plan assets + $37 actual return + contributions − $22 benefits paid = $395 ending balance plan assets. Solving for the contributions, we get $53. (Study Session 5, LOS 17.b)

16. **C** The higher expected return reduces pension expense. Lower pension expense results in higher net income. Higher net income results in higher retained earnings. Neither the PBO nor the funded status is affected by the expected return on plan assets. (Study Session 5, LOS 17.d)

17. **C** Amount reported under IFRS:

Service cost	$37
Interest cost[1]	$10.4
Past service cost	$80
Pension cost on P&L	$127.4 million

[1]Interest cost = discount rate × beginning funded status = 0.06 × (500 − 327)

(Study Session 5, LOS 17.c)

18. **B** Total periodic pension cost can be calculated by summing the changes in the PBO for the period (excluding benefits paid) and then subtracting the actual return on assets. The change in the PBO (excluding benefits) is $157 (635 reported 20X8 PBO + 22 benefits paid − 500 reported 20X7 PBO). Subtract the actual return to get economic pension expense of $120 (157 change in PBO excluding benefits paid − 37 actual return).

Alternatively, total periodic pension cost is equal to contributions minus change in funded status. 20X8 funded status was −240 (395 plan assets − 635 PBO) and the funded status for 20X7 was −173 (327 plan assets − 500 PBO). Contributions were $53 (calculated in Question 21). Thus, total periodic pension cost is $120 [53 − (−67)]. (Study Session 5, LOS 17.c)

19. **C** The target payout ratio approach to estimating a company's expected dividend uses the following formula:

    increase in dividends = increase in earnings × target payout ratio × adjustment factor

    Rearranging the formula to solve for the target payout ratio, we obtain:

    $$\text{target payout ratio} = \frac{\text{increase in dividends}}{\left(\text{increase in earnings} \times \text{adjustment factor}\right)}$$

    Managers at MavsHD want to move toward the target payout ratio over a period of 8 years, which makes the adjustment factor equal to: 1 / 8 = 0.125. The expected dividend increase is given as $250,000, and the increase in earnings can be computed as the difference between expected earnings and earnings from the prior year: 153,000,000 – 145,000,000 = $8,000,000. Plugging each of these figures into the previous formula, the target payout ratio is calculated as:

    $$\text{target payout ratio} = \frac{250,000}{\left(8,000,000 \times 0.125\right)} = 0.25 = 25\%$$

    (Study Session 7, LOS 23.g)

20. **C** Paying a premium price for the shares (i.e., a price higher than the current market price of the stock) will reduce the value of the remaining shareholders' shares. However, this value reduction is actually transferred to the selling shareholders since they receive more than the market value per share for selling their shares. (Study Session 7, LOS 23.k)

21. **C** $\Delta P = D(1 - T_D) / (1 - T_{CG}) = 2.25(1 - 0.15) / (1 - 0.396) = 3.17$

    (Study Session 7, LOS 23.d)

22. **C** Investors do not like instability in the dividends paid by a company. Any volatility in dividends is seen as a negative sign by investors, and the company's stock price would be punished as a result of varying dividends. According to the bird-in-the-hand theory, investors prefer the assurance of receiving a higher dividend today rather than waiting for returns in the form of capital appreciation. Because of the uncertainty associated with capital appreciation and the relative certainty of dividends, the bird-in-the-hand theory predicts that investors will reward dividend paying companies with a lower cost of equity and, thus, a higher equity value. A repurchase does not provide the same type of assurance since it is an unpredictable and possibly one-time event. (Study Session 7, LOS 23.b,c,g)

23. **A** If the company plans on spending $160 million on net investments, then only 60% of the funds need to come from retained earnings. Therefore, MavsHD needs 0.6 × 160 = $96 million in retained earnings. Net income is projected to be $153 million, leaving $57 million (153 – 96) available to pay dividends. Thus, the dividend payout ratio would equal 57 / 153 = 37.3%. (Study Session 7, LOS 23.g)

24. **B** Under a residual dividend policy, a firm determines the optimal capital budget and then uses retained earnings to fund the optimal capital budget, paying out what is left over to shareholders. Because the amount of distributable earnings is not known in advance and is determined as a function of the capital budget, the dollar dividend paid to shareholders will fluctuate widely from year to year. However, the firm will be able to use internally generated funds to a greater extent when deciding how to fund the optimal capital budget. It is not true, however, that the residual dividend policy will reduce the firm's cost of capital. Investors do not like unpredictable dividends and will penalize the company in the form of a higher required return on equity to compensate for the additional uncertainty related to dividend payments. (Study Session 7, LOS 23.g)

25. **C**   BMC is a mature company. The most appropriate model for valuation is the single-stage Gordon growth model.

	In $ millions
EBIT (operating income)	3,290.0
Interest expense	600.0
Earnings before tax	2,690.0
Tax at 30%	807.0
Earnings	1,883.0
Dividends at 72%	1,355.8
Dividend per share	1.36

Cost of Equity:	
CAPM beta	0.90
Risk-free rate	4.0%
Market risk premium	5.0%
Discount rate	(0.90)(5.0%) + 4.0% = 8.5%

LT growth rate = 3.4% (given)

$$\frac{1.36 \times (1.034)}{(0.085 - 0.034)} = \$27.57$$

(Study Session 9, LOS 28.c; and Study Session 10, LOS 30.c)

26. **A**   MSC is best valued using a two-stage growth model. For the first three years, dividends grow at 25.0%; after Year 3, dividends grow at 3.4%. Calculate the Year 4 dividend and use this to find the terminal value, which is treated as additional cash flow in Year 3.

Value of Dividend	In $ millions
Year 0	278.0
Year 1	347.50
Year 2	434.38
Year 3	542.97
Terminal value (Year 3 cash flow)	(542.97 × 1.034) / (0.094 – 0.034) = 9357.18

Cost of Equity:	
CAPM beta	1.12
Adjusted beta	1.12(2/3) + 1.00 (1/3) = 1.08
Market risk premium	5.0%
Discount rate	(1.08)(5.0%)+ 4.0% = 9.4%

Using a financial calculator, CF0 = 0; CF1 = 347.50; CF2 = 434.38; CF3 = 542.97 + 9357.18 = 9,900.15; I/Y = 9.4; solve for NPV = $8,241.77 million.

Divide $8,241.77 million by 250 million shares results in $32.97 per share.

(Study Session 9, LOS 28.d; and Study Session 10, LOS 30.l)

27. **C** SGC is a growing company that has no dividend history, so the dividend discount model would be inappropriate. Residual income is appropriate for companies with high quality earnings. The value of SGC stock is best estimated using free cash flow model, as we are told that earnings are erratic but cash flows are stable. (Study Session 10, LOS 30.a)

28. **B** Using the Pastor-Stambaugh model to calculate SGC's cost of equity:

0.04 + (1.20 × 0.05) + (0.50 × 0.02) + (−0.20 × 0.04) + (0.20 × 0.045) =11.10%

$$\$28.45 = \frac{\$1.60(1.30)}{0.111} + PVGO$$

$28.45 = $18.74 + PVGO
PVGO = $9.71
PVGO/Price = $9.71 / $28.45
= 34.13%

(Study Session 9, LOS 28.c; and Study Session 10, LOS 30.e)

29. **B** If the justified fundamental leading P/E ratio is 14.1X, then the justified fundamental trailing P/E ratio is (14.1) × (1.034) = 14.6X.

	In $ millions
EBIT (operating income)	3,290.0
Interest expense	600.0
Earnings before tax	2,690.0
Tax at 30%	807.0
Earnings	1,883.0
Shares outstanding	1000.0
EPS	$1.883

Based on the current market price, the trailing price-to-earnings is $26.50 / $1.883 = 14.1X. This means that the fundamental value is greater than the market price; the stock is undervalued. (Study Session 10, LOS 30.f)

30. **A** Using the H-model, valuation of SGC is:

$$V_0 = \frac{D_0 \times (1 + g_L)}{r - g_L} + \frac{D_0 \times H \times (g_S - g_L)}{r - g_L}$$

$$= \frac{\$0.80 \times (1.034)}{0.12 - 0.034} + \frac{\$0.80 \times 8 / 2 \times (0.30 - 0.034)}{0.12 - 0.034}$$

$$= \$19.55$$

(Study Session 10, LOS 30.p)

31. **B** Normalizing EPS using the method of average EPS is accomplished by averaging the EPS over the six-year period from 2010–2015:

   EPS(normalized) = (1.90 + 1.65 + 0.99 + 1.35 + 0.77 + 1.04) / 6 = 1.283. The P/E ratio based on this normalized EPS is 26.5 / 1.283 = 20.649. (Study Session 11, LOS 32.e)

32. **A** Normalizing EPS (for 2016) using the method of average return on equity is accomplished by (1) averaging the ROE over the six-year period from 2010-2015, and then (2) multiplying the average ROE times the 2015 BVPS. ROE(average) = (0.178 + 0.178 + 0.122 + 0.177 + 0.114 + 0.160) / 6 = 0.155. EPS(normalized) = 0.155(10.66) = 1.652. The P/E ratio based on this normalized EPS is 26.5 / 1.652 = 16.04.
   (Study Session 11, LOS 32.e)

33. **A** Book values are more likely to be positive than EPS. Thus, the P/B ratio suffers less often from the problem where P/E ratios are not meaningful because of a negative EPS. The other two advantages given are actually disadvantages associated with using P/B ratios. (Study Session 11, LOS 32.c,d)

34. **A** Aims is correct about both ratios. For example, let's take the trailing P/E ratio, which is P_0/E_0. Multiplying by the net profit margin results in $P_0/E_0 \times E_0/S_0 = P_0/S_0$. If the justified P/E is $(1 - b)(1 + g) / (r - g)$, the justified P/S is $(E_0/S_0) (1 - b)(1 + g) / (r - g)$. Multiplying the leading P/E ratio by the ROE results in $P_0/E_1 \times E_1/B_0 = P_0/B_0$. If the justified P/E is $(1 - b) / (r - g)$, the justified P/B is $ROE(1 - b) / (r - g)$. This becomes $(ROE - b \times ROE) / (r - g)$. Since $b \times ROE = g$ (from sustainable growth equation), the equation becomes $(ROE - g) / (r - g)$. (Study Session 11, LOS 32.h)

35. **A** Both criteria are poorly applied by the associate. Generally, a lower PEG ratio is considered desirable, not a higher one. The difference in the trailing and leading P/E ratios could be due to transitory elements in the current year's income in the denominator of the trailing P/E. In a constant growth model (admittedly a strong assumption), the leading P/E will naturally be smaller than the trailing P/E because earnings are growing by g. (Study Session 11, LOS 32.e,r)

36. **C** Comment 1 about EBITDA ratios is incorrect. EBITDA is a pre-interest variable, so it is a flow available to all suppliers of capital, not just common shareholders. The comment about dividend yields is reasonable. (Study Session 11, LOS 32.m,n)

37. **C** Statement 1: McDonnell is correct. Private firms are usually smaller than public firms and, thus, thought to be riskier. Accordingly, private firms are usually assigned higher risk premiums and required returns than public firms. The lack of access to liquid public equity markets can also limit a private firm's growth.

   Statement 2: McDonnell is correct that small private firms may not be able to attract as many qualified applicants for top positions as public firms. This may reduce the depth of management, slow growth, and increase risk at private firms. She is, however, incorrect that private firm managers and investors have a shorter-term view. Public firm shareholders often focus on short-term measures such as quarterly earnings and the consistency of such. Public management may therefore take a shorter-term view than they otherwise would. So it is private firms that should be able to take a longer-term view.

   Furthermore, in most private firms, management has substantial equity ownership. In this case, external shareholders cannot exert as much control, and the firm may be able to take a longer-term perspective. (Study Session 11, LOS 34.a)

38. **C** McDonnell and Lutge will use the investment value of Albion Biotechnology to determine what the firm is worth to Thorngate. Investment value is the value to a specific buyer and may be different for each investor due to different cash flow estimates, perceived firm risk, discount rates, financing costs, and synergies that lead to decreased costs.

Market value is frequently used in real estate and other real asset appraisals where the purchase will be levered. Intrinsic value is the value that should be the market value once other investors arrive at this "true" value.

McDonnell and Lutge are determining the firm's value to Thorngate. The firm is not publicly traded so there is no market for its shares at the present time.

Furthermore, combining Albion with Thorngate's current pharmaceutical firm would result in advances that no pharmaceutical competitor could match. The synergies appear to be unavailable to other potential buyers (i.e., the value that McDonnell and Lutge will determine is specific to Thorngate and is not a value determined in a market of many buyers and sellers). (Study Session 11, LOS 34.c)

39. **A** In a strategic transaction, a firm is acquired based in part on the synergies it brings to the acquirer. A financial transaction occurs when there are no synergies. The previous suitor of Balanced, a competitor in the same industry, was a strategic buyer and could realize the synergistic cost savings of $1,200,000.

Thorngate currently does not own a manufacturing firm, so it would be a financial buyer. Thorngate will not be able to realize any synergistic cost savings, so these are not included in the free cash flow to the firm (FCFF) estimates in the following tables.

The calculations are as follows.

Pro forma Income Statement	
Revenues	$23,540,000
Cost of goods sold	$17,655,000
Gross profit	$5,885,000
SG&A expenses	$5,400,000
Pro forma EBITDA	$485,000
Depreciation and amortization	$235,400
Pro forma EBIT	$249,600
Pro forma taxes on EBIT	$74,880
Operating income after tax	$174,720
Adjustments to Obtain FCFF	
Plus: Depreciation and amortization	$235,400
Minus: Capital expenditures	$297,000
Minus: Increase in working capital	$231,000
FCFF	–$117,880

©2017 Kaplan, Inc.

The following provides a line by line explanation for the above calculations.

Pro forma Income Statement	Explanation
Revenues	Current revenues times the growth rate: $22,000,000 × (1.07)
Cost of goods sold	Revenues times one minus the gross profit margin: $23,540,000 × (1 − 0.25)
Gross profit	Revenues times the gross profit margin: $23,540,000 × 0.25
SG&A expenses	Given in the question
Pro forma EBITDA	Gross profit minus SG&A expenses: $5,885,000 − $5,400,000
Depreciation and amortization	Revenues times the given depreciation expense: $23,540,000 × 0.01
Pro forma EBIT	EBITDA minus depreciation and amortization: $485,000 − $235,400
Pro forma taxes on EBIT	EBIT times tax rate: $249,600 × 0.30
Operating income after tax	EBIT minus taxes: $249,600 − $74,880
Adjustments to Obtain FCFF	
Plus: Depreciation and amortization	Add back noncash charges from above
Minus: Capital expenditures	Expenditures cover depreciation and increase with revenues: $235,400 + 0.04 × ($23,540,000 − $22,000,000)
Minus: Increase in working capital	The working capital will increase as revenues increase 0.15 × ($23,540,000 − $22,000,000)
FCFF	Operating income net of the adjustments above

(Study Session 11, LOS 34.e)

40. **A**   The free cash flow method can accommodate multiple stage growth assumptions and is the most appropriate. The firm's growth is expected to slow considerably in the years ahead, so the constant growth assumption of the capitalized cash flow method would be inappropriate. The capitalized cash flow method is a single-stage model.

 The excess earnings method is useful when there are intangible assets to value, but that does not appear to be a concern in the valuation of Balanced. The firm's assets appear to be largely tangible (consisting of equipment and the factory). (Study Session 11, LOS 34.f)

41. **B**   Lutge is using the guideline transactions method (GTM) because his database uses the price multiples from the sale of entire public and private companies. The interest in Jensen is a noncontrolling equity interest, so a discount for lack of control (DLOC) will be applied to its valuation. A discount for lack of marketability (DLOM) will also be applied because the Jensen interest cannot be easily sold.

 The DLOC is backed out of the control premium.

$$DLOC = 1 - \left[\frac{1}{1 + \text{Control Premium}} \right]$$

$$DLOC = 1 - \left[\frac{1}{1 + 0.187} \right] = 15.75\%$$

The total discount includes the discount for lack of marketability (DLOM).

Total discount = 1 − [(1 − DLOC)(1 − DLOM)]

Total discount = 1 − [(1 − 0.1575)(1 − 0.24)] = 36.0%

(Study Session 11, LOS 34.i,k)

42. **A** Statement 1: McDonnell is correct. Using data from the smallest cap segment of public equity to get the size premium may include a distress premium that is not applicable to a healthy private firm such as Jensen. If so, the estimated size premium will be too large, resulting in a discount rate that is too high and an undervaluation of the Jensen equity interest.

    Statement 2: McDonnell is correct. Using the CAPM and estimating beta from public firm data may not be appropriate for private firms that have little probability of going public or being acquired by a public firm. In the build-up method, an industry risk premium is added to the risk-free rate along with an equity risk premium, the small stock premium, and a company-specific risk premium.

    (Study Session 11, LOS 34.g,k)

43. **B** If the spot curve is upward sloping, the forward curve will be upward sloping and lie above the spot curve. (Study Session 12, LOS 35.a)

44. **C** $f(1,1) = [(1.0029)^2/(1.0013)] − 1 = 0.00450$ or 0.45%. (Study Session 12, LOS 35.b)

45. **A** If the spot rate curve after one year has passed is the same as the one-year forward curve from one year ago, the total return on a bond of any maturity over that year will be the one-year spot rate. In other words, the return on a bond over one year is always equal to the one-year spot rate if spot rates evolve as predicted by today's forward curve. (Study Session 12, LOS 35.c)

46. **A** In a "riding the yield curve" strategy, given an upward-sloping yield curve, investors purchase bonds with maturities longer than their investment horizon. As the bond approaches maturity, its price will increase, generating superior returns for the investor. (Study Session 12, LOS 35.d)

47. **A** Volatility at the long-maturity end is thought to be associated with uncertainty regarding the real economy and inflation, while volatility at the short-maturity end reflects risks regarding monetary policy. (Study Session 12, LOS 35.l)

48. **C**

Theoretical Shift A	KRD	% Change
Short term (2yr) +70bps	0.50	−0.35
Medium term (5yr) +0bps	1.20	0.00
Long term (15yr) +50bps	0.80	−0.40
		−0.75
Theoretical Shift B		
Short term (2yr) +30bps	0.50	−0.15
Medium term (5yr) +30bps	1.20	−0.36
Long term (15yr) +30bps	0.80	−0.24
		−0.75
Theoretical Shift C		
Short term (2yr) −10bps	0.50	+0.05
Medium term (5yr) +40bps	1.20	−0.48
Long term (15yr) +50bps	0.80	−0.40
		−0.83

(Study Session 12, LOS 35.k)

49. **B** Jacobs needs to offset the returns on the S&P 500 Index. She is currently receiving the returns on the index (which means if there is a negative return on the Index, Jacobs must make a payment), so she will need to enter into a swap in which she pays the index and receives a fixed rate. (Study Session 14, LOS 40.c)

50. **C** Calculate the contract rate on a fixed-rate receiver equity swap using the following formula:

$$C_N = \frac{1 - Z_N}{\left(Z_1 + Z_2 + \ldots + Z_N\right)}$$

Note that this is the same formula for determining the fixed interest rate on an interest rate swap. The discount (Z) factors are given in Exhibit 1. Therefore, the contract rate is:

$$C_N = \frac{1 - 0.8251}{\left(0.9690 + 0.9242 + 0.8718 + 0.8251\right)} = 4.9\%$$

(Study Session 14, LOS 40.c)

51. **A** Value to payer = (sum of discount factors) × (SFR$_{new}$ – SFR$_{old}$) × (days / 360) × notional

= 2.7377 × (0.05 – 0.045) × (360 / 360) × \$10,000,000 = \$136,885

Since Jacob is a fixed rate receiver, value to Jacob = \$–136,885.

Note: The value of equity side is not relevant because the valuation is immediately after settlement. Hence the change in index value net of fixed rate payment was already settled. Discount factors are as calculated below:

Term (yr)	LIBOR	DF
1	4.10%	0.9606
2	4.70%	0.9141
3	5.29%	0.8630
Sum		2.7377

(Study Session 14, LOS 40.d)

52. **C** N(d$_2$) is interpreted as the risk-neutral probability that a *call* option will expire in the money. N(–d$_2$) is interpreted as the risk-neutral probability that a *put* option will expire in the money. (Study Session 14, LOS 41.g)

53. **B** Statement 3 is correct, but Statement 4 is incorrect. Under the Black model, a call option is conceptualized as a futures component minus a bond component. (A put option is comprised of a bond component minus a futures component.) (Study Session 14, LOS 41.h,i)

54. **C** The credit risk underlying the equity swap is associated with the swap counterparty, not the companies in the equity index. This credit risk arises from the possibility that the counterparty to the swap will be unable or unwilling to make payments to Jacobs if the equity return is less than the fixed rate on the swap (i.e., the counterparty owes a payment to Jacobs). (Study Session 13, LOS 39.a)

55. **C** While almost any private equity real estate investment will be unique (if for no other reason than that they must be in different locations), residential properties tend to have the fewest unique characteristics. Transactions-based indices tend to be more useful for residential commercial property benchmarking than for nonresidential commercial properties due to the large amount of data required for many properties and the unique features of many nonresidential commercial properties. (Study Session 15, LOS 43.b)

56. **C** Commercial uses with higher management involvement, such as restaurants, hotels, shopping centers, also have higher operational risks. One way to check this given the specifics in this case is to look at management fees as a percentage of effective gross income for the three properties.

Property #1   3.97%   = (\$145,000 / \$3,652,000)

Property #2   3.99%   = (\$172,500 / \$4,327,500)

Property #3   4.06%   = (\$138,288 / \$3,407,557)

Therefore, Property #3 would be expected to have greater operational risk. (Study Session 15, LOS 43.d)

57. **B**   Property #2 is an older office building with unique characteristics that could not be easily reproduced using current architectural designs and materials. Therefore, the cost approach would be less appropriate than the income approach as a basis for appraisal. The sales comparison approach would also be less suitable as the property is relatively unique. (Study Session 15, LOS 43.e)

58. **B**   DCF valuation based on a required return of 9.5% is:

	NOI	Present Value
Year 1	$1,706,500	$1,558,447.49
Year 2	$1,774,760	$1,480,169.30
Year 3	$1,845,750	$1,405,822.60
Year 4	$1,919,580	$1,335,210.50
Year 5	$1,996,364	$1,268,145.64
Terminal value	$27,150,550	$17,246,780.74
Property #1 value		$24,294,576.27

Selected Calculation:
Terminal value is computed by applying the terminal cap rate to NOI in year 6. To estimate NOI for year 6, we need a growth rate estimate. We are not given the growth rate directly, but given the discount rate of 9.5% and the terminal cap rate of 7.5%, we can estimate the growth rate to be 2%.

$$TV_5 = \frac{NOI_5(1+g)}{C_t}$$

$$= \frac{\$1,996,364(1+0.02)}{0.075} = \$27,150,550.40$$

Note: Make sure that you use the uneven cash flow function to compute NPV using your financial calculator. (Study Session 15, LOS 43.g)

59. **A**   The maximum loan amount will typically be based on the lower of loan-to-value (LTV) or debt service coverage ratio. Based on LTV of 70%, ALIC would be willing to loan $21 million ($30 million × 0.70). Based on a debt service coverage ratio of 1.5x, ALIC will loan just under $20.7 million. ALIC will be willing to loan only an amount equal to the lower of these two measures.

The calculation for maximum debt service based on a minimum debt service coverage ratio of 1.5x is:

$$\text{Maximum debt service} = \frac{NOI_1}{DSCR}$$

$$= \frac{\$1,706,500}{1.5} = \$1,137,666.67$$

Maximum debt service on an interest-only loan can be used to calculate the maximum loan amount:

$$\text{Maximum loan} = \frac{\text{Maximum debt service}}{\text{Interest rate}}$$

$$= \frac{\$1,137,666.67}{0.055} = \$20,684,848.48$$

(Study Session 15, LOS 43.m)

60. **B** AIP should earn a higher return on equity by financing part of its purchase price with a mortgage because the cost of mortgage funds (5.5%) is less than the required return on equity (9.5%). Including the mortgage funding in a weighted-average cost of capital (WACC) will increase the value over the purchase price required if only equity funding is used. (Study Session 15, LOS 43.l)

©2017 Kaplan, Inc.

Exam 2
Afternoon Session Answers

To get valuable feedback on how your score compares to those of other Level II candidates, use your Username and Password to gain Online Access at schweser.com and choose the menu item *"Practice Exams Volume 2 (Enter answers from book)."*

61. A	81. B	101. C
62. B	82. B	102. A
63. A	83. B	103. A
64. B	84. A	104. B
65. A	85. A	105. C
66. B	86. C	106. A
67. B	87. C	107. C
68. A	88. C	108. C
69. A	89. B	109. B
70. C	90. A	110. A
71. C	91. C	111. B
72. B	92. C	112. C
73. C	93. B	113. A
74. B	94. B	114. A
75. B	95. A	115. B
76. A	96. C	116. B
77. C	97. C	117. C
78. C	98. B	118. A
79. B	99. C	119. B
80. A	100. A	120. B

Exam 2
Afternoon Session Answers

61. **A** Vakil obtained permission from Blue Lotus to use the past performance and, therefore, is not violating the Standard IV(A): Duties to Employer: Loyalty. By not crediting the entire team in the management of Xeta fund, Vakil violated Standard III(D): Performance Presentation. (Study Session 1, LOS 2.a,b)

62. **B** By taking the models without permission from his past employer, Vakil violated Standard IV(A) – Duties to Employer: Loyalty. Vakil also failed to disclose using his past employer's model, violating Standard I(C) – Professionalism: Misrepresentation. The models are proprietary but do not constitute material nonpublic information (insider information). (Study Session 1, LOS 2.a,b)

63. **A** By discussing his research with Dutt, including recommending a specific stock, Vakil violated his duty to his employer by disclosing sensitive business information to outsiders. However, the information is not material nonpublic information and, thus, is not a violation under Standard II(A) – Integrity of Capital Markets: Material Nonpublic Information. (Study Session 1, LOS 2.a,b)

64. **B** By transacting in Sandhirst stock, Dutt did not rely on any material nonpublic information and, therefore, is not in violation of Standard II(A) – Material and Nonpublic Information. However, her investment in the retail ETF relies on material nonpublic information about Frapco. (Study Session 1, LOS 2.a,b)

65. **A** Trading for oneself or causing others to trade based on material nonpublic information is a violation under Standard II(A) – Material and Nonpublic Information. (Study Session 1, LOS 2.a,b)

66. **B** Because the Snead hedge funds may not be suitable for all clients, Vakil violated Standard III(D) Duties to Clients: Suitability. No clients were treated unfairly and there was no market manipulation. (Study Session 1, LOS 2.a,b)

67. **B** The p-value is the probability that the null hypothesis, H_0: slope = zero, is true. The decision rule is to reject the null hypothesis if the p-value is less than the significance level (i.e., there is only a very small chance that the null hypothesis is correct). The p-value for the R_M slope is less than the significance level, and the p-value for the VMG slope is greater than the significance level. Therefore, the R_M slope is statistically significant (reject the null hypothesis that the R_M slope equals zero) and the VMG slope is not statistically significant (cannot reject the null hypothesis that the VMG slope equals zero). (Study Session 3, LOS 10.a)

68. **A** The equation for the R^2 equals the regression sum of squares divided by the total sum of squares. The total sum of squares equals the regression sum of squares plus the error sum of squares. Therefore, the R^2 equals:

$$R^2 = \frac{\text{regression sum of squares}}{\text{regression sum of squares} + \text{error sum of squares}}$$

The problem states that the R^2 equals 0.80. Because the R^2 exceeds 50%, the regression sum of squares must exceed the error sum of squares. (Study Session 3, LOS 10.g)

69. **A** Conditional heteroskedasticity refers to regression errors whose variance is not constant. If there is conditional heteroskedasticity, the variance changes as function of the independent variables. The squared residual (i.e., residual is the estimated error) is used to proxy the error variance. A low R^2 in equation (2) indicates that the slopes in equation (2) are very close to zero, indicating that the error variance is unaffected by the independent variables. For instance, if all the slopes in equation (2) equal zero, then the error variance equals the intercept (a_0, which is constant over time). (Study Session 3, LOS 10.k)

70. **C** According to Recommendation 1 provided by Lockhart, the inflation change variable is highly correlated with the Wilshire index returns (one of the independent variables). If Sawyer includes the inflation change variable along with the Wilshire index returns, the regression will be plagued by multicollinearity (the inclusion of correlated independent variables). Multicollinearity causes the standard errors for the regression parameter estimates to be biased upward, which, in turn, causes the t-statistics to be biased downward (deflated). (Study Session 3, LOS 10.l)

71. **C** According to Recommendation 2, the data should not be pooled across all 36 months. The sample clearly is split into two parts: pre-Reg FD and post-Reg FD. Sawyer should run separate regressions for each subperiod, or should employ dummy variables to control for the structural shift related to the passage of Reg FD. In either case, by pooling across the two very different sample periods, Sawyer's regression is an example of a misspecified functional form. (Study Session 3, LOS 10.m)

72. **B** Sawyer is incorrect with respect to Claim 1 and is correct with respect to Claim 2. If the omitted variables are correlated with the included variables, then the omitted variable regression parameter estimates [i.e., from equation (1)] will be biased and inconsistent. Desirable properties, on the other hand, are unbiasedness and consistency. An estimator is unbiased if the expected value of the estimate equals the true population value. An estimator is consistent if the estimate approaches the true population value as the sample size increases. The existence of omitted variables (that are correlated with the included variables) destroys both of these desirable properties. (Study Session 3, LOS 10.m)

73. **C** Because YTC operates independently and makes its own financing decisions, the local currency (AUD) should be the functional currency. When the local currency is the functional currency, the subsidiary's financial statements are consolidated with the parent's financial statements using the current rate method. Under the current rate method, all of the income statement items are translated using the average rate for the year. To calculate the percent change in net income, we must translate these items for 2016 and 2015 and then calculate the rate of change.

2015 translated net income = 25 / 1.30 = 19.23

2016 translated net income = 12 / 1.45 = 8.28

growth in net income = (8.28 / 19.23) – 1 = –56.94%

(Study Session 5, LOS 18.d)

74. **B** Under the temporal method, the nonmonetary assets and liabilities are remeasured at historical rates. Thus, only the monetary assets and liabilities are exposed to changing exchange rates. Therefore, under the temporal method, exposure is defined as the subsidiary's net monetary asset or net monetary liability position. A firm has net monetary assets if its monetary assets exceed its monetary liabilities. If the monetary liabilities exceed the monetary assets, the firm has a net monetary liability exposure.

Since very few assets are considered to be monetary (mainly cash and receivables), most firms have net monetary liability exposures. If the parent has a net monetary liability exposure when the foreign currency (AUD) is appreciating, the result is a loss. Conversely, a net monetary liability exposure coupled with a depreciating currency will result in a gain. (Study Session 5, LOS 18.d)

75. **B** total asset turnover = revenue / total assets

Note that no calculations are necessary to answer this question. Revenues are translated using the same average exchange rate in the temporal and current rate methods. The only difference in the total asset turnover ratio must therefore be in the denominator (i.e., total assets). Under the current rate method, assets are translated using the current rate. Under the temporal method, monetary assets are translated using the current rate, and nonmonetary assets are translated using the historical rate. Because the historical rate is lower than the current rate, the nonmonetary assets (and therefore total assets) will have a higher value under the temporal method. A higher asset value means a lower total asset turnover ratio under the temporal method. The calculation of the total asset turnover ratio using both methods is provided for reference below:

	Temporal		Current Rate	
Cash	20 / 1.50 =	13.33	20 / 1.50 =	13.33
Accounts receivable	460 / 1.50 =	306.67	460 / 1.50 =	306.67
Inventories	30 / 1.20 =	25.00	30 / 1.50 =	20.00
Prepaid expenses	25 / 1.20 =	20.83	25 / 1.50 =	16.67
Fixed assets	400 / 1.20 =	333.33	400 / 1.50 =	266.67
Total assets		699.16		623.34
Revenues	870 / 1.45 =	600.00	870 / 1.45 =	600.00
Total asset turnover	600.00 / 699.16 =	0.86	600.00 / 623.34 =	0.96

(Study Session 5, LOS 18.d)

76. **A** AUD revenue growth rate = $(870 / 765)^{1/2} - 1 = 6.64\%$

Revenues are translated at average rate:

2014 USD revenues = 765 / 1.40 = 546.43; 2016 USD revenues = 870 / 1.45 = 600

USD revenue growth rate = $(600 / 546.43)^{1/2} - 1 = 4.79\%$

The USD revenue growth rate is 1.85% lower than the local currency (AUD) revenue growth rate. (Study Session 5, LOS 18.i)

77. **C** Under both the current rate and temporal methods, the revenues for the Ukrainian subsidiary would be translated using the average rate. Cost of goods sold (COGS) would be translated using the historical rate for the temporal method and the average rate for the current rate method. Note that because local currency prices are expected to be constant in Ukraine, there will be no difference between LIFO and FIFO since all beginning, purchased, sold, and ending inventory will have the same cost. When a currency is depreciating, the COGS based on historical cost (temporal method) will be higher than COGS translated at the average rate (current rate method) since the average rate will incorporate the historical exchange rate and the most recent (depreciated) exchange rate, decreasing the COGS. For instance, if COGS in the local currency is 10 and the historical and average exchange rates are 1 and 1.5 (local currency per reporting currency), then COGS under the temporal method will be 10 and under the current rate method will be 6.67. Since translated sales are the same under both methods, gross profit and the gross profit margin will be higher under the current rate method.
(Study Session 5, LOS 18.f)

78. **C** U.S. accounting standards define a hyperinflationary economy as one in which the 3-year cumulative inflation rate exceeds 100%. The Indian economy can be characterized as hyperinflationary. The inflation rate over the past three years can be calculated as follows:

year 1 inflation = $[(1 + 0.3464) / (1 + 0.020)] - 1 = 32\%$

year 2 inflation = $[(1 + 0.2915) / (1 + 0.025)] - 1 = 26\%$

year 3 inflation = $[(1 + 0.2566) / (1 + 0.030)] - 1 = 22\%$

cumulative 3-year inflation = $(1.32)(1.26)(1.22) - 1 = 103\%$

U.S. accounting standards allow the use of the temporal method, with the functional currency being the parent's reporting currency, when a foreign subsidiary is operating in a hyperinflationary environment. IFRS accounting standards allow the parent to translate an inflation-adjusted value of the nonmonetary assets and liabilities of the foreign subsidiary at the current inflation rate, removing most of the effects of high inflation on the value of the nonmonetary assets and liabilities in the reporting currency. In a hyperinflationary environment, the parent company can reduce translation losses by reducing its net monetary assets or increasing its net monetary liabilities. In order to do this, the parent should issue debt denominated in the subsidiary's local currency and invest the proceeds in fixed assets for the subsidiary to use in its operations.
(Study Session 5, LOS 18.g)

79. **B** Historically, two accounting methods have been used for business combinations: (1) the purchase method and (2) the pooling-of-interests method. However, over the last few years, the pooling method has been eliminated from U.S. GAAP and IFRS. Now, the acquisition method is required.

The pooling-of-interests method, also known as uniting-of-interests method under IFRS, combined the ownership interests of the two firms and viewed the participants as equals—neither firm acquired the other. The assets and liabilities of the two firms were simply combined. Key attributes of the pooling method include the following:
- The two firms are combined using historical book values.
- Operating results for prior periods are restated as though the two firms were always combined.
- Ownership interests continue, and former accounting bases are maintained.

Note that fair values played no role in accounting for a business combination using the pooling method—the actual price paid was suppressed from the balance sheet and income statement. (Study Session 5, LOS 16.c)

80. **A** If the target of a merger has unused tax losses accumulated, the merged company can use the tax losses to immediately lower its tax liability, thus increasing its net income (Correct). The Internet operation of The Daily is insignificant compared to the overall merger value. Any improvement in the cost structure of the Internet operation will not have a significant impact on overall earnings. In addition, the high-growth characteristics of the Internet segment would not warrant a cost restructuring of the operations (Incorrect). (Study Session 8, LOS 26.b)

81. **B** First, we must separate the synergistic value from the combined value of the firm as follows:

$$V_{AT} = V_A + V_T + S - C$$

where:
V_{AT} = the combined value of the firm
V_A = the value of the acquirer before the merger
V_T = the value of the target before the merger
S = the synergistic value from the merger
C = the cash paid to the target

Rearranging the formula, the synergistic value can be isolated as follows:

$$\begin{aligned} S &= V_{AT} - V_A - V_T + C \\ &= 17{,}500 - (68 \times 117.6) - (35 \times 213.1) + (45 \times 213.1) \\ &= 17{,}500 - 7{,}996.8 - 7{,}458.5 + 9{,}589.5 \\ &= \$11{,}634.2 \text{ million} \end{aligned}$$

Next, calculate the acquirer's gain as follows:

$$\text{acquirer's gain} = S - (P_T - V_T)$$

where:
S = the synergistic value from the merger
P_T = the price paid for the target
V_T = the value of the target before the merger

$$\begin{aligned} \text{acquirer's gain} &= 11{,}634.2 - [(45 \times 213.1) - (35 \times 213.1)] \\ &= 11{,}634.2 - (9{,}589.5 - 7{,}458.5) \\ &= \$9{,}503.2 \text{ million} \end{aligned}$$

(Study Session 8, LOS 26.k)

82. **B** total shares = 63.0 + 117.6 = 180.6 million

$$V_{AT} = 7{,}996.8 + 7{,}458.5 + 11{,}634.2 - 0 = 27{,}089.5$$

new share price = 27,089.5 / 180.6 = 150.0

(Study Session 8, LOS 26.k,l)

83. **B** The legal action based on antitrust is the only choice given that is a post-offer defense. Staggered boards, restricted voting rights, and poison puts are all pre-offer defenses that would not be possible after the tender offer has been made. (Study Session 8, LOS 26.f)

84. **A**   A hostile merger occurs when the management of a merger target is opposed to the proposed merger. In such a situation, the acquiring company may initiate a bear hug in which the merger proposal is delivered directly to the board of directors of the target company. Voyager has initiated a bear hug in the hopes of gaining board support for the proposed merger before management can react to the proposal. If the bear hug is unsuccessful, the acquirer may appeal directly to the target's shareholders through a tender offer in which the acquirer offers to buy shares directly from shareholders or through a proxy fight in which a proxy solicitation is used to convince shareholders to elect a board of directors chosen by the acquirer. The board of directors would then replace the target's management and allow the merger to move forward. A white knight is a takeover defense, not a type of merger. (Study Session 8, LOS 26.e)

85. **A**   The required rate of return for Aussie Shipping is:

$$r = R_F + \beta_i[E(R_M) - R_F] = 5.2\% + 1.20(4.5\%) = 10.6\%$$

The estimated intrinsic value using the Gordon growth model is:

$$V_0 = \frac{D_0(1+g)}{r-g} = \frac{2.20 \times (1.05)}{0.106 - 0.05} = \frac{2.31}{0.056} = \text{AUD } 41.25$$

The intrinsic value exceeds the market price of AUD 33.50, so the firm should buy.

(Study Session 10, LOS 30.c)

86. **C**   The values of the next three dividends are:

$$D_1 = 4.00(1.40) = 5.60$$

$$D_2 = 4.00(1.40)^2 = 7.84$$

$$D_3 = 4.00(1.40)^2(1.06) = 8.3104$$

The terminal value of the stock (at the beginning of the final constant growth phase) is:

$$V_2 = \frac{D_3}{r-g} = \frac{8.3104}{0.12 - 0.06} = 138.507$$

The present value of the first two dividends plus the terminal value of the stock is:

$$V_0 = \frac{5.60}{1.12} + \frac{7.84}{1.12^2} + \frac{138.507}{1.12^2}$$

$$V_0 = 5.00 + 6.25 + 110.42 = £121.67$$

(Study Session 10, LOS 30.l)

87. **C**   The first three dividends remain at:

$$D_1 = 4.00(1.40) = 5.60$$

$$D_2 = 4.00(1.40)^2 = 7.84$$

$$D_3 = 4.00(1.40)^2(1.06) = 8.3104$$

You need to find a rate of return that gives a value closest to £90. Trial and error is a sound approach to finding the answer, and the test wise candidate should use the values given as multiple-choice answers. Basically substitute 12%, 13%, or 14% into the valuation equation:

$$V_0 = \frac{5.60}{1+r} + \frac{7.84}{(1+r)^2} + \frac{8.3104 / (r - 0.06)}{(1+r)^2}$$

For r = 12%, V_0 = £121.67

For r = 13%, V_0 = £104.11

For r = 14%, V_0 = £90.96

The answer, to three decimal places, is 14.085%. (Study Session 10, LOS 30.l,m)

88. **C**   PVGO is the part of a stock's total value that comes from future growth opportunities. It is estimated as $V_0 = E_1/r + PVGO$, where E_1/r is the no-growth value per share. Note that earnings are divided by *r*, not dividends. The reason for this is that a no-growth firm should distribute all of its earnings as dividends. (Study Session 10, LOS 30.e)

89. **B**   Sustainable growth is growth that can be achieved by retaining some earnings and keeping the capital structure (debt to equity) constant. (Study Session 11, LOS 32.o)

90. **A**   Given the assumptions of a constant growth model, the justified forward P/E is smaller than the justified trailing P/E. The equations for the two concepts are:

forward P/E: $\dfrac{P_0}{E_1} = \dfrac{D_1 / E_1}{r - g} = \dfrac{1 - b}{r - g}$

trailing P/E: $\dfrac{P_0}{E_0} = \dfrac{D_0(1 + g) / E_1}{r - g} = \dfrac{(1 - b)(1 + g)}{r - g}$

The trailing P/E will equal the forward P/E times (1+g).

The other two phrases from the investment banker are correct. (Study Session 10, LOS 30.f)

91. **C**   A decrease in the value of available-for-sale securities that bypasses the income statement would artificially increase net income and, consequently, ROE. Book value is unaffected as the decrease is accounted for in the OCI section of shareholders' equity. (Study Session 11, LOS 33.k)

92. **C** $WACC = \left(\dfrac{MVD}{MVD + MVCE}\right) \times \left[r_d\left(1 - \text{tax rate}\right)\right] + \left(\dfrac{MVCE}{MVD + MVCE}\right)r$

r_d = debt coupon given as 7.0%

tax rate = 40% (given in Exhibit 1)

r = equity cost = 0.15 (given in Exhibit 2)

MVD = market value of debt = book value of debt for YD = 12

MVCE = market value of common equity = $15.50 × 18.6 = $288.3

$WACC = \left(\dfrac{12}{12 + 288.3}\right) \times \left[0.07\left(1 - 0.40\right)\right] + \left(\dfrac{288.3}{12 + 288.3}\right) \times 0.15 = 0.146$

(Study Session 6, LOS 20.a; Study Session 9, LOS 28.g)

93. **B** $WACC = WACC \times capital = 0.12 \times 200 = 24$

      $EVA = NOPAT - \$WACC = 42 - 24 = 18$

      (Study Session 11, LOS 33.a)

94. **B** $V_0 = B_0 + [(ROE - r) \times B_0] / (r - g)$

      book value = equity / total shares

      book value = 131 / 18.6 = 7.04 (from Exhibit 1)

      r = cost of equity = 0.15 (given in Exhibit 2)

      ROE = 0.17 (given in Exhibit 2)

      g = 0.10 (given in Exhibit 2)

      $V_0 = 7.04 + [(0.17 - 0.15) \times 7.04] / (0.15 - 0.10) = 9.86$

      (Study Session 11, LOS 33.f)

95. **A**   It is difficult for a company to maintain a high ROE because of competition. The persistence factor will be lower for those companies. A company that has a low dividend payout has greater growth opportunities than a company with a high dividend payout. The greater growth opportunities should support a higher persistence factor. (Study Session 11, LOS 33.h)

96. **C**   Statement 1 is correct. The multistage residual income model uses continuing residual income to denote the long-run residual income. Based on reversion to the mean, and increasing competition for YD, continuing residual income would be expected to decline to zero over time. Statement 2 is correct. Based on the residual income model formula, $V_0 = B_0 + (ROE - r) \times B_0 / (r - g)$. If ROE = r, then $V_0 = B_0$. (Study Session 11, LOS 33.d,j)

97. **C**   The present value of expected loss measure in credit analysis uses risk-neutral probabilities in calculating expected value of loss. The adjustment to probabilities to account for the risk of the cash flows is the risk premium. (Study Session 13, LOS 38.a)

98. **B**   Under the structural model's debt option analogy, owning a company's debt is economically equivalent to owning a riskless bond that pays K dollars at time T, plus simultaneously selling a European put option on the assets of the company with maturity T and strike price K. (Study Session 13, LOS 38.d)

99. **C**   The relevant assumption is that the value of the assets (at maturity) has a *lognormal* distribution. (Study Session 13, LOS 38.f)

100. **A**

Time to Cash Flow	Cash Flow	Risk-Free Spot Rate	Credit Spread (%)	Total Yield (%)	PV (risk-free rate)	PV (total yield)
0.5	20	1.50%	0.20%	1.70%	19.85	19.83
1	20	1.75%	0.25%	2.00%	19.65	19.60
1.5	20	2.00%	0.30%	2.30%	19.41	19.32
2	1020	2.25%	0.35%	2.60%	975.12	968.32
				Total	$1,034.03	$1,027.07

Present value of expected loss = PV(risk-free rate) – PV (total yield)

= 1,034.03 – 1,027.07 = $6.96

(Study Session 13, LOS 38.h)

101. **C** Evaluating credit risk for an ABS should include the probability of loss because the probability of default does not apply. When there are defaults within the collateral pool of an ABS, the losses are absorbed according to the waterfall provisions in the ABS structure. The probability of default applies to sovereign debt. (Study Session 13, LOS 38.i)

102. **A** Market participants typically prefer to use the swap-rate curve as a benchmark (rather than a government bond yield curve) for the following reasons:
- The availability of swaps and the equilibrium pricing are driven only by the interaction of supply and demand. It is not affected by technical market factors that can affect government bond yields.
- The swap market is not regulated by any government, which makes swap rates across different countries more comparable.
- Swap curves across countries are also more comparable than sovereign bond yield curves because swap curves reflect similar levels of credit risk, while sovereign bond yield curves also reflect credit risk unique to each country's government bonds.
- The swap curve typically has yield quotes at 11 maturities between 2 and 30 years. The U.S. government bond yield curve typically only has on-the-run issues trading at four maturities between 2 and 30 years.

(Study Session 12, LOS 35.f)

103. **A** First, calculate the conversion ratio: $\text{conversion ratio} = \dfrac{\text{par value}}{\text{conversion price}} = \dfrac{1,000}{55.56} = 18$

Now, calculate market conversion price:

$\text{market conversion price} = \dfrac{\text{market bond price}}{\text{conversion ratio}} = \dfrac{947}{18} = 52.61$

Finally, calculate the market conversion premium per share as the difference between the market conversion price and the market price of the stock:

market conversion premium = 52.61 – 50.00 = 2.61

(Study Session 13, LOS 37.o)

104. **B** Minimum value of a convertible = Max (straight value, conversion value)
Straight value = $917 (given)
Conversion value = 18 × $50 = $900
Minimum value of the convertible = $917

(Study Session 13, LOS 37.o)

105. **C** The 7-year, 7.25% convertible bond has a market price of $947 (given) and, therefore, does not qualify (as it is below par). A similar option-free bond would be worth less (given in the case as $917). A similar callable bond would be worth even less. This value is not given but would be below $917 and, therefore, below par. A 7-year bond extendible by five years would be valued the same as an equivalent 12-year putable bond with an European put option that is exercisable in seven years. The value of the putable bond is given as $1,052; this bond meets the criteria. (Study Session 13, LOS 37.a)

106. **A** If interest rates are not expected to change then the straight value of the bond will not change (ignoring the change in value resulting from the passage of time). If the straight value does not change, then downside risk is indeed limited to the difference between the price paid for the bond and the straight value. If, however, interest rates rise as the price of the common stock falls, the conversion value will fall and the straight value will fall, exposing the holder of the convertible bond to more downside risk.
(Study Session 13, LOS 37.q)

107. **C** OAS, or option-adjusted spread, is the constant spread that is added to each node in an interest rate tree to force the model value to equal the market price of the bond. OAS might be more appropriately called the "option-removed spread" (i.e., the spread added after the option feature is removed). Because the option feature is removed via adjustment to cash flows, bonds with similar credit and liquidity risk should have similar OAS. (Study Session 13, LOS 37.g)

108. **C** Decreasing volatility of common stock prices would devalue any options related to the stock. The convertible bond contains an embedded call option on the stock, which would experience a decrease in value. Increasing interest rate volatility would increase the value of options related to interest rates. MediSoft's convertible bond is also callable and the value of the call on the bond would increase. The total value of the convertible bond is as follows: convertible bond value = straight value + call on stock − call on bond. The combined effect of the changes in the values of the options is a decrease in the value of the convertible bond. Thus the statement regarding the volatility effects on MediSoft's convertible bonds is incorrect. The value of the putable bond can be summarized as follows: putable bond value = option-free value + put on bond. The increase in put option value resulting from the increase in interest rate volatility would increase the value of the putable bond. Therefore, the statement regarding the volatility effects on MediSoft's putable bonds is also incorrect. (Study Session 13, LOS 37.p)

109. **B** Walker is entering into a 6 × 8 forward rate agreement (FRA), which represents a 2-month (60-day) loan that will begin six months (180 days) from now. The relevant LIBOR rates for this contract are 180-day and 240-day LIBOR. To calculate the contract rate on the 6 × 8 FRA, first un-annualize the 180- and 240-day rates as follows:

$$R_{180} = 0.0452 \left(\frac{180}{360} \right) = 0.0226 \qquad R_{240} = 0.0511 \left(\frac{240}{360} \right) = 0.0341$$

Next, calculate the rate on the 6 × 8 FRA as follows (note we are using the 180-day and 240-day LIBOR rates to find the 60-day rate that lies between them):

$$FRA_{6\times8} = \left(\frac{1 + R_{240}}{1 + R_{180}} \right) - 1 = \left(\frac{1.0341}{1.0226} \right) - 1 = 0.0112$$

The 0.0112 or 1.12% rate represents a 60-day rate. Annualizing the rate will yield the following:

$$FRA_{6\times8} = 0.0112 \left(\frac{360}{60} \right) = 0.0675 = 6.75\% \approx 6.8\%$$

(Study Session 14, LOS 40.a)

110. **A** For this question, we must find the value of the FRA three months (90 days) after the inception of the contract. First find the contract rate on a new FRA. Since we are 90 days past the inception of the original contract an equivalent new contract would be a 3 × 5 FRA, which would represent a 2-month (60-day) loan that would begin three months (90 days) from now. Thus, the relevant LIBOR rates are going to be 90-day and 150-day LIBOR. Calculate the FRA rate the same way as in the previous question:

$$R_{90} = 0.0512 \left(\frac{90}{360} \right) = 0.012800 \qquad R_{150} = 0.0596 \left(\frac{150}{360} \right) = 0.024833$$

$$FRA_{3\times5} = \left(\frac{1 + R_{150}}{1 + R_{90}} \right) - 1 = \left(\frac{1.024833}{1.012800} \right) - 1 = 0.011881$$

$$FRA_{3\times5} = 0.011881 \left(\frac{360}{60} \right) = 0.07129 = 7.129\%$$

Now take the difference between the new FRA rate and the original rate (given as 6.0% in the question) on an un-annualized basis and multiply by the notional principal (i.e., the amount that will be borrowed).

$$\left[(0.07129 - 0.06) \left(\frac{60}{360} \right) \right] \times \$1,275,000 = \$2,399$$

Finally, discount this difference to the present using the 150-day LIBOR rate.

$$\frac{\$2,399}{\left[1 + \left(0.0596 \times \frac{150}{360} \right) \right]} = \$2,340$$

(Study Session 14, LOS 40.b)

111. **B** Using the Black model, the call option is valued as $C_0 = e^{-rT}[F_T N(d_1) - XN(d_2)]$.
(Study Session 14, LOS 41.i)

112. **C** The company will need to sell silver in eight months. Thus, if the price of silver is expected to fall over that time frame, Walker should be short a forward contract on the price of silver to lock in a higher selling price now. Walker will also need to convert Australian dollars to U.S. dollars after the extracted Australian silver is sold. Thus, he is effectively long Australian dollars and will need either a short currency forward contract on Australian dollars or equivalently a long currency forward contract on U.S. dollars if he expects the Australian dollar to depreciate. (Study Session 14, LOS 40.a)

113. **A** If the exercise rate on a cap and floor is same, a long cap and short floor can be used to replicate a payer swap. If the value of such long cap and short floor is same, their (common) exercise rate should be equal to the swap fixed rate. (Study Session 14, LOS 41.j)

114. **A** In answering this question, you must first compute the contract rate for a zero value (arbitrage free) 7 × 10 FRA (i.e., the FRA expires in 210 days and the underlying loan expires in 300 days). The contract rate for the 7 × 10 FRA is computed as follows:

$$R_{210} = 0.0603\left(\frac{210}{360}\right) = 0.0352 \qquad R_{300} = 0.0641\left(\frac{300}{360}\right) = 0.0534$$

$$FRA_{7\times10} = \left(\frac{1+R_{300}}{1+R_{210}}\right) - 1 = \left(\frac{1.0534}{1.0352}\right) - 1 = 0.0176$$

$$FRA_{7\times10} = 0.0176\left(\frac{360}{90}\right) = 0.0704 = 7.04\%$$

Since the contract rate on an arbitrage free is higher than the desired rate of 6.95%, Walker must establish a position in an off-market FRA. He will need a long position because he will be borrowing at the contract rate, not lending. Since having a contract rate that is lower than the market rate (6.95% < 7.04%) is valuable to the long, Walker will have to make a payment to the short position at the contract inception. (Study Session 14, LOS 40.b)

115. **B** What Yeung has identified as Constraint 1 is properly classified as a return objective and not a constraint. Investment constraints are factors that restrict investment choices. Constraint 2 is an example of time horizon constraint. Constraint 3 is an example of liquidity constraint. (Study Session 16, LOS 47.e)

116. **B** Macroeconomic models are based on surprises in macroeconomic data. Principal component analysis is used to identify the factors of a statistical factor model, which cannot necessarily be described using conventional economic variables. Fundamental factor models use firm-specific valuation metrics such as PE with standardized sensitivities. (Study Session 16, LOS 48.d)

117. **C** Information ratio for Lincoln fund = IR = active return/active risk = (7.6% – 6.5%) / 5% = 0.22

Sharpe ratio of benchmark = SR_B = (6.5% – 3%) / 11% = 0.32

The optimal amount of active risk can be calculated as:

σ^*_A = (IR/SR_B) × σ_B = (0.22 / 0.32) × 11.0% = 7.56%

The weight of the active Lincoln portfolio should be 7.56% / 5.0% = 1.51, and the weight on the benchmark portfolio would be 1 – 1.51 = –0.51. (Study Session 17, LOS 51.d)

118. **A**   The highest Sharpe ratio can be calculated using the relation $SR_p^2 = SR_B^2 + IR^2$:

$$SR_p = \sqrt{SR_B^2 + IR^2} = \sqrt{0.32^2 + 0.22^2} = 0.388$$

Thus, the highest Sharpe ratio that can be achieved by combining the active and passive portfolios is approximately 0.39. (Study Session 17, LOS 51.d)

119. **B**   An asset whose value is negatively correlated to the investor's utility from future consumption provides a poor hedge against bad consumption outcomes. That is, the asset pays off more when the investor's utility is low. Such assets would command a higher risk premium. (Study Session 17, LOS 50.c)

120. **B**   For countries with high expected economic growth rates, real rates will be high. Investors will be less concerned about the future, and the inter-temporal rate of substitution will be *low*. Also, investors will want to increase current consumption and, hence, will borrow more and save less. (Study Session 17, LOS 50.c)

Exam 3
Morning Session Answers

To get valuable feedback on how your score compares to those of other Level II candidates, use your Username and Password to gain Online Access at schweser.com and choose the menu item *"Practice Exams Volume 2 (Enter answers from book)."*

1. B	21. B	41. B
2. C	22. B	42. A
3. C	23. A	43. C
4. B	24. C	44. C
5. C	25. B	45. B
6. B	26. B	46. B
7. C	27. A	47. A
8. C	28. C	48. B
9. C	29. A	49. C
10. C	30. B	50. B
11. A	31. B	51. A
12. C	32. C	52. B
13. A	33. A	53. B
14. B	34. A	54. A
15. A	35. B	55. A
16. C	36. A	56. A
17. C	37. A	57. C
18. A	38. A	58. A
19. C	39. B	59. C
20. A	40. A	60. C

1. **B** Topel recommended the stock to his superiors, but they chose not to buy it. While Topel should not buy the stock in advance of his recommendation, he is not prohibited from purchasing it for himself should the company choose not to act. Kennedy's research may have been thorough, and there is no evidence that she violated the reasonable-basis Standard. However, the loyalty Standard requires that Kennedy put Samson Securities' interest before her own and not deprive her employer of her skills and abilities. Since Kennedy spent five days of company time researching Koral Koatings, the company has a right to benefit from her research. (Study Session 1, LOS 2.a)

2. **C** The Koons's gift does not violate Standard I(B). According to the standard, gifts from clients are different from gifts from other parties because the potential for obtaining influence to the detriment of other clients is not as great. Therefore, according to the standard, Garvey may accept the Koons's gift as long as she discloses it to her employer, which she did.

   The Jones's gift is a bonus from a job that does not compete with Garvey's work for Samson, and as such, does not violate the Standard. The fact that Jones is a Samson client is irrelevant in terms of this gift, as there is no information in the vignette about Garvey providing investment-related services for Jones. (Study Session 1, LOS 2.a)

3. **C** Topel's purchases of Vallo do not violate Standard II(A) because it was not based on material nonpublic information, and he has no duty to keep the information to himself. Therefore, Garvey's purchase of Vallo for her own account is also consistent with Standard II(A).

   The brokers discussing Metrona mentioned that their star analyst came out with a report with a "buy" recommendation that morning, which suggests that the information has already been made public. Therefore, Garvey's purchase of Metrona for her own account is consistent with Standard II(A). (Study Session 1, LOS 2.a)

4. **B** Garvey's idea for a growth estimate is interesting, but a number of factors affect the growth rate of a beverage company, many arguably more so than GDP growth. In addition, it is not sufficient to use two years worth of quarterly data (eight observations) to estimate a regression model and forecast growth over the following three years. The research was not thorough enough to satisfy Standard V(A).

   Standard I(C) as it deals with plagiarism was not violated because the consensus GDP estimates were derived from a recognized reporting service. (Study Session 1, LOS 2.a)

5. **C** In the first statement, Garvey accurately calls herself a Level III CFA candidate, but she is not permitted to project when she will receive the charter, as she must still meet the work and eligibility restrictions and pass the Level III exam. Therefore, the first statement violates Standard VII(B).

   In the second statement, the use of the CFA mark as a noun also violates the Standard VII(B). (Study Session 1, LOS 2.a)

6. **B** Nagoree is obligated to disclose conflicts in any matter that may potentially affect the member's ability to make an unbiased recommendation. The Research Objectivity Policy of the Research Objectivity Standards (ROS) requires that a formal written policy be established on the independence and objectivity of research, and this policy should require disclosure of any conflicts of interest. Additionally, Standard VI(A) Disclosure of Conflicts requires this disclosure to employer, clients, and prospective clients. (Study Session 1, LOS 3.b)

7. **C** Standard I(B) Professionalism: Independence and Objectivity prohibits members and candidates from accepting any gift that reasonably could be expected to compromise their independence and objectivity. The purpose of the gift appears to be to ensure that Islandwide continues to do business with Quadrangle and can be seen, therefore, as a clear attempt to influence her choice of brokers in the future. (Study Session 1, LOS 2.a)

8. **C** Standard II(A) Integrity of Capital Markets: Material Nonpublic Information prohibits members and candidates who possess material nonpublic information to act on or cause others to act on that information. Information disclosed to a select group of analysts is not made "public" by that fact. (Study Session 1, LOS 2.a)

9. **C** Standard I(B) Professionalism: Independence and Objectivity indicates that gifts from clients are seen to less likely affect a member's independence and objectivity, and only disclosure is required. The offer from Baker is based on future performance and is seen to carry greater risk of affecting objectivity because preferential treatment for one client could be detrimental to others. Thus, according to Standard IV(B) Duties to Employer: Additional Compensation Arrangements, Harris must disclose the offer to her employer (in writing) and receive the employer's permission before accepting the offer from Baker. (Study Session 1, LOS 2.a)

10. **C** Michaels has not violated Standard II(B) Integrity of Capital Markets: Market Manipulation by either of these actions. In neither case is there the intent to mislead market participants. A large buy program may well increase the price of a stock. The trading desk has informed market participants that they will create additional liquidity for a period of 90 days after the offering and created no expectation that the liquidity of the stock will permanently remain at that level. (Study Session 1, LOS 2.a)

11. **A** According to Standard IV Duties to Employers, Swamy must secure written permission before undertaking the investment advisory work for the symphony because this work competes with her employer and could create a conflict of interest, as she is receiving compensation in the form of season tickets. Her service on her brother-in-law's board may be subject to employer rules about outside employment but is not covered by the Standard because there is no likely competition or potential conflict with her employer. The question says *most likely*, so it is important to focus on the key difference between the two outside activities. Both are compensated; the fact that one is cash and the other tickets is irrelevant. The key difference is that for the symphony, Swamy is acting as an investment advisor for a large endowment, which clearly competes with her employer's business. (Study Session 1, LOS 2.a)

12. **C** Standard III(B) Fair Dealing requires that shares of an oversubscribed IPO be prorated fairly to all subscribers. Arbitrarily increasing the allocation to the "problem client" is a violation, as is the resulting underallocation to the remainder of the firm's clients. (Study Session 1, LOS 2.a)

13. **A** We must start by calculating the JPY/EUR spot rate. This is a simple algebra problem. We know that the JPY/USD spot rate is 120 and the EUR/USD spot rate is 0.7224. Dividing JPY/USD by EUR/USD leaves us with JPY/EUR. Plugging in the numbers, we get a JPY/EUR spot rate of 166.113 (= 120 / 0.7224). Next, we estimate the JPY/EUR spot rate two years from now using the relative PPP formula (for two years) given that EUR inflation is expected to be 5% higher (per year) than JPY inflation:

$$E(S_1) = S_0 \times (1 - 0.05)^2 = 166.113(0.95)^2 = 149.92$$

(Study Session 4, LOS 13.g)

14. **B** Using the international Fisher relation, we can solve for the inflation forecasts in Japan and Europe, given interest rate differentials and the U.S. inflation forecast:

$$R\ nominal_A - R\ nominal_B = E(inflation_A) - E(inflation_B)$$

For Japan: $7.00\% - 3.88\% \neq 3\% - 0\%$

For Eurozone: $9.08 - 7.00 \neq 5\% - 3\%$

Both implied inflation rates are inconsistent with the forecasts from the econometrics department. (Study Session 4, LOS 13.e)

15. **A** Uncovered interest rate parity forecast:

The U.S. interest rate is higher by $7\% - 3.88\% = 3.12\%$.

$$120 \times (1 - 0.0312) = 116.26$$

(Study Session 4, LOS 13.g)

16. **C** Under Mundell-Fleming model, an expansionary monetary policy would lead to depreciation of the JPY. Under a fixed exchange rate regime, to counteract the depreciation of the JPY, the Japanese government has to support its currency by purchasing it in the market. This action is limited by its foreign currency reserves. (Study Session 4, LOS 13.k)

17. **C** This question requires you to look at deviations from international parity conditions and then determine whether those deviations will tend to work to the advantage of the customer. In this problem, you are given the necessary information to examine parity conditions using relative purchasing power parity (RPPP). For the JPY, RPPP tells us that, since the spot rate one year ago was 116 and U.S. inflation was 3% higher than Japan's, the spot rate today should be:

$$S_{today(assuming\ RPPP\ held)} = S_{last\ year}(1 - 0.03) = 116(0.97) = 112.52$$

Since the expected spot rate today, based on RPPP (i.e., 112.52), is not equal to the actual spot rate today (i.e., 120), RPPP did not hold over the past year. Since the actual rate is higher than the rate forecast by RPPP, the long-term trend based on deviations from international parity conditions will be for the rate to fall and the JPY to appreciate. Hence, using deviations from parity conditions as indicators of future currency movements, the bank should recommend that the JPY exposure be left unhedged.

Using the same RPPP process for the EUR exposure, we can calculate an RPPP spot rate today of 0.7340 (given that the rate was 0.72 one year ago and that U.S. inflation was lower by 2%).

$$S_{today\,(assuming\;RPPP\;held)} = S_{last\;year}(1 + 0.02) = 0.72(1.02) = 0.7344$$

Again, RPPP did not hold (i.e., the actual rate today, 0.7224, is not equal to the RPPP rate that should exist today given the inflation rates). However, for the EUR case, the RPPP expected spot is higher than the actual spot, indicating that the EUR may be currently overvalued and, thus, more likely to depreciate in the future. EUR exposure should be hedged. (Study Session 4, LOS 13.g)

18. **A**   The carry trade is a leveraged strategy that involves borrowing in a low-yielding currency (the "funding" currency) and investing in a higher-yielding currency (the "investment" currency), while leaving the exchange rate risk unhedged. The return distribution of the carry trade is *negatively* skewed, with *fat* tails (relative to a normal distribution). (Study Session 4, LOS 13.i)

19. **C**   Subsidiaries whose operations are well integrated with the parent will use the parent's currency as the functional currency. When the functional currency is the same as the parent's presentation currency (reporting currency), as it is in this case, the temporal method is used. Therefore, Statement 1 is incorrect.

Self-contained, independent subsidiaries whose operating, investing, and financing activities are primarily located in the local market will use the local currency as the functional currency. When the functional currency is not the same as the parent's presentation currency (reporting currency), as in this case, the current rate method is used. Therefore, Statement 2 is incorrect. (Study Session 5, LOS 18.d)

20. **A**   Sales will be lower after translation because of the depreciating U.S. dollar. (Study Session 5, LOS 18.e)

21. **B**   Depreciation expense and COGS are remeasured at the historical rate under the temporal method. Under the current rate method, depreciation and COGS are translated at the average rate. Because the U.S. dollar is depreciating, depreciation expense and COGS are lower under the current rate method. (Study Session 5, LOS 18.e)

22. **B**   Since the subsidiary's operations are highly integrated with the parent, the temporal method is used. Accordingly, a loss of CAD 31,200 is recognized in the parent's income statement (see balance sheet and income statement worksheet below). However, no calculations are actually necessary to answer this question. The parent has a net monetary asset position in the subsidiary (monetary assets > monetary liabilities). Holding net monetary assets when the foreign currency is depreciating will result in a loss. Under the temporal method, the loss is reported in the income statement. Only choice B satisfies this logic. (Study Session 5, LOS 18.e)

The Canadian dollar is the functional currency because the subsidiary is highly integrated with the parent. Therefore, the temporal method applies.

Step 1: Remeasure the balance sheet using the temporal method.

	2018 (USD)	Rate	2018 (CAD)
Cash and account receivables	775,000	1.32	1,023,000
Inventory (given in Item 9)	600,000	Given	810,000
PP&E (net)	730,000	1.50	1,095,000
Total assets	2,105,000		2,928,000
Accounts payable	125,000	1.32	165,000
Long-term debt	400,000	1.32	528,000
Common stock	535,000	1.50	802,500
Retained earnings	1,045,000	(a)	1,432,500
Total liabilities and shareholders' equity	2,105,000		2,928,000

(a) Retained earnings is a plug figure that makes the accounting equation balance CAD 2,928,000 assets – CAD 165,000 accounts payable – CAD 528,000 long-term debt – CAD 802,500 common stock = CAD 1,432,500.

Step 2: Derive net income from the beginning and ending balances of retained earnings and dividends paid as follows:

	CAD	
Beginning retained earnings	1,550,000	Given Item 6
Net income	(83,250)	Calculate
Dividends paid in the year	(34,250)	(25,000 × 1.37 historical rate)
Ending retained earnings	1,432,500	From Step 1

Step 3: Remeasure the income statement using the temporal method.

	2018 (USD)	Rate	2018 (CAD)
Sales	1,352,000	1.35	1,825,200
Cost of goods sold (given Item 11)	(1,205,000)	Given	(1,667,250)
Depreciation expense	(140,000)	1.50	(210,000)
Remeasurement loss		(b)	(31,200)
Net income	7,000	From Step 2	(83,250)

(b) The remeasurement loss is a plug that is equal to the difference in net income of – CAD 83,250 and income before remeasurement of –CAD 52,050 (CAD 1,825,200 sales – CAD 1,667,250 COGS – CAD 210,000 depreciation).

23. **A**   The local currency (the USD) is depreciating, so the historical rate will be higher than the current rate. Fixed asset turnover (sales divided by net PP&E) will be higher under the current rate method. Net PP&E will be translated at the lower current rate, and because sales are the same under both methods, the ratio will be higher.

      If you want to do the calculations, net PP&E under the current rate method is USD730,000 × 1.32CAD/USD = CAD 963,600, and fixed asset turnover is CAD 1,825,200/CAD 963,600 = 1.9 times. Fixed asset turnover under the temporal method is CAD 1,825,200/CAD 1,095,000 = 1.7 times. (Study Session 5, LOS 18.e)

24. **C**   Return on assets prior to translation will be different than the ratio after translation because the numerator (net income) is translated at the average rate, and the denominator (assets) is translated at the current rate using the current rate method.

      Net profit margin will be the same because both the numerator (net income) and the denominator (sales) are translated at the average rate using the current rate method. (Study Session 5, LOS 18.f)

25. **B**   The excess of purchase price over the pro-rata share of the book value of Optimax is allocated to PP&E. The remainder is goodwill.

Purchase price (in thousands)	$300
Less: Pro-rata share of Optimax	210 [$600 Optimax book value × 35%]
Excess of purchase price	90
Less: Excess allocated to PPE	70 [($1,200 fair value – $1,000 book value) × 35%]
Acquisition goodwill	$20

      (Study Session 5, LOS 16.c)

26. **B**   Under the equity method, Wayland recognizes its pro-rata share of Optimax's net income less the additional depreciation that resulted from the increase in fair value of Optimax's PP&E.

Pro-rata share of Optimax's net income	$87,500 [$250,000 × 35%]
Less: Additional depreciation from PPE	7,000 [($200,000 / 10 years) × 35%]
Equity income	$80,500

      Wayland's investment account on the balance sheet increased by its equity income and decreased by the dividends received from the investment.

Beginning investment account	$300,000
Equity income from Optimax	80,500
Less: Dividends received	35,000 [$100,000 dividends × 35%]
Ending investment account	$345,500

      (Study Session 5, LOS 16.b)

27. **A**   Since all of the profit from the intercompany transaction is included in Optimax's net income, Wayland must reduce its equity income of Optimax by the pro-rata share of the unconfirmed profit. Since half of the goods remain, half of the profit is unconfirmed. Thus, Wayland must reduce its equity income $2,625 [($15,000 total profit × 50% unconfirmed) × 35% ownership interest]. (Study Session 5, LOS 16.b)

28. **C** Under IFRS 9 (new standards), equity investments that are held for trading must be measured at fair value through profit or loss. Other equity investments can be measured at fair value through profit or loss or fair value through OCI and the choice is irrevocable. Debt securities that meet the business model and cash flow characteristic test must be measured at amortized cost *except when such measurement results in accounting mismatch in which case the debt securities can be classified as fair value through profit or loss.* (Study Session 5, LOS 16.a)

29. **A** Under the current standards, IFRS typically does not allow reclassification of investments into and out of fair value through profit or loss category and reclassification of investments out of held-for-trading category. U.S. GAAP does permit securities to be reclassified into or out of held-for-trading or designated at fair value. (Study Session 5, LOS 16.a,b)

30. **B** The change in market value for the period and dividends received from the investment are recognized in the income statement for trading securities. In 2018, there was a $25,000 unrealized gain on the original 25,000 shares [25,000 shares × ($76 – $75)] and a $10,000 unrealized loss on the shares purchased in 2018 [5,000 shares × ($76 – $78)]. Wayland received $30,000 in dividends from Vanry (30,000 shares × $1 per share). For 2018, the income statement impact is a $45,000 profit ($25,000 unrealized gain on original shares – $10,000 unrealized loss on increase in shares + $30,000 dividends received). (Study Session 5, LOS 16.a,b)

31. **B** Residual income models are appropriate when expected free cash flows are negative for the foreseeable future.

Residual income models are applicable even when dividends are volatile. (Study Session 11, LOS 33.j)

32. **C** A high persistence factor will be associated with low dividend payments, which is exactly the case with Schubert.

A low persistence factor will be associated with significant levels of nonrecurring items. However, Schubert has very few nonrecurring items (which would suggest a high persistence factor). (Study Session 11, LOS 33.h)

33. **A**

Beginning book value (B_{t-1})	$32.16 ($4,181,000 / 130,000)

Beginning book value = Total Equity
            = Common shares + Retained earnings
            = 2,100,000 + 2,081,000 = $4,181,000

Earnings per share forecast (E_t)	$4.50 (given)
Dividend forecast ($D_t = E_t$ × payout ratio)	$0.23 ($4.50 × 5%)
Forecast book value per share ($B_{t-1} + E_t - D_t$)	$36.43
Equity charge per share ($r \times B_{t-1}$)	$4.12 (0.128 × $32.16)
Per share RI_t [($E_t - (r \times B_{t-1})$)]	$0.38 ($4.50 – $4.12)

(Study Session 11, LOS 33.c)

34. **A** Economic value added (EVA) is calculated as follows:

$WACC = WACC × total capital (beginning of 2018)

Note that total capital = net working capital + net fixed assets OR
book value of long-term debt + book value of equity

$= 0.119 × (\$6,200,000 + \$3,281,000) = \$1,128,239$

$$\begin{aligned} EVA &= NOPAT - \$WACC \\ &= EBIT(1-t) - \$WACC \\ &= \$1,868,000(1-0.30) - \$1,128,239 \\ &= \$179,361 \end{aligned}$$

market value of the company (year-end 2018) = market value of the equity + market value of the debt

$$= (\$36 × 130,000) + (0.95 × 6,211,000)$$
$$= \$10,580,450$$

market value added (MVA) = market value – total capital

$$= \$10,580,450 - (\$6,211,000 + \$2,100,000 + \$2,081,000) = \$188,450$$

(Study Session 11, LOS 33.a)

35. **B** $$g = r - \frac{\left[B_0 × (ROE - r)\right]}{V_0 - B_0}$$

$B_0 = [(2,100,000 + 2,081,000)] / 130,000 = \$32.16$

r = cost of equity = 12.8%

$$g = 0.128 - \frac{[32.16 × (0.14 - 0.128)]}{36 - 32.16}$$

$$= 0.0275 = 2.75\%$$

(Study Session 11, LOS 33.g)

36. **A** The clean surplus relationship (i.e., ending book value = beginning book value + net income – dividends) may not hold when items bypass the income statement and affect equity directly. Foreign currency gains and losses under the current rate method bypass income statement and are reported under shareholders equity as CTA. Changes in the market value of trading securities are included in net income and do not violate the clean surplus relationship. Changes in working capital do not bypass the income statement. [Usually, changes in working capital do not affect the income statement. When they do (e.g., inventory writeoffs, bad debts, etc.), the income statement will not be bypassed.] (Study Session 11, LOS 33.k)

37. **A** According to the H-model:

$$V_0 = \frac{D_0(1+g_L)}{r-g_L} + \frac{D_0 H(g_S - g_L)}{r-g_L} = \frac{\$1 × (1+0.04)}{0.12 - 0.04} + \frac{\$1 × 3 × (0.08 - 0.04)}{0.12 - 0.04} = \$14.50$$

(Study Session 10, LOS 30.l)

38. **A** The key assumption underlying the H-model is that the dividend growth rate declines linearly from a high rate in the first stage to a long-term level growth rate. (Study Session 10, LOS 30.i)

39. **B** The relationship we need to evaluate is $V_0 = \dfrac{E_1}{r} + PVGO$.

   This expression can be rewritten as $PVGO = V_0 - \dfrac{E_1}{r} = \$18 - \dfrac{\$0.90}{0.12} = \$10.50$.

   (Study Session 10, LOS 30.e)

40. **A** The P/E ratio can become unreliable for ranking purposes when earnings are close to zero. When this happens, the P/E will be unrealistically large and its reciprocal, the earnings yield (E/P), will instead approach zero. Therefore, Statement 1 is correct. A high E/P suggests an underpriced security, and a low (or negative) E/P suggests an overpriced security. Therefore, Statement 2 is incorrect. (Study Session 11, LOS 32.d)

41. **B** Earnings must be adjusted to reflect the nonrecurring extraordinary item restructuring costs and asset write downs.
   Adjusted 2018 earnings before tax = \$30,400,000 + \$189,100,000 = \$219,500,000.
   Adjusted 2018 after-tax earnings = \$219,500,000 × (1 − 0.34) = \$144,870,000.
   2018 underlying EPS = \$144,870,000 / 106,530,610 = \$1.36

   (Study Session 11, LOS 32.c)

42. **A** FDS has a price-to-sales ratio in 2018 of: $\dfrac{\$18}{\left(\dfrac{\$6,435,900,000}{106,530,610}\right)} = \dfrac{\$18}{\$60.41} = 0.30$.

   Because its price-to-sales ratio is less than the industry average of 0.50, FDS is relatively underpriced. (Study Session 11, LOS 32.h,k)

43. **C** Notice that in this case, $g_S = g_L$ and, accordingly, the H-model simplifies to the Gordon growth model. We can then solve for the unknown rate:

   $$r = \dfrac{D_0\left(1+g_L\right)}{V_0} + g_L = \dfrac{\$1.25 \times \left(1+0.06\right)}{\$25} + 0.06 = 0.113 = 11.3\%$$

   (Study Session 10, LOS 30.m)

44. **C** Among the choices given, the only drawback to the P/S ratio is that it is susceptible to manipulation if management should choose to act aggressively with respect to the recognition of revenue. (Study Session 11, LOS 32.c)

45. **B**   UHS trailing P/E = \$25 / \$0.82 = 30.49

UHS trailing PEG = 30.49 / 6% = 5.08

Trailing industry P/E = 22.50

Trailing industry PEG = 22.50 / 10% = 2.25

The PEG ratio for UHS exceeds that of the industry. This implies that UHS's growth rate is relatively more expensive than is the industry's growth rate. We can therefore conclude that on the basis of the PEG ratio, UHS stock is overvalued.

UHS P/S = \$25 / (\$7,400,100,000 / 95,366,000) = 0.32

Industry P/S = 0.50

Relative to the industry, the P/S ratio for UHS stock is low, and it would therefore be considered as undervalued.

Conflicting results between different ratios is common in practice. When this occurs, an analyst must look deeper to arrive at a reliable conclusion. An important consideration in this case is whether or not there has been any manipulation of sales and/or earnings. The estimation of the dividend growth rate is also an important factor. (Study Session 11, LOS 32.h,i)

46. **B** $\text{Average ROE} = \dfrac{0.032 + 0.040 + 0.045 + 0.039}{4} = 0.039$

$\text{BVPS}_{2018} = \$25.58$

$\text{Normalized EPS} = \overline{\text{ROE}} \times \text{BVPS}_{2018} = 0.039 \times \$25.58 = \$1.00$

(Study Session 11, LOS 32.e)

47. **A**   Beta = 0.8
4-year average ROE = 3.9% (See previous solution)
8-year dividend growth forecast = 6%
Predicted P/E = 5 − (10 × 0.8) + (3 × 3.9%) + (2 × 6%) = 20.7
(Study Session 11, LOS 32.i)

48. **B**   The belief that there are patterns of persistence or reversals in returns provides the rationale for valuation using relative strength indicators. There has been a considerable amount of empirical research in this area. Research suggests that the investment horizon is also an important determining factor in the appearance of these patterns.
(Study Session 11, LOS 32.p)

49. **C**   Statement 1 is correct. If the volatility of interest rates decreases, the call option is less valuable, which increases the value of the callable bond. Recall that $V_{\text{callable}} = V_{\text{noncallable}} - V_{\text{call}}$. Statement 3 is also correct. The value of the noncallable bond increases by more than the callable bond because as yield falls, the value of the call goes up. As the call value increases, the callable value (noncall value − call option value) goes up by less than the noncall value. (Study Session 13, LOS 37.d,e)

50. **B** Statement 2 is incorrect because the noncallable bond value *will be affected* by a change in the *level* of interest rates.

Statement 4 is correct because higher interest rate volatility will increase the value of the embedded put option and increase the value of the puttable bond. (Study Session 13, LOS 37.d,e)

51. **A** The answer is 1.56 and is found by taking the difference between the value of the callable and the noncallable bonds: Call option value = 99.77 − 98.21 = 1.56. *Note: This is an example of a basic question that you should get right! Don't give up these points or lose time by starting a complicated calculation. The question might be as easy as it seems.* (Study Session 13, LOS 37.b)

52. **B** In this case, the bond is callable and putable at the same price (100). Because Walters states that the embedded options (the issuer's call option and the holder's put option) will be exercised if the option has value (i.e., is in-the-money), the value of the bond must be 100 (plus the interest) at all times. Why? If rates fall and the computed value goes above 100, the company will call the issue at 100. Conversely, if rates increase and the computed value goes below 100, the bondholder will "put" the bond back to the issuer for 100.

The OAS is a constant spread added to every interest rate in the tree so that the model price of the bond is equal to the market price of the bond. In this case, using the interest rate lattice, the model price of the callable bond is greater than the market price. Hence, a positive spread must be added to every interest rate in the lattice. When a constant spread is added to all the rates such that the model price is equal to the market price, you have found the OAS. The OAS will be positive for the callable bond. (Study Session 13, LOS 37.f,g)

53. **B** The answer is 93.26. This value of the non-callable bond at node A is computed as follows:

$$\text{value} = \frac{\left[0.5 \times \left(V_{up} + \frac{\text{coupon}}{2}\right)\right] + \left[0.5 \times \left(V_{down} + \frac{\text{coupon}}{2}\right)\right]}{\left(1 + \frac{\text{interest rate}}{2}\right)}$$

$$= \frac{\left[0.5 \times \left(91.73 + \frac{6}{2}\right)\right] + \left[0.5 \times \left(96.17 + \frac{6}{2}\right)\right]}{\left(1 + \frac{0.0791}{2}\right)} = 93.26$$

(Study Session 12, LOS 36.d)

54. **A**   The correct value is 100.00. The computed value of the callable bond at node A is obtained as follows:

$$\text{value} = \frac{\left[0.5 \times \left(100 + \frac{6}{2}\right)\right] + \left[0.5 \times \left(100 + \frac{6}{2}\right)\right]}{\left(1 + \frac{0.0315}{2}\right)} = 101.4$$

However, when working with a callable bond, you have to remember that the value of the bond at any node is the lesser of (1) the bonds computed value or (2) the call price. So, we have:

$$\text{value} = \text{Min}\left[100, \frac{\left[0.5 \times \left(100 + \frac{6}{2}\right)\right] + \left[0.5 \times \left(100 + \frac{6}{2}\right)\right]}{\left(1 + \frac{0.0315}{2}\right)}\right] = 100$$

In this case, since the computed value (101.4) is greater than the call price (100), the nodal value is $100. (Study Session 13, LOS 37.f)

55. **A**   Statement 1 is correct. Credit ratings tend to be stable over time and across business cycles, which has the effect of reducing price volatility in the debt market. (Study Session 13, LOS 38.c)

56. **A**   Statement 2 is correct. (Study Session 13, LOS 38.a)

57. **C**   One of the assumptions of structural models is that default risk is constant during the life of the bond and hence does not change over business cycles or in response to changing economic variables. (Study Session 13, LOS 38.f)

58. **A**   Statement 4 is correct. Probability of default does not apply to asset-backed securities because ABS do not default when an underlying collateral defaults. For this reason, probability of loss is used in place of probability of default for ABS. (Study Session 13, LOS 38.i)

59. **C**

Time to Cash Flow	Cash Flow	Risk-Free Spot Rate	Credit Spread (%)	Total Yield (%)	PV (Risk-Free Rate)	PV (Total Yield)
0.5	25	0.23%	0.80%	1.03%	24.97	24.87
1	1,025	0.25%	0.85%	1.10%	1,022.44	1,013.79
			Total		$ 1,047.41	$ 1,038.66

PV(risky $1,025) = 1,025/e^{(1*0.011)} = $1,013.787
Present value of expected loss = PV(risk-free rate) − PV(total yield)
     = 1,047.41 − 1,038.66 = $8.75

(Study Session 13, LOS 38.h)

60. **C**   While Thompson's statement about reduced form models imposing assumptions on the output of structural models is correct, Thompson is incorrect about balance sheet composition being required; reduced form models do not require a specification of the company's balance sheet structure. (Study Session 13, LOS 38.f)

Exam 3
Afternoon Session Answers

To get valuable feedback on how your score compares to those of other Level II candidates, use your Username and Password to gain Online Access at schweser.com and choose the menu item *Practice Exams Volume 2 (Enter answers from book)."*

61. B	81. C	101. B
62. A	82. B	102. C
63. A	83. A	103. A
64. C	84. C	104. A
65. A	85. B	105. A
66. B	86. C	106. A
67. C	87. C	107. C
68. A	88. A	108. B
69. B	89. B	109. B
70. C	90. B	110. B
71. B	91. A	111. C
72. A	92. C	112. C
73. B	93. C	113. C
74. C	94. A	114. A
75. A	95. A	115. C
76. C	96. C	116. B
77. C	97. A	117. A
78. A	98. A	118. B
79. A	99. C	119. B
80. A	100. B	120. C

Exam 3
Afternoon Session Answers

61. **B** Fisher should take the natural log of the dependent variable so that the data in Exhibit 1 are transformed and can be better modeled using a linear regression. From the plot, it appears that the data follow a log-linear trend. If the natural log is taken of the dependent variable, the data will be more linear so that it is readily modeled in a regression. The transformed data will plot as follows:

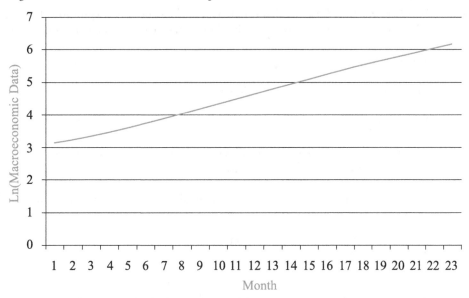

(Study Session 3, LOS 10.k, l and 11.a)

62. **A** The most likely problem in Fisher's regression of the emerging market data is that the error terms appear to be positively correlated in Exhibit 2. The first few error terms are positive, then negative, and then positive. This indicates serial correlation, which is common in trend models. As Fisher regresses the macroeconomic data against a time variable, she is using a trend model. In a trend model, the Durbin Watson statistic can be used to detect serial correlation. (Study Session 3, LOS 10.k)

63. **A** The use of the Durbin Watson statistic is inappropriate in an autoregressive regression, which is what Weatherford is using. The Durbin Watson statistic is appropriate for trend models but not autoregressive models. To determine whether the errors terms are serially correlated in an autoregressive model, the significance of the autocorrelations should be tested using the *t*-statistic. (Study Session 3, LOS 11.d)

64. **C**   Weatherford is using an autoregressive first-order regression model in which this period's silver price is regressed on the previous period's price. The regression is of the form:

$$X_t = b_0 + b_1 X_{t-1}$$

The most likely problem in this regression is that the data is not covariance stationary. In the plot of the data, the mean of the data does not appear to be constant (it is much higher in the middle period.) The estimate of the lag one slope coefficient is close to 1.0, which also suggests that the data is nonstationary.

To definitively test this, the Dickey Fuller test should be used, where the null hypothesis is that $b_1 - 1$ is equal to zero. If the null hypothesis is not rejected, we say that the data has a unit root and is nonstationary. (Study Session 3, LOS 10.l and 11.f, k, n)

65. **A**   Weatherford should use the first differences of the data in the regression. That is, instead of using the actual price levels, she should use the change in the data rather than levels:

$$Y_t = X_t - X_{t-1}$$

Then the appropriate regression will be:

$$Y_t = b_0 + b_1 Y_{t-1}$$

The transformed time series data will have a mean reverting level and be covariance stationary. (Study Session 3, LOS 11.j)

66. **B**   To determine the mean reverting level, we divide the intercept by one minus the slope coefficient:

$$\text{mean-reverting level} = \frac{b_0}{1-b_1} = \frac{2.00}{1-(-0.09)} = 1.83$$

The one-step-ahead predicted value is calculated by substituting the current value into the regression equation:

$$\hat{y}_{t+1} = b_0 + b_1(y_t) = 2.00 + (-0.09)(-0.80) = 2.072$$

The two-step-ahead predicted value is then calculated by substituting the one-step-ahead predicted value into the regression equation:

$$\hat{y}_{t+2} = b_0 + b_1(\hat{y}_{t+1}) = 2.00 + (-0.09)(2.072) = 1.81$$

(Study Session 3, LOS 11.d, e)

67. **C**   Investments in financial assets are classified as held-to-maturity, held-for-trading, designated at fair value, and available-for-sale. Held-to-maturity applies to debt securities only. Held-for-trading securities are debt or equity securities that are expected to be sold in the near term. Since the investment in Odessa is long-term, the securities are classified as available-for-sale. (Study Session 5, LOS 16.a)

68. **A**   Since Iberia owns 40% of Midland (5 million shares owned / 12.5 million total shares outstanding), the equity method is used. Under the equity method, Iberia reports its pro-rata share of Midland's net income (€5 million loss × 40% = €2 million loss). Changes in market value are ignored under the equity method.

Iberia's investment in Odessa is classified as available-for-sale since the investment is considered long-term. Dividend income from available-for-sale securities is recognized in the income statement (€3 dividend × 1 million shares = €3 million). The changes in market value are reported in shareholders' equity.

Investment income from Midland and Odessa is €1 million (€3 million dividend income from Odessa – €2 million pro-rata loss from Midland). (Study Session 5, LOS 16.a)

69. **B**   Under the equity method, the balance sheet carrying value is increased by the pro-rata earnings of the investee and decreased by the dividends received from the investee. The balance sheet value at the end of 2008 is €88 million [€80 million + (€30 million Midland 2008 net income × 40%) – (€10 million dividend × 40%)]. The balance sheet value at the end of 2009 is €84.4 million [€88 million – (€5 million loss × 40%) – (€4 million dividend × 40%)].

Available-for-sale securities are reported on the balance sheet at fair value. Thus, the fair value of Odessa is €17 million (€17 × 1 million shares).

As a result of its investment in Midland and Odessa, Iberia will report investment assets of €101.4 million (€84.4 million book value of Midland + €17 million fair value Odessa). (Study Session 5, LOS 16.a)

70. **C**   Profit from intercompany transactions must be deferred until the profit is confirmed through use or sale to a third party. Since all of the goods purchased from Midland have been sold to third parties, all of the profit from the intercompany sale has been confirmed. Thus, no adjustment is needed. (Study Session 5, LOS 16.a)

71. **B**   Under U.S. GAAP, all entities can account for their equity method investments at fair value. Under IFRS, the fair value option is only available for venture capital firms/ mutual funds and similar entities. (Study Session 5, LOS 16.b)

72. **A**   In a profitable year, net profit margin (net income/sales) will be higher under the equity method because sales are lower under the equity method. Acquisition includes the sales figures for both the parent and subsidiary, while the equity method only includes the sales figure for the parent company. Net income is the same under both methods. Therefore, the statement is correct. (Study Session 5, LOS 16.c)

73. **B**   Lower expected rate of return on plan assets (i.e., 8% instead of 10%) would not affect the PBO or the total periodic pension cost. PBO is the present value of benefits earned to date and is unaffected by changes in expected return on plan assets (but is sensitive to changes in discount rate). Total periodic pension cost is affected by *actual* return on plan assets and not the *expected* return on plan assets. (Study Session 5, LOS 17.d)

74. **C** Benefits paid can be determined by reconciling ending PBO to beginning PBO:

Beginning PBO	1,022
+ Current service cost	118
+ Past service cost	36
+ Interest cost	82
+ Acturial Loss	128
(–) benefit paid	188
(=) Ending PBO	1,198

(Study Session 5, LOS 17.b)

75. **A** ending fair value of plan assets

= beginning fair value + contributions + actual return – benefits paid

= 896 + 102 + 214 – 188 = 1,024 million

(Study Session 5, LOS 17.b)

76. **C** Total periodic pension cost = employer contributions – change in funded status

= 102 – [ending funded status – beginning funded status]

= 102 – [(1,024 – 1,198) – (896-1,022)] = $150 million

or

total periodic pension cost = current service cost + past service cost + interest cost + actuarial loss – actual return on plan assets = 118 + 36 + 82 + 128 – 214 = $150 million.

(Study Session 5, LOS 17.c)

77. **C** Under IFRS, periodic pension cost reported in P&L would consist of current and past service cost plus/minus net interest expense/income. Net interest income is computed as the discount rate multiplied by beginning funded status.

periodic pension cost in P&L = 118 + 36 – 0.08[896 – 1,022] = 164.08

Note that since the beginning funded status is negative, there is a net interest cost.

(Study Session 5, LOS 17.c)

78. **A** PBO will increase with a higher rate of compensation growth. A higher rate of compensation growth will also increase the total periodic pension cost as well as the periodic pension cost in P&L by increasing both the service and interest costs. Under IFRS, the net interest cost is computed as the discount rate multiplied by beginning funded status. The beginning PBO for the next period would be higher due to the higher compensation growth assumption and hence the net interest cost will be higher. (Study Session 5, LOS 17.d)

79. **A**   Hinesman's comment is correct. Studies have shown, that on average, companies with strong corporate governance systems have higher measures of profitability and generate higher returns for shareholders.

Randall's comment is also correct. The lack of an effective corporate governance system increases risk to an investor. Four main risks of not having an effective corporate governance system include asset risk and liability risk, as well as the two risks described by Randall: financial disclosure risk and strategic policy risk. (Study Session 8, LOS 25.a,h)

80. **A**   According to corporate governance best practice, the audit committee should consist only of independent directors; it should have expertise in financial and accounting matters (for purposes of the exam, at least two members of the committee should have relevant accounting and auditing experience); the internal audit staff for the firm should report directly to the audit committee; and the committee should meet with external auditors at least once annually without management present. (Study Session 8, LOS 25.e)

81. **C**   Using a target debt-to-equity ratio of 1:1, the $150 million in capital spending for 20X1 will be financed with $75 million in internal equity and $75 million in debt. The total dividend is the remaining internal equity of $112.5 − $75 = $37.5 million, or $37.5 / 56.25 = $0.67 per share. (Study Session 7, LOS 23.n)

82. **B**   FCFE = cash flow from operations − FcInv + net borrowings

20X0: FCFE = 115 − 43 + 22 = 94

20X1: FCFE = 132 − 150 + 75 = 57

FCFE coverage ratio = FCFE / (dividends + share repurchases)

20X0: 94 / (42.88 + 42) = 1.11

20X1: 57 / (45 + 3) = 1.19

(Study Session 7, LOS 23.m)

83. **A**   Kazmaier received a score of 25% because it was in compliance with global best practice with respect to only one of the four criteria.

Criterion 1:   Global best practice recommends that three-quarters (75%) of the board members be independent. Of the nine total board members, only five are independent. Kazmaier fails this criterion.

Criterion 2:   Global best practice recommends that the Chairman of the Board be independent. Since Kazmaier's Chairman is also the CEO, Kazmaier fails this criterion.

Criterion 3:   Global best practice recommends that the entire board of directors stand for reelection annually. Since it appears that Kazmaier has staggered board elections, Kazmaier fails this criterion.

Criterion 4:   Global best practice requires independent board members to meet in separate sessions at least annually. Although quarterly meetings between independent directors are preferable, the fact that they happen annually means Kazmaier passes this criterion.

(Study Session 8, LOS 25.e)

84. C   Nagy's three rationales all correctly describe common advantages of share repurchases. (Study Session 7, LOS 23.k)

The complete solution to Questions 85 to 90 is as follows (in thousands):

	Years			
Cost Item	**0**	**1**	**2**	**3**
Cost	(400)			
Sale of old*	30			
Revenue		175.0	175.0	175.0
Less: operating cost		25.0	25.0	25.0
Less: depreciation (400,000 × MACRS%)		132.0	180.0	60.0
EBT		18.0	(30.0)	90.0
– Tax (40%)		7.2	(12.0)	36.0
NI		10.8	(18.0)	54.0
+ Depreciation		132.0	180.0	60.0
+ Sale				10.0
+ Sale tax shield**				7.2
= CF		142.8	162.0	131.2

NPV (@ 20%) = –62,574

IRR = 8.796%

Therefore, REJECT, because the NPV < 0, IRR < 20%.

Using the calculator: CF0 = –370, C01 = 142.8, C02 = 162, C03 = 131.2, I = 20, CPT → NPV –62,574, CPT → IRR = 8.796.

** Sale tax shield		*Sale of old
BV =	28 (= 400 × 0.07)	BV = 0
–sale	–10	Sale = 50
Loss	18	Gain = 50
Tax shield = loss × tax rate = 18 × 0.4 = 7.2		Tax (40%) = 20
Net impact of sale = $10 sale proceeds + $7.2 tax shield = 17.2		Net proceeds = 30

85. B   See solution above. Alternatively, initial outlay = FCInv + WCInv – Sal_0 + $T(Sal_T – B_0)$ = 400 + 0 – 50 + 0.4(50 – 0) = 400 – 50 + 20 = $370. (Study Session 7, LOS 21.a)

86. C   See solution above. Alternatively, CF_1 = (S – C)(1 – T) + DT = (175 – 25)(0.6) + (0.4)(0.33)(400) = 90 + 52.8 = $142.8. (Study Session 7, LOS 21.a)

87. C   See solution above. Alternatively, CF = –(175 – 25)(0.4) + 400(0.45)(0.4) = –60 + 72 = +$12. (Study Session 7, LOS 21.a)

88. A   See solution above. Alternatively, CF_3 = (175 – 25)(0.6) + (400)(0.15)(0.4) = 90 + 24 = $114. TNOCF = Sal_T + WCInv – $T(Sal_T – B_T)$ = 10 + 0 – 0.4(10 – 28) = 10 + 7.2 = $17.2. CF_3 + TNOCF = $114 + $17.2 = $131.2 (Study Session 7, LOS 21.a)

89. **B** NPV will be underestimated because the reduction in inventory should reflect a cash inflow at the beginning of the project. Even if the inventory builds back up to its previous level at the end of the project (resulting in a cash outflow), the cash inflow will be larger than the present value of the cash outflow. (Study Session 7, LOS 21.a)

90. **B** If the NPV is less than zero, the IRR must be less than the discount rate of 20% (so 8.8% is the only possible answer), and the project should be rejected. The actual calculations of NPV and IRR are shown in the solution, but these calculations are not necessary to answer the question. (Study Session 7, LOS 21.a)

91. **A** The equity risk premium is estimated as:

ERP = [1 + i] × [1 + REg] × [1 + PEg] – 1 + Y – RF

where:
i = the expected inflation rate = 2.6%
REg = expected real growth in GDP = 3.0%
PEg = relative value changed due to changes in P/E ratio = –0.03
Y = yield on the market index = 1.7%
RF = risk-free rate of return = 2.7%
ERP = (1.026) × (1.030) × (0.97) – 1 + 0.017 – 0.027 = 0.015 = 1.50%

Note: We do not add the risk-free rate because we are computing the equity risk premium and not the required rate of return. Conversely, we can compute the required rate of return and then subtract the risk-free rate to obtain the equity risk premium.

(Study Session 9, LOS 28.b)

92. **C** Historical estimates are subject to survivorship bias. If the data are not adjusted for the effects of non-survivors, returns (based only on survivors) will be biased upwards. (Study Session 9, LOS 28.b)

93. **C** Using CAPM, the required return is:

required rate of return = risk-free rate + (beta × equity risk premium)

required return for NE = 2.7% + (0.83 × 5.2%) = 7.02%

(Study Session 9, LOS 28.c)

94. **A** With the Fama-French model, the required return is:

required rate of return = risk-free rate + β_{MKT} (market risk premium) + β_{size} (size risk premium) + β_{value} (value premium)

required rate of return for NE = 2.7% + 0.83(5.2%) + (–0.76)(3.2%) + (–0.04)(5.4%) = 4.37%

(Study Session 9, LOS 28.c)

95. **A** adjusted beta = (2/3)(0.83) + (1/3)(1.0) = 0.89. (Study Session 9, LOS 28.c)

96. **C** The recommended method for estimating the beta of a nonpublic company from the beta of a public company is as follows: (1) Unlever the beta for the public company, using the public company's debt/equity ratio. (2) Relever (adjust upward) this beta using VixPRO's debt/equity ratio to get the estimated equity beta for VixPRO. (Study Session 9, LOS 28.d)

97. **A** Nolte is long in the underlying stock, so she should short call options, and she can use any of the options to delta hedge. The hedge ratio (the number of calls per share) is (1 / delta), so any of these four short call positions will hedge her long position in the stock:

$$\frac{1}{0.54} \times 5,000 = 9,259 \text{ 1-month call options}$$

$$\frac{1}{0.58} \times 5,000 = 8,621 \text{ 3-month call options}$$

$$\frac{1}{0.61} \times 5,000 = 8,197 \text{ 6-month call options}$$

$$\frac{1}{0.63} \times 5,000 = 7,937 \text{ 9-month call options}$$

(Study Session 14, LOS 41.l)

98. **A** The hedge must be continually rebalanced, even in the unlikely event that the stock price doesn't change, because the option's delta changes as time passes and the option approaches maturity. If she simultaneously buys an equivalent amount of put options, the overall position (including the calls, the puts, and 5,000 shares of Pioneer) will no longer be delta hedged. (Study Session 14, LOS 41.l)

99. **C** Gamma risk arises when the price of the underlying jumps abruptly (as opposed to smoothly). (Study Session 14, LOS 41.m)

100. **B** Delta hedged portfolio consists of long position in stocks and short position in call options. Because the gamma of long stock position is zero and the gamma of short call is negative, the net gamma of a delta hedged portfolio is negative.

As the stock price increases, call delta increases and we need fewer calls. As we reduce the number of short calls, the net gamma increases (becomes less negative). (Study Session 14, LOS 41.m)

101. **B** Both the 3-month and the 9-month put options are correctly priced according to put-call parity. Note that you are given the continuously compounded risk-free rate, so you have to use the continuous version of put-call parity.

$$P_0 = C_0 - S_0 + \frac{X}{e^{R_f^c \times T}}$$

$$P(3\text{-month}) = \$5 + \frac{\$40}{e^{0.05 \times 0.25}} - \$40 = \$4.50$$

$$P(9\text{-month}) = \$8.81 + \frac{\$40}{e^{0.05 \times 0.75}} - \$40 = \$7.34$$

Therefore, she's correct that the 3-month put is not mispriced, but incorrect in her conclusion that the 9-month put is mispriced. (Study Session 14, LOS 41.a)

102. **C** $S_0 = \$60$, $S^+ = 60(1.15) = \$69$, $S^- = 60(0.85) = \$51$, $X = \$60$. $C^+ = 69 - 60 = \$9$, $C^- = 0$.

$$h = \frac{C^+ - C^-}{S^+ - S^-} = \frac{9-0}{69-51} = 0.5$$

$$C_0 = hS_0 + \frac{(-hS^+ + C^+)}{(1+R_f)} = 0.5(60) + \frac{(-0.5)(69)+9}{(1.05)} = \$5.71$$

Because the current call price of $6.90 is higher than the no-arbitrage price, an arbitrage profit can be earned by writing calls and buying 0.5 shares per call written. (Study Session 14, LOS 41.c)

103. **A** The semi-annual fixed payment is calculated as

$$\frac{1-0.9285}{0.9840+0.9676+0.9488+0.9285} = 0.01867$$, which, when annualized, is 3.73%.

(Study Session 14, LOS 40.c)

104. **A** Floating rate applicable for the first settlement was determined at the inception of the swap (i.e., 3.25%). The net amount owed by the fixed payer of the swap would be $(0.038 - 0.0325)/2 \times \$30,000,000 = \$82,500$. (Study Session 14, LOS 40.c)

105. **A** After the first settlement date, there are three more settlements remaining, at 180, 360, and 540 days.

The sum of the discount factors for those three dates = $0.9820 + 0.9596 + 0.9336$ = 2.8752. We are told that the original swap fixed rate is 4.0%, and the new swap fixed rate is given as 4.62%.

Value to the payer = $\Sigma DF \times (SFR_{new} - SFR_{old}) \times$ (days / 360) × notional principal

= $2.8752 \times (0.0462 - 0.04) \times (180 / 360) \times \$30,000,000 = \$267,394$.

(Study Session 14, LOS 40.d)

106. **A** CHF notional = $0.97 \times 10,000,000$ = CHF 9,700,000

$$\text{CHF fixed rate} = \frac{(1-0.9838)}{(1.0033+1.0055+1.0030+0.9980+0.9926+0.9838)} \times \left(\frac{360}{180}\right) = 0.541\%$$

Periodic CHF payment $= (0.00541) \times (180 / 360) \times 9.7 \text{ million} \approx \text{CHF } 26,200$

(Study Session 14, LOS 40.d)

107. **C** A long position in a payer swaption decreases in value as rates decrease, and a short position increases. A long position in a receiver swaption increases in value as rates decrease, and a short position decreases.

Therefore, to exploit the anticipated drop in rates, Black should go short in the payer swaption or long in the receiver swaption. (Study Session 14, LOS 41.j)

108. **B** Value of fixed-rate bond = 0.015(0.9840) + 0.015 (0.9676) + 1.015 (0.9488) = 0.9923
Value of equity swap immediately after settlement = par value = $1
Value of pay fixed, receive equity swap = $1 − $0.9923 = $0.0077 (per $1 notional)
Value for $5 million notional = $38,500
(Study Session 14, LOS 40.d)

109. **B** Invested capital in the fund was $20 million + $100 million = $120 million. Committed capital was $120 million + $100 million = $220 million. Since the fund was sold for $180 million, the fund earned a profit of $180 million − $120 million = $60 million.

Under the total return using invested capital method, carried interest is paid to the GP only after the portfolio value exceeds invested capital (by 30% as specified by IGS). Since the $180 million exceeds ($120 million)(1.3) = $156 million, the GP is entitled to carried interest. Carried interest is calculated as:

$180 million − $120 million = $60 million. 20% of $60 million is $12 million.

(Study Session 15, LOS 43.h,i)

110. **B** The DCF method and relative value approach would be less appropriate for Sverig. Given that Sverig is a startup venture capital firm, it would be difficult to assess its future cash flows and there are likely few comparables to benchmark against. Given that L'Offre has been in existence for over a century, it likely has relatively stable and predictable cash flows. Several comparables would also likely exist in the same industry. This would make either the DCF method or relative value approach an appropriate valuation technique. (Study Session 15, LOS 45.i)

111. **C** Market risk is the uncertainty in long-term macroeconomic factors, such as changes in interest rates and foreign exchange rates. If these changes adversely affect the private equity fund firms, both the fund's investors (limited partners) and the firms' managers could see their equity stake and investment declining. Agency risk refers to the possibility that the managers of the portfolio (investee) companies may place their personal interests ahead of the interests of the firm and of private equity investors. (Study Session 15, LOS 45.g)

112. **C** The GP's share in profits is referred to as carried interest and is generally set at 20% of net profits after fees. A tag-along, drag-along clause would give management the right to sell an equity stake upon sale by the private equity owners.

   Ratchet specifies the equity allocation between the limited partners (LPs) and management. Distribution waterfall specifies how profits will flow to the LPs and also the conditions under which the GP may receive carried interest. (Study Session 15, LOS 45.b)

113. **C** First, the $400 million terminal value must be discounted two years at 30% to the second round of financing:

$$POST_2 = \frac{\$400 \text{ million}}{(1.3)^2} = \$236.686 \text{ million}$$

   The second-round pre-money valuation (PRE_2) is calculated by netting the $40 million second-round investment from the $POST_2$ calculation:

$$PRE_2 = POST_2 - INV_2 = \$236.686 \text{ million} - \$40 \text{ million} = \$196.686 \text{ million}.$$

   Finally, the PRE_2 valuation must be discounted back 4 years at 40% to arrive at the $POST_1$ valuation:

$$POST_1 = \frac{\$196.686 \text{ million}}{(1.4)^4} = \$51.199 \text{ million}$$

   (Study Session 15, LOS 45.j)

114. **A** Calculating the number shares for Sverig's first-round investors requires a three-step approach where:

   - f_1 is the fractional ownership for first-round investors.
   - INV_1 is the initial investment in Sverig by the private equity partners.
   - S_e is the number of shares owned by Sverig's founders.
   - S_{pe} is the number of shares owned by the private equity LPs.

   Step 1: Determine the fractional ownership for first-round investors (f_1):

$$f_1 = \frac{INV}{POST_1} = \frac{\$20 \text{ million}}{\$51.199 \text{ million}} = 39.06\%$$

   First-round investors thus own approximately 39.06% of the firm.

©2017 Kaplan, Inc.

Step 2: Determine the number of shares first-round investors need to receive their fractional ownership:

$$S_{pel} = S_e \left(\frac{f_1}{1-f_1} \right) = 5,000,000 \left(\frac{0.3906}{1-0.3906} \right) = 3,204,792$$

To obtain a 39.06% stake in Sverig, first-round investors would have to receive 3,204,792 shares.

Step 3: Determine the stock price after the first round of financing (P_1):

$$P_1 = \frac{INV_1}{S_{pel}} = \frac{\$20 \text{ million}}{3,204,792} = \$6.24$$

(Study Session 15, LOS 45.j)

115. **C** $E(R_P) = 0.6E(R_{WMB}) + 0.4E(R_{REL}) = 0.6(9\%) + 0.4(10.8\%) = 9.72\%$

(Study Session 16, LOS 48.d)

116. **B** $\beta_{P,INF} = 0.6\beta_{WMB,INF} + 0.4\beta_{REL,INF} = 0.6(-2.2) + 0.4(-1.0) = -1.72$

(Study Session 16, LOS 48.d)

117. **A** $8 = E(R) + (-0.9 \times 0.5) + (1.2 \times 0.5) + (0.5)$

$E(R) = 7.35\%$

(Study Session 16, LOS 48.d)

118. **B** Consider portfolio A comprising 50% portfolio X and 50% portfolio Z. Portfolio A will have an expected return of 12.5% and a factor sensitivity of 1.25. A long position in portfolio A and short position in portfolio Y will have an expected return of 0.5% with zero factor sensitivity.

(Study Session 16, LOS 48.b)

119. **B** Active risk squared = active factor risk + active specific risk

(Study Session 16, LOS 48.e)

120. **C** Credit spreads tighten during times of economic expansions. During such times, lower-rated bonds outperform higher-rated bonds. (Study Session 17, LOS 50.f)

Notes

Notes

Notes

Notes

Notes